DISCARD

THE DINING CAR

Also by Eric Peterson

Life as a Sandwich

THE DINING CAR

ERIC PETERSON

huckle
berry
house

LAKE TAHOE, NV

Published by Huckleberry House, Lake Tahoe, Nevada
Interior & Cover Design by Kathleen Wise
Edited by Jennifer Silva Redmond
Cover image: Martin Harvey/Photolibrary/Getty Images

The Dining Car
First edition
Library of Congress Control Number: 2016949902
ISBN 978-0-9824860-1-6
10 9 8 7 6 5 4 3 2 1

Printed in the USA

The Dining Car is available from Amazon, at select bookstores, through Ingram, and directly from the publisher.

Books may be purchased in quantity and/or special sales by contacting the publisher, Huckleberry House, at HuckleberryHouseBooks.com

To my brother, Christopher John Peterson

And in memoriam:

To Lucius Beebe and Charles Clegg

ON THAT COOL SUMMER EVENING, the captains of industry headed down the hill early, eager to grab seats in the open-air amphitheater. The rustic bowl, fashioned from hewn logs and surrounded by towering redwoods, seated more than a thousand and was at the heart of Mount Hollow, the Saratoga Club's exclusive all-male retreat high in the Santa Cruz Mountains. The guest speaker's appearance that night promised to be the pinnacle event of the summer.

I was alone on the upper reaches of the property, tending bar at a camp called Biscuit Shooters, washing glasses and cleaning up, when the headlights of a golf cart announced the arrival of a new guest. The cart slid to a heavy stop in the gravel turnout at the mouth of the sturdy bridge to our camp, and a fat man tumbled drunkenly from the passenger seat. He held a magnum of Pérignon Cuvée aloft and gave a shout of surprise as he fell backward into a swale of redwood sorrel, poison oak, and ferns. With a cracking of branches, the forest consumed him.

An Isuzu stake bed truck pulled up behind the golf cart. Two Mount Hollow staffers jumped from the cab and bolted for the edge of the canyon, where they and the driver of the golf cart tried pulling the man from the foliage.

"Fish heads!" the man railed. "Unhand me! I am Professor John Henry Cluttermush, dean of the Harvard Divinity School!" After a summer of overcast days and drizzly nights, the black soil was boggy as used coffee grounds, the carpet of sodden leaves was covered with a slick moss, and one by one the rescuers lost their footing and went over like bad manners at Buckingham Palace. "I'll dynamite this infernal place!" our new lodger shouted.

He was eventually rescued from the underbrush, and the same staffers went to work unloading his luggage from the back of the truck. In near darkness, they hauled a steamer trunk, two Louis Vuitton suitcases, a Neiman Marcus garment bag, and three leather valises up a meandering path to the guest's assigned sleeping quarters. The tall, portly man followed his luggage up the trail, walking with the help of a silver-headed stick.

The fifteen platforms that comprised the sleeping quarters at Biscuit Shooters camp were identical in size and furnishings: a white canvas top draped eight feet above two cots, two small bedside stands, and a single kerosene lamp. The man saw his tent and balked.

"This is an insult!" he said, backing away. "Tell the billiard committee I sleep alone!"

A staffer got on his walkie-talkie, and soon a camp supervisor arrived on scene in a second golf cart.

The focal point of Biscuit Shooters was its bar, an open timber structure with three log cabin walls, a semicircular granite bar top, two dishwashers, a Sub Zero refrigerator, and a liquor inventory that would be the envy of any San Francisco nightclub. An original Picasso hung where, in most other taverns, you'd find a flat-screen TV.

The well-lit bar was a beacon in the night to the new lodger. Crossing the expansive deck, he tripped over a chaise and nearly went headlong into the stone fireplace. My instinct was to cut him off, but at Mount Hollow, such judgment calls were prohibited. I was staff, a bug in the dirt. I slept separately. I ate separately. Cell phones and e-mail were off-limits. As a condition of employment I'd been forced to sign a nondisclosure agreement. With my bank account hovering at zero, I needed the work.

The man settled on an end barstool. With critical eyes he scanned the lines of bottles behind me. His mouse-gray hair was neatly parted on one side. He had a head like a Clydesdale, a strong Roman nose, and prodigious jowls. I judged him to be in his late sixties.

"Welcome to Biscuit Shooters," I said. "You're Mr. Whitehead's guest. We've been expecting you."

"Where's that tosspot Billy?"

"Everyone's down at the evening program."

The man frowned. "I'll take a Tanqueray martini, up, bone-dry, with olives," he said. "And while you're at it, let's bring out the heavy artillery. How about a shot of that '63 Fonseca Port?

"Road dust," he added, by way of explanation. The diamonds in his pinkie ring twinkled as he gathered a fistful of cashews from the bowl before him and released them into his gaping mouth.

"Rough trip?" I said.

He made a grumpy face. "It's the port of call. Two days here will pickle my liver and lay me bare to hantavirus."

Two days? I pictured that mountain of luggage.

"I feel like I've been cudgeled with a polo mallet," he said.

Apparently the camp supervisor had the authority to reassign sleeping quarters. Beyond the deck I could make out the vague figures of two staff members emptying the tent of a Kansas City millionaire and moving the steamer trunk in.

"I make a point of knowing my bartenders," the man said. "You're new."

"My first summer here, Mr.—"

"Button. Horace Button." He extended a hand.

"I'm Jack," I said.

We shook across the bar. For a man with a fairy name he had a crushing handshake.

"So tell me, Jack, who's speaking at the amphitheater tonight?" Horace asked.

Did he really not know?

"Russell Rawlins," I said. "The U.S. senator."

Horace grunted. With the wave of a hand he dismissed the man who was determined to be the next leader of the free world. Russ Rawlins served as senate majority leader and was his party's presumed front-runner for the presidential nomination.

"Not your cup of tea?" I said.

"My boy, I enjoy many flavors of tea," Horace said. "But I have an aversion to swindlers of grandmothers." He raised the snifter of port in my direction, nodded starchily, and downed the contents in a single swallow. He banged the empty snifter on the bar.

I filled a silver shaker with gin. "You aren't what I'd expect of the dean of Harvard Divinity School."

Horace studied my ringless hands, and then he looked up at me with impish eyes. "A useful diversionary tactic I've developed through the years. It discourages harassment by Mormons and Dutch madams." He shifted on the barstool and squared his shoulders to me. "What about you, Jack? What's a strapper like you doing hidden away in Katmandu? You should be down in the Valley, chasing girls."

I shook the shaker until my fingers were numb with cold, smiling politely.

You don't care about my story.

You couldn't hold a candle to my story.

"Too busy looking after Mr. Whitehead and his friends," I said. I poured the thickened gin into a waiting martini glass and finished with a flourish—a snap of the wrist that reassured me I was in charge.

Horace brought the drink to his lips, took a long sip, and closed his eyes. Perhaps it was the wood smoke from the fireplace getting to him. It often drifted like a gray fog across the bar. He opened his eyes, and I became the object of his shrewd stare.

"I admire the diplomacy, Jack," he said, "but I'll warn you: the roaring campfires and old-growth forest bring out the inner Viking in these hyenas and jackals. I'd watch my back if I were you."

Prescient words.

TWO

"DON'T TELL BILLY," Horace said.

A box of cigars stood open on the bar counter. Horace filled the voluminous pockets of his hunting jacket and retired to a fireside chaise. In the hour since his arrival, I'd learned that he was a muckety-muck at the Western food, travel, and lifestyle magazine *Sunshine Trails*, the flagship of Billy Whitehead's publishing conglomerate.

A damp fog had blown in from the ocean, turning the night cold. Horace lay on the chaise, swaddled in a thick woolen blanket. He scribbled in longhand on a yellow legal pad, pausing every so often to gaze in thought at the embers swirling above the rock chimney. He and I had a tacit understanding—I kept the silver shaker next to him full of gin, and he attended to his writing without further demands. If he noticed my limp or the scar on my face he didn't mention it.

The camp was quiet. I leaned against the counter behind the bar and pulled a folded envelope from my back pocket, where I'd carried it for almost a year. I studied her name embossed on the back flap and below it the Palo Alto address I associated with her and with those heady days.

> Jack,
> I've received your letters, and I have purposely declined your calls. In fact, I am ambivalent about writing this letter, afraid you'll misinterpret its intention, yet at the same time quite concerned by the path you are on. I am petrified to think my inaction could hasten your distress. Perhaps it's egotistical to think my words could influence any human being, even someone to whom I was once engaged. If that's the case, I apologize for

wasting your time. But I fear you will do yourself harm. As I have said before, I think you should seek professional help.

From the direction of the amphitheater came shouts—the familiar din of boys being let out of school. I filled a glass with water and took a long drink. In a matter of minutes, I knew, Biscuit Shooters would be slammed.

The world doesn't care how fast you run or how many college records you hold—I certainly don't, and I never did. A lifetime of brain damage and crippling arthritis is a sickening price to pay for a temporary paycheck and some transitory adulation. You're still running, Jack—running from everything you ever stood for. The test of a real man is adversity and how he deals with it. I'm sorry for your pain and your loss, but I am also indebted to those two intruders, for they made me realize the terrible mistake I was making.

I have important things to accomplish—we're on this earth ever so briefly and I've been blessed with this magnificent opportunity. When the time is right I intend to settle down with a loving man. You are not that man. You are a self-absorbed, whimpering baby. Your self-induced morass is pitiful. I challenge you, Jack, to find your purpose in life. I can only hope that someday you will grasp the unselfish nature of love and learn to value someone's soul above your own.

May you move on and, in the process, find happiness and peace.

Please cease all further communication with me. I loathe the thought of seeking a restraining order against a man I once loved.

Sincerely,
Bianca James

The sounds of the revelers grew near. And then, like harbingers of a military action, men were stepping onto the deck, their faces ruddy from the uphill walk. In their ski parkas they looked inflated, like a scouting party of sausages.

I put the letter away.

Venture capitalists, celebrity lawyers, magnates of industry, editors, fiction writers, and the high-tech glitterati—they lined up four- and five-deep at the bar, laughing and shouting and reveling in their rollicking privilege. Drink orders came one on top of the other in the clipped monotones of serious boozers: "scotch soda"; "Goose rocks";

"bourbon splash." In this crowd, no one called for a sissy drink. Asking a bartender to take time to blend a margarita or muddle a mojito would've held up the line and, worse, identified the patron an amateur. Even with the straightforward drink orders I quickly found myself in the weeds.

Billy Whitehead, captain of the Biscuit Shooters camp, came behind the bar to lend a hand. He was in his forties, whey-faced and physically soft. In my two months at Mount Hollow I'd never seen Billy lift a finger to help anyone.

He called to me in a panic.

"Jack," he said, "why the hell are these club sodas so damn flat?"

He held a small, clear bottle.

"That's still water, Mr. Whitehead," I said. "The club sodas are behind you."

My good friend Dr. Henry Rose—he'd gotten me the job at Biscuit Shooters—also stepped behind the bar to help with the crowd. Dr. Rose was in his early eighties. His unruly white hair hinted at scientific genius, but making drinks for a legion of noisy strangers befuddled him. He began uncorking bottles of a big, rich Sonoma Zinfandel and pouring out glasses of wine. Someone said that one of his patients owned the winery.

I was passing two drinks across the bar when a voice called out, "Hiya, King Kong! How 'bout a double vodka tonic?" The crowd parted for a tall, elderly man in a yellow Lands' End ski jacket. At first I took him for just another loudmouth—he had laughably, beautifully coiffured white hair and the red face of a heavy drinker—but as my hands started working I looked again. Standing before me was Senator Russell Rawlins, featured Mount Hollow lecturer and possibly the next president of the United States.

The sycophants and bootlickers swarmed around him: "Bang-up job on the talk, Senator!"; "Right on all counts, Russ!" The senator autographed anything anyone put in front of him.

Billy pushed past me to shake the senator's hand. "Hey, terrific talk, Senator Rawlins. You knocked it out of the park." His outstretched arm hung over the bar like a malfunctioning gate at a railroad crossing.

Senator Rawlins glanced impatiently at the line behind him and told

Billy, "Listen, sport, there's a lot of thirsty guys out here. Let's get busy."

It wasn't often that the publisher and majority owner of a media empire was mistaken for a service worker. Billy's face suggested he might burst into tears.

A convivial drinker clapped Senator Rawlins on the back. "Wonderful talk, Russ. How long you staying on the mountain?"

"That depends," Senator Rawlins said. "I'll get back to you after I've experienced some of this legendary tail."

The men around him laughed boorishly. It was Mount Hollow's poorly kept secret: when the men of wealth and influence arrived at this Edenic spot each summer, they were closely followed by a posse of prostitutes who set up shop in rented cabins in small, nearby mountain towns like Ben Lomond and Bonnie Doon. A herd of men, I'd noticed, always headed down the hill around midnight. It was said that a line of taxis waited just outside the camp gate.

Word spread quickly that the senator was at Biscuit Shooters. The crowd swelled. I don't remember making another double vodka tonic for him, but I was working hard behind the bar, and if one of his minions had been sent to fetch another drink, it would have escaped my notice. I poured wine, I put up drinks, I tossed bottles into the well. An hour later another commotion swept across the deck. Senator Rawlins and his entourage were leaving.

"Wait, is that Horace Button I see?" Senator Rawlins said, stopping abruptly.

Horace was sitting at the end of the bar. He sipped his martini, eyes fixed straight ahead.

Senator Rawlins made his way over. "Hey, Horace, how's the gossip business?"

Horace cut the senator a curt glance. "I'll let you know if I hear anything."

"Oh, I forgot," Senator Rawlins said. "Operas, ballet, anything with men in tights—that's your specialty, right?"

Horace kept his gaze averted.

Senator Rawlins played to the crowd. He raised his head and looked around in mock bewilderment. "I'm confused. I thought they didn't allow bitches in this place."

Horace took another casual sip of gin.

With an icy smile, Senator Rawlins said, "Speaking of bitches, how's your sister? Still serving the cretins and hayseeds of Nevada?"

Horace set his drink down. "I wouldn't know. I avoid Washington these days. It has a bad stench."

Senator Rawlins jabbed an indignant finger at Horace's breastbone. "Next time you see her, tell her she's on the wrong side of this Al-Umer er Raisuli deal. Those people are reformers. They're all about education."

"Even if I saw her," Horace said, "I wouldn't dignify your lies."

"This administration's got it right. She'll see."

"It must be a terrible burden," Horace said. "Whoring yourself out for money, destined to be a footnote in history."

Senator Rawlins leaned in close to Horace. "Screw you, pal. You're the footnote in history. You're the biggest whore on this planet." He started to leave, and then turned back to Horace. "Know what's wrong with this country? Resources are scarce. People are fat. They need to cut back."

"Sell it to the nut jobs, Russ," Horace said. "You're delusional."

In a flash Senator Rawlins was upon Horace. He had him in a head-lock and was trying to wrench him off the barstool. Frantic shouts, toppled barstools clattering noisily on the concrete floor—the place erupted. Men were pushing and shoving, grabbing wildly at sleeves and shoulders. Glassware was swept to the floor and shattered at the feet of the scrum, which moved clumsily behind the bar. Under the pile, Horace raised his arms, fending off blows. I shouldered my way through the men and stripped Horace from the senator's grasp, at which time I had the honor of being punched in the throat by the senior senator from the great state of Rhode Island. A drunken, white-haired man throwing a haymaker is an embarrassing thing to see. He stays back on his heels and lands the hook with the force of a schoolgirl.

"You call that a punch?" I said.

"Asshole!" Senator Rawlins lunged at me.

I stiff-armed him. He wailed as he crumpled onto the rubber floor mat behind the bar. The puffy yellow jacket rode over his head like a duvet.

Suddenly I was staring down a multitude of gun barrels: pistols, shotguns, and at least one MP5 submachine gun. I should have challenged the bastards to shoot me on the spot.

"Collect your guy," I said to the resolute eyes behind the barrels, "and get out of my bar."

At half past eleven I was circulating around the empty deck, straightening patio furniture and gathering dirty glasses, when a golf cart skidded to a stop at the footbridge. A member of the camp staff delivered a note. I was to report to Major McCracken's office, in the log cabin next to the amphitheater, the next morning at eight o'clock sharp. Major McCracken was Mount Hollow's year-round general manager. Every employee reported to a supervisor. Every supervisor reported to a director. And all the directors reported to Major McCracken.

I ARRIVED AT MAJOR MCCRACKEN'S OFFICE five minutes early. He sat behind a heavy desk in the middle of a cold, dank room. Intent on ignoring me, he cleared his throat, and I took this as an invitation to sit in the chair across from him. I sat in silence and studied this solemn servant of the wealthy, marveling at his graceless manners. White-haired and sunburned, with wire-framed glasses, dressed in a khaki shirt and concentrating on the papers in the pool of light in front of him, he could have been a military general planning to invade a foreign country.

On the wall behind him a Bavarian cuckoo clock announced the hour. Major McCracken set down his pen, straightened his papers, and peeled off his glasses. He shifted in his chair and looked at me, and I understood instantly why the papers on his desk had commanded his full attention. His left eye was glass.

"Tell me I'm looking at Jack Marshall," Major McCracken said, focusing on me with his one good eye. "Jack Marshall from Biscuit Shooters."

I almost laughed. His left eye was trained on the floor behind me and appeared astonished, as if an enormous rat were sauntering into the room.

"Yes," I said, resisting the urge to look around. "Sir," I added.

"Can you guess why I called you here this morning?" Major McCracken said.

"I really don't know, sir."

Major McCracken leaned forward and narrowed his right eye at me. The left side of his face was as lifeless as his gaping eyeball. "My telephone rang at ten o'clock last night. Do you know who it was?"

"I have no idea."

"Senator Rawlins's chief of staff." Major McCracken's face turned crimson. "Do you know why he was calling?"

"I don't."

"The senator has a *lump* on his forehead, a *raspberry* the size of a *grapefruit*. This man was our guest and you assaulted him! Now he's walking around like a goddamned Greek Cyclops!" Major McCracken pounded the desk.

"With all due respect, sir," I said, "if I'd wanted to assault him, he'd be dead."

"Save the he-man stuff for someone else. You have no idea… last night… they damn near hauled you off to the penitentiary in chains!" Major McCracken's voice broke. He looked away. It took him a moment to regain his composure. "Now, son, do you want to guess again why you're here?"

"You're letting me go."

Major McCracken sat back and steepled his fingers. "That's right. I'm letting you go."

"For the record," I said, "I barely touched him."

"They wanted to press charges. This club intervened on your behalf." He eyed me venomously. "Now, as far as anyone's concerned, last night never happened. You're to keep your trap shut. You remember that, boy. Our membership roster is thick with lawyers. A word about this to anyone and we'll sue you till Holy Jesus and all hell come raining down on you from Big Muskie buckets. Here. Take it!"

He picked up an envelope and flung it at me. The envelope fluttered in the air, stalled, and fell to the floor beside my chair.

"I want you off this mountain within the hour," he said.

Inside the envelope was my final paycheck.

I WAS HEADING FOR MY TENT to pack up my things when Horace hailed me from the bar. He was sitting with Dr. Rose. They both wanted Bloody Marys. Dr. Rose was infuriated to learn I'd been fired, but Horace took perverse delight in hearing the details of my story.

"'Till Holy Jesus and all hell come raining down on you from Big Muskie buckets'?" Horace beamed. "He actually said that?"

"What's a Muskie bucket?" Dr. Rose asked.

"If memory serves me right it's the world's biggest steam shovel," Horace said. "Our good major must've been a Seabee."

"If that's the case then his steam shovel's full of crap," Dr. Rose said. "These people are about as enlightened as a grilled cheese sandwich. The irony is that a year from now, Major McCracken would probably be working for Jack."

"What makes you say that?" I said to Dr. Rose.

"We're spiritual beings, here to experience the gamut of what it means to be human," he said. "I know you, Jack. Once you find your dharma, there'll be no stopping you."

My dharma? I glanced skeptically at Dr. Rose. I found his New Age philosophy incomprehensible.

"A teaspoon of horseradish and a dollop of Grey Poupon," Horace said. "That a boy, Jack. Precision is the hallmark of a good bartender."

I set the Bloody Marys on the bar.

"This place is nothing but a giant outdoor men's can anymore," Dr. Rose said. "I'll tell you why it's gone downhill. Because the sons are never as interesting as the fathers."

"Yonder approaches Exhibit A,'" Horace said, nodding.

Billy Whitehead walked quickly toward the bar. He wore a white tennis sweater draped across his back, the arms tied loosely around his neck.

"Dammit, Jack. Why are you still here? And what did you say to piss off Major McCracken?"

"Dickens, Billy. You fired the bartender?" Horace said.

"Let's just say it was a high-level request."

"It's grossly unfair," Dr. Rose said. "Where do I lodge my complaint?"

"Don't bother, Henry," Billy said. "It's already settled."

"My God, Billy," Horace said. "This lad saved my life and you're casting him out like an old shoe."

Billy looked at me. "Really, Jack. You must gather your things and leave pronto. I don't understand why you're still behind that bar."

Horace said, "Remember, Billy, I have yet to file my summer dispatch from the Hollow."

"You'll think of something to write about, I'm sure."

"I hear a big-shot senator came to town. Anything interesting happen?"

Billy sized up Horace warily. "You wouldn't dare."

"'Slacker Senator Gets Bum's Rush from Saratoga Club Bar.' Has a good ring to it, don't you think?"

"That isn't funny."

"Rumble in the jungle. Intoxicated politico takes a fall in the first. Zigged when he should have zagged."

"Mother is a big supporter of Senator Rawlins."

"I don't work for your mother, Billy."

"No, but you work for me, and you'll leave the senator out of it. Last night was an aberration, a powerful man letting his hair down. The sooner we forget it, the better." Billy checked his wristwatch and sighed.

"You got a bus to catch?" Horace said.

Billy said, "I'm supposed to be down at the amphitheater, directing a rehearsal of Folies Bergère."

"That tiresome old rerun?" Horace said. "How many times can you ask people to sit through fat cats of industry dressed in drag?"

Billy gave Horace a loopy smile. "I still have some juicy roles to cast. Stay an extra day and I can make you the dowager Duchess of Marylebone."

"Tempting," Horace said. "But I'd rather be holed up on the *Pioneer Mother* with a case of whiskey and Wanda's cooking."

I looked at Horace.

Wanda?

Billy turned to me. "I need water and some aspirin."

"We can always recycle the story about the wild boar charging through the camp," Horace said. "Remember that one, Billy? How you single-handedly trapped the beast in a garbage pail and turned it over to the chef for a *cuissot de sanglier rôti?*"

I popped the cap on a bottle of aspirin and filled a Collins glass with water. I set them both on the bar in front of Billy.

"After this, Jack, promise me you'll leave," he said. "I gave the senator's chief of staff my word—"

"Or we can retell the story of the bees in the bathhouse," Horace said. "How all the members bolted for the door. Except for you, Billy. You had the presence of mind to throw a shower curtain over the whole swarming mess, and then you tiptoed wet and naked like a cunning Indian through the forest, and you set the hive loose on a rival camp. Our hero, Billy Whitehead. A man apart, the sum of all excellences, the life of every party—"

"All right, Horace. Cut it out." Billy popped the aspirin into his mouth.

"Only none of it was true, was it, Billy? Tell Jack. I'm your one-man press agency. Without me you wouldn't know a javelina from a mackerel, a *cuissot de sanglier rôti* from crêpes suzettes. You're a line jumper, a silver-spooner, the byproduct of an old man bending his secretary over a boardroom credenza."

"That's crude. I can't believe you sometimes."

"'The Accident.' Isn't that what they called you when you were eighteen and working in the mailroom?"

"Honestly, Horace. Must you be such an insufferable jackass?"

"It's you, Billy. You bring out the best in me. *Painus in the buttocks,* isn't that the medical term, Henry?"

"What makes me so mad is he didn't do anything wrong," Dr. Rose said. "There must be something we can do for poor Jack, here."

"I'll enjoy another excellent Bloody Mary," Horace said, signaling for a drink.

"I'm serious," Dr. Rose said. "He's getting a bum rap."

"I have the perfect solution," Horace said.

We all looked at Horace.

"The *Pioneer Mother* needs a bartender," Horace said. "What do you say, Billy? I suspect Jack has the chops for it."

"Wanda can handle it," Billy said quickly.

"Are you kidding? She'd need eight arms. She's a chef, not an octopus."

"This is no time to be adding overhead."

"You're determined to destroy everything your father and I ever built."

"Not destroy. Modernize."

"For God's sake, Billy. I've got a book coming out and a full calendar of events. We can't show up in Denver and start canceling my appearances for lack of manpower."

Billy hesitated.

"For once in your life, do the right thing," Horace said. "Give Jack the job. You'll get the hero's treatment in my dispatch from the Hollow. And I won't say a word about Russ Rawlins."

"Thinly disguised extortion."

"Quid pro quo. It's how the world works."

Billy looked from Horace to me and back to Horace.

"All right," Billy said. "But it's strictly temporary. No per diem, no benefits."

Triumphant, Horace turned to me. "What do you say, Jack? Major-domo on the *Pioneer Mother*?"

I didn't understand.

"A boat?" I said.

"A Pullman," Horace said. "Bartender on my private railroad car."

Billy checked his watch again and grimaced. "I should just cast a dozen strippers and be done with it."

"That's it!" Horace clapped once and pointed to Billy. "Your summer escapade. You'll smuggle in a posse of starlets posing as men masquerading as women, and you'll bring down the house with a racy burlesque number. I'll start drafting the column *tout de suite*. Orgy at the Hollow! The wives will howl! Your reputation will remain intact!"

Billy looked sick. "God help me. And God help *Sunshine Trails*."

Special to *Sunshine Trails*
"Window on the West," by Horace Button
"Dispatch from the Hollow"

SANTA CRUZ COUNTY, CA—Every summer, an iron veil of secrecy cloaks the goings-on at Mount Hollow, the Saratoga Club's posh mountain retreat, where the titans of industry, entertainment and affairs of state gather for an invitation-only, off-the-record bacchanalian debauch of monumental proportions. The seditious, scurrilous characters who compose the Club's membership are, after all, no strangers to the centaur in the mirror.

But for a feat of sheer moxie, the summer sweepstakes goes to our own Billy Whitehead, publisher and plenipotentiary of *Sunshine Trails* magazine, irrepressible prankster, most eligible bachelor and party host extraordinaire.

The details of the story are just beginning to emerge, but already it's got the afflicted socialites and rhinoplasty crowd of the Second Wives Club crying foul. And on this I must weigh in: there is merit to the home team's grievance.

Mount Hollow tradition is firm. No women allowed.

Our *enfant terrible*, Billy, never one to color inside the lines, has for the past several years been tapped to write and produce the Hollow's annual Folies Bergère, a stage extravaganza-cum-debacle featuring a questionable cast of Club members playing the roles of Roman spearmen,

Greek gods, marauding Vikings and Elizabethan-era queens. As the night progresses and Old Reprehensible takes its toll, it isn't uncommon to see a spear carrier or a marauding Viking take a tumble down the steep dirt hill that serves as upstage to the great outdoor amphitheater. Tradition dictates that the show always closes with a dancing pack of unsightly female impersonators.

Rules, as they say, are meant to be broken. In a brilliant and clandestine maneuver befitting a raid on Baghdad, our boy Billy imported a dozen starlets from San Francisco's Orpheum Theater, where they were appearing as the chorus in the award-winning Broadway stage musical *Mamma Mia!* Flaunting his considerable talent for turning the sublime into the ridiculous, Billy cast these comely starlets in the role of unsightly female impersonators.

Suffice it to say the curtain calls were nearly endless, once the members of the audience—standing room only, most of them stewed—realized the unclad girls cavorting on the stage and singing Abba songs were... well, girls. From the foggy peaks of the Santa Cruz Mountains you could hear my dearly departed friend and fellow *Sunshine Trails* cofounder, Lincoln Whitehead—Billy's proud papa—laughing from heaven.

The Rules Committee promptly fined Billy a case of Dom Pérignon, on general principle. They levied the stiff fine without delay, taking their proportionate shares within the confines of cut-crystal champagne flutes, which they carried up the hill to Billy's camp, Biscuit Shooters, where the post-Folies party raged. I am told the same dozen starlets, some quite undraped, served as the live patio entertainment, singing Broadway tunes till dawn.

At least, that's the rumor. Like any good guest of the Hollow, I'm keeping my head down on this one.

Signed,
Your ace reporter,
HB

AT 8:45 ON A MONDAY MORNING, I locked my pickup truck in the parking lot of a nondescript warehouse in San Jose. My duffel contained a week's worth of clothes, several ties, a blue blazer, and a crisp white waiter's jacket—American pima cotton, XXL, $65.

I found the old Pullman parked on a rail spur alongside the warehouse. She looked forlorn and out of place—a museum artifact shunted to a back lot for lack of development funds. Her name, *Pioneer Mother*, was painted along the sides in a bold serif font I've always associated with Wells Fargo. Her forest-green paint, black mansard roof, and Victorian architectural flourishes brought to mind a haunted house on wheels.

My steps slowed as I approached the railcar. I didn't need any more ghosts in my life.

A green-and-white striped canopy adorned the roof above the railroad car's rear platform. It gave the Pullman the air of a country club veranda—a place for drinking gin Rickeys and watching the world go by.

The open platform led to a heavy door. I grasped the handhold and mounted the first step.

"Hello," I said. "Anyone here?"

The door opened. A woman in a white chef's uniform stepped out. She wore a red bandana on her head and clutched a butcher knife. She looked to be in her late twenties—an older woman, in my book. She had green eyes and a pretty mouth.

"This is private property," she said.

"I'm Jack Marshall. I think you're expecting me."

She sized me up.

"You're early," she said.

The railcar's interior evoked an old Virginia City whorehouse: gilded mirrors, red velvet drapes, glass chandeliers. The gleaming mahogany woodwork smelled of teak oil. From a vent in the ceiling, a chilly breeze tousled my hair. We passed through the observation lounge, which had two sets of opposing parlor chairs, each pair of chairs separated by identical rosewood side tables and lamps. The formal dining table sat eight. A built-in breakfront was filled with mementos and books.

The cook was tall for a woman, made taller by her thick-soled kitchen clogs. The strands of hair sprouting from her bandana were dishwater blond. She invited me to have a seat at the table.

"Set your bag on the floor," she said, sitting at the head of the table. She wore no makeup that I could discern. The bridge of her nose contained a slight, irregular hump, as if it had once been broken. She kept the butcher knife in her lap.

"You got a résumé?" she said.

"Do I need one?"

"Call me old school. I like to know who's applying for the job."

Applying?

I walked her through my experience as a bartender: a few college bars around Palo Alto, a hotel bar in South San Francisco, the camp steward job at Mount Hollow.

"That the one that didn't end so hot?" The line of ballpoint pens in the pocket on her shoulder made her seem like my interrogator. Her eyes kept shifting to the scar on my face.

I shrugged. "Anyway. Here I am."

"What do you know about fine dining?"

I smiled. "I've eaten in a lot of nice restaurants."

"I've farted in denim," she said. "But that doesn't make me a rodeo cowboy."

I sat back and gazed at her, stifling a smile. "Look, I know my way around a bar. That seemed good enough for your boss."

"There's a lot more to this job than fixing drinks."

"Maybe you should take it up with Mr. Button. He made it pretty clear. I'm supposed to be the new majordomo."

"Majordomo?" She burst out laughing.

My face grew hot.

She said, "He was hammered, wasn't he?"

"Not necessarily," I said.

She narrowed her eyes. "Discreet. Good quality in a bartender. Especially around this madhouse."

Wanda Nordquist was her name. The job, she said, was mine.

"Don't read a lot into it," she said. "Let's just say your timing is right."

My tour of the old Pullman began with the walk-behind bar. Three leather barstools faced forward. From my post behind the bar I had a clear view of the dining table and observation lounge. Through the wide picture windows I surveyed the panorama around the railcar: the windowless walls of the warehouse; the rusty railroad track that curved through the industrial park; the tanks and towers of the Oberski & Martin asphalt plant.

"How old is this thing?" I said.

"Originally built in 1932," Wanda said. "She's had four different owners, including a Vanderbilt. *Sunshine Trails* bought it in the early seventies. Nixon used it once for an Army-Navy game."

"Does it take a lot of upkeep?"

"There's always another project. Last year we upgraded the appliances and installed the new bar counter."

I ran my hand over the granite surface of the bar. I inspected the small refrigerator, dishwasher, and wine chiller beneath the bar top. They looked new.

"No ice maker?" I said.

"We get our ice from Amtrak," Wanda said. "It's in the contract. Here, I'll show you the galley."

A side-by-side refrigerator, a four-burner propane stove, a convection oven—it all fit into an area the size of a walk-in closet. Storage lockers ran up to the ceiling.

"You actually cook in here?" I said.

"Three meals a day."

A pass-through window linked the galley to the bar.

"I cook, you serve, we both clean," she said. "That's how it works."

She showed me the linen cabinet. Great stacks of neatly folded white cloth packed the shelves.

"Everything we do here is white tablecloth, no exceptions," she said. "Breakfast, lunch, and dinner."

I caught a whiff of the fresh linen: orange blossom and jasmine. Or was that Wanda's fragrance?

A narrow hallway led to the rest of the railcar. I had to turn at an angle and duck a shoulder to keep from knocking the glass sconces off the wall.

"This is our powder room," Wanda said, opening the first door. The powder room was small and clean, done in a white and black-veined marble.

"Elegant," I said.

"And Mr. Button's stateroom…" Wanda opened the next door. The walls of the small bedroom were intricately trimmed in bird's-eye marquetry. A queen-size bed was shoehorned against one wall. Next to the bed stood a built-in writing desk with an old IBM Selectric type-writer on it. The stateroom had its own private lavatory.

"Does he use the typewriter?" I said.

"All the time," Wanda said. "As a general rule you'll find Mr. Button doesn't interact with anything manufactured since 1985. That goes for people, too. He has an intense aversion to children."

"And no TVs?"

"Strictly forbidden. His only surrender to technology has been satellite radio. He likes background music with his meals—classical, mostly."

Wanda opened the next door. "Here's our community shower."

The walk-in shower was ornamented in a magnificent gold tile. A carved Louis XVI vanity and a wooden dressing bench were situated on the wall opposite the shower.

"Stunning," I said.

"I shower at night, you shower in the morning. Mr. Button has exclu-sive use of the shower between eight in the morning and eight at night.

It's one of his quirks. He sometimes showers twice a day."

"Sobering up?"

"That and washing off the grit and soot from the tracks. He spends a lot of time out on the open platform while we're running. It gets pretty dirty out there."

She opened the next door. "Our guest stateroom..."

The room was a mirror image of Horace's bedroom—without the typewriter on the writing desk.

"Do you get many guests?"

"I've been here two years. Mr. Whitehead has done a handful of trips. Mr. Button's physician, Dr. Rose, probably does one or two trips a year."

"I know Dr. Rose."

"Nice old guy. Anyway, he and Mr. Whitehead are the exceptions. For the most part, Mr. Button is very protective of his privacy. He's like a cat."

"I've heard of private jets and yachts," I said. "But never a private railroad car."

"A yacht's the best comparison," Wanda said. "Only we go pretty much anywhere Amtrak goes." She opened the last door off the hallway. "Crew's quarters. This is you and me, Majordomo."

In train talk it was called a double bedroom, but in reality it was as Spartan and tightly packed as its moniker was airy and spacious. A small sofa converted into a bed at night. From the looks of it I couldn't sit on the sofa and stretch out my legs without meeting the upholstered bulkhead that constituted the far wall. A second bed—mine—dropped on a track from above and became the upper berth.

"We're supposed to share this?"

"Only to sleep. Go in."

I had to be careful where I placed my feet. Wanda's duffel bag lay on the floor, unzipped and spilling clothes. Wanda entered the bedroom behind me and shut the door, revealing the door to a private lavatory. She opened that door and clicked a silver toggle switch. A light flickered and then came on. The lav was little more than a heavy stainless steel wash basin suspended above a toilet, all squeezed into a space the size of a phone booth. It appeared too narrow for me to even stand in.

"Are you kidding?" I said.

"You'll get used to it," Wanda said. She showed me how pressing the small silver paddles on either side of the sink brought hot or cold water to the faucet. She also showed me how tipping the wash basin up and stowing it in the wall emptied water from the bowl and made the toilet accessible. A push button triggered the toilet to flush.

"Pretty slick engineering," I said. "For 1932."

"Make a habit of closing the lid before you flush," Wanda said. "It's a pretty powerful system. It can come back in your face. You'll only make that mistake once."

She stepped back into the bedroom and opened the door to a narrow cabinet recessed into the wall next to the sofa. "This is our closet." It was already crammed with clothes—hers. "Feel free to hang your stuff," she said. "Whatever fits."

I glanced at the door to the hallway—my escape route. In a mirror on the back of the door I saw Wanda studying me.

"And you're okay with this?" I said, turning to face her. "Sharing a bedroom with a complete stranger?"

"It's not so bad," she said. "With the hours we work, we actually spend very little time in here. If you have time to sleep, believe me, you'll want to sleep."

A laptop computer sat on the floor next to Wanda's duffel.

"Is this your computer?" I said.

Her face hardened. "It belongs to the magazine. It serves a very specific purpose."

"What's that?"

"It's none of your business. So I'd appreciate if you keep your hands off it."

"Sorry. Didn't mean to pry."

"On the road Mr. Button maintains a precise schedule. Breakfast at nine. Lunch at one. He naps from two to three. The first cocktail is always served at six o'clock sharp. Dinner is after eight. Then he retires to the lounge, usually for cognac and a cigar. These are hard trips. Be prepared to work a lot of late nights."

"Do you enjoy being stuck on this thing?"

"I enjoy meeting exceptionally high standards and getting paid for it. Not necessarily in that order. All right, Majordomo. Quiz time. The oyster fork. You're setting the table. Which side does it go on?"

I didn't have a clue.

"Trick question," I said. "It goes on top."

Wanda rolled her eyes. "Just what I was afraid of. You and I have a lot of work to do. And very little time."

SEVEN

WE STOOD ON THE RAILROAD CAR'S open platform. Wanda closed the door, locked the dead bolt, and set an alarm. With the thick ring of keys in her hand she could have been my jailer.

After more than two hours of cleaning bathrooms, mopping and vacuuming floors, and polishing mahogany, that's what my time on the *Pioneer Mother* was beginning to feel like—a jail sentence.

"Where you from originally, Majordomo?" Wanda said.

"Midland, Texas."

"Good work ethic."

"Thanks," I said. "What about you? Where're you from?"

"That's a hard one to answer. Come on. I'll show you the warehouse."

Under the hot midday sun I followed Wanda down a dirt path to the warehouse adjacent to the tracks. She opened a side door. Inside the cool building, she punched a code into a keypad, disarming the security system, and turned on the lights high above us.

"We keep this as a depository for supplies," Wanda said. "It also serves as a base of operations for the crew and provides power to the railcar while she's in storage."

I had come full circle. I was back at the janitor's shed of my teenage years: the mops and brooms; the open shelves of cleaning products; behind a thick wire screen, the dusty shop with its long workbenches, table saws, and metal lathes. At the front of the warehouse, beyond a series of dry storage lockers, were three small offices. Wanda unlocked the door to her office and turned on the fluorescent lights. Her desk was neat and well-organized, attended by a black task chair on casters. A bookcase filled with cookbooks stood against a wall. The rectangular window provided an unobstructed view of the warehouse floor.

Wanda went to the desk and turned on a reading lamp. "Just give me a few minutes," she said. "Then we'll hit the road."

"Mind if I look around?" I said.

"Help yourself."

I soon saw why the building had a state-of-the-art alarm system.

One dry storage locker contained an astonishing supply of top-shelf liquor. A climate-controlled wine room, kept at a constant 55 degrees, held at least two dozen cases of rare wines: French Sauternes, Grand Cru Burgundies, red Bordeaux—two cases of Château Lafite-Rothschild — some Napa Valley Cabernets and Russian River Chardonnays. Stacked cases of champagne reached nearly to the ceiling.

Beyond the wine room a cedar-paneled walk-in humidor held at least a dozen boxes of expensive cigars: Cohibas, Davidoffs, Arturo Fuentes, Romeo y Julietas. The cigars I saw were from the Dominican Republic or Nicaragua. I looked for Cuban cigars, but none of the boxes said *Habana*.

"Impressed?" Wanda said, when I returned to her office.

"Amazing."

"We'll pull the wines and the liquor after we get the shopping done."

I sat in a visitor's chair while Wanda finalized her shopping lists. I studied her profile, trying to picture her in a cocktail dress or a bathing suit. Seeing beyond the shapeless white chef's jacket tested my imagination.

I scanned the office for clues about her personal life. Except for a whiteboard listing work orders for the railcar, the walls were bare. Two framed pictures sat on the bookcase. The larger of the two was a photo of Wanda and Horace standing on the open platform of the *Pioneer Mother*. They looked happy. The other picture, much smaller, was a black and white photo of a young man. He stared past the camera with a serious expression. He had slicked-back hair and wore a natty suit.

"Was your grandfather an immigrant?" I said.

Wanda stopped writing and looked up.

"My grandfather?"

"That old picture on the bookshelf. Is that your grandfather?"

Wanda glanced at the photo and then back to me.

"Oh, no," she said. "That's just Max—back when he was young."

"Who's Max?"

"Long story. Another time, maybe."

She put down her pen, closed the last cookbook, and switched off her light. She tossed me a set of keys. "Let's hit it, Majordomo. You drive. I'll tell you where to go."

Her Jeep Cherokee was parked in front of the warehouse, near my pickup.

For the next two hours we crisscrossed the city of San Jose, stocking up on provisions. Wanda was no pushover when it came to dealing with the meat, seafood, and produce vendors. She rejected mussels for their cracked shells, oregano leaves for not having been freshly dried on the branch, and frogs' legs for being too big.

"Big frogs' legs?" I said. "Is that a problem?"

"The intensity of the flavor diminishes as the legs grow larger," Wanda said. She got the attention of the Vietnamese proprietor behind the counter by tapping a finger on a corner of the white butcher paper that held the frogs' legs.

"Smaller, Sang," she said. "You must have some that are smaller."

Sang hurried over, nodding. "Sure, sure, smaller."

Many of the vendors inquired about Wanda's famous client. Clearly, they took pride in satisfying Horace Button's personal chef. I followed Wanda in and out of markets, up and down the aisles, pushing the grocery carts. She worked her way through her lists. I lugged the provisions out to the Jeep in heavy cardboard boxes.

We stopped for lunch at a storefront Mexican restaurant in a strip mall. Wanda had me keep the engine running and the air conditioning on full blast as we ate our fish tacos over the hood of the Jeep—our rolling refrigerator.

"Good lunch," I said.

"Enjoy it," Wanda said. "You won't taste Mexican like this until we're back in California." A piece of shredded cabbage peeked from a corner of her mouth. She wiped it away with a thin paper napkin. "So, Majordomo, you married?"

"Engaged." I flinched at the sound of my own lie. "It's been called off, actually."

"Cold feet?"

"Hers, not mine."

"Think she'll come around?"

"Maybe. Hope so."

Wanda shifted her gaze to the four-lane boulevard, where an articulated city bus was pulling away from a bus stop.

"What about you?" I said. "Married?"

"No. Almost engaged at one point," she said. "But also called off."

"What happened there?"

Her eyes darkened suddenly. She looked away and brought the napkin quickly to her mouth. "If you don't mind, I'm not prepared to get into it right now."

So there you had it. She didn't want to talk about her personal life any more than I wanted to discuss mine.

Fine with me. Considering the close quarters of the old Pullman, it was easy to see that an indiscreet, gabby co-worker would be intolerable.

Our destination was Denver—the North American Food and Wine Literary Festival. *Sunshine Trails* was a major sponsor of this annual, end-of-summer event. On our calendar were two dinner parties, several breakfast and lunch meetings, the filming of an interview with a national newsmagazine show, and, on our last night, a post-midnight champagne reception. That would follow a tribute dinner in Horace's honor, recognizing him for his groundbreaking work and its impact on the contemporary food and wine scene. The dinner was being held at the literary festival's host hotel, the Grand Harvey.

By five o'clock we had the railcar fully stocked. We were running on generator power, waiting for the Union Pacific yard locomotive that would move us to a special interchange point, where we'd be attached to the night's northbound Amtrak train and taken to the Oakland yard.

Wanda made the most of our downtime by drilling me on the dos and don'ts of formal table service.

"Serve from the left, clear from the right," she said. "Keep your body open to the guest. Avoid showing the back of your hand. As you serve the entrée, rotate the plate until the protein is at six o'clock." She turned a dinner plate clockwise until her hand was at the six o'clock position. The dinner plate was an original piece from the Twentieth Century Limited, a famous steam-era flyer that ran between New York and Chicago. I'd later learn that Horace was a collector of fine china from historic passenger trains.

"When pouring water, never touch the lip of the water pitcher to the rim of the guest's glass," Wanda said. "Clear by the course and never until everyone has finished eating. Touch only the stems of stemware and the handles of flatware. When serving coffee, position the handle loop at four o'clock to the guest."

"Are you serious?" I said. "Who cares where the coffee cup points?"

"I care," Wanda said.

My lesson was cut short when a Union Pacific locomotive loomed in the back window.

A barrel of a man wearing clear safety goggles, a blue hard hat, and a loose Pendleton over a dirty T-shirt entered the observation lounge. The trainman conferred with Wanda. I followed him out to the open platform and watched, transfixed, as the crew coupled the locomotive to our old Pullman.

Wanda called me inside and we walked to the head-end of the railroad car, where she showed me how to release the hand brake, a chain-and-lever mechanism in the vestibule.

"Any questions, Majordomo?"

"Do you always wait until we're hooked to the engine, or can you do it before?"

"Always after. If you release it before and the coupling isn't good, we'll go flying down the track like a billiard ball."

I monitored our departure from the open platform.

The engine's horn sounded and we began to move.

In an instant, my apprehension about being stuck aboard this rolling crucible vanished in the wake of my childlike excitement. The wooden railroad ties creaked under our old Pullman's heavy trucks. We picked up speed. The familiar landmarks of the *Sunshine Trails* warehouse and the Oberski & Martin asphalt plant receded in the distance. The tall locomotive swayed from side to side. Dusty wind whipped my face.

Wanda summoned me inside. "Enough loafing, Majordomo. Time for your next lesson." She had already draped a white linen tablecloth over the dining table.

"Setting the table is really very simple if you always follow the same routine," she said. "Put the plates down in this order: dinner plate, salad plate, bread plate." She set down plates as she spoke. "The napkin, properly folded, goes in the center of the dinner plate, like this. Next, the forks and spoons. You should place the knives and forks so the ends of their handles are aligned exactly one inch from the edge of the table." She used the pad of a thumb to measure the inch. She wore no rings on her slender fingers. She held up a small fork with three curved tines. "This is the oyster fork. It goes to the right of the dinner plate, outside the soup spoon. Remember that. Mr. Button likes his oysters." She arranged the remaining utensils at the top of the table setting. "Bread knives and dessert spoons point left. The dessert fork points right."

"Is this an open-book test?"

She looked at me sternly. "Don't get smart. Mr. Button boards first thing in the morning. This is probably the most demanding trip of the year, and I can't afford to have you screwing it up."

By pointing a dessert fork in the wrong direction? For a man who swigs Pérignon Cuvée from a magnum and falls backward into canyons?

I bit my tongue.

"Stemware goes left to right in this order"— she began placing glasses across the table —"water glass, red wine, white wine, cordial, champagne flute." She looked like a croupier putting down markers on a craps table.

I was concentrating on the dizzying array of fine china, flatware, and crystal stemware on the table in front of me, trying to memorize the whole complicated arrangement, when a lurch of the railcar caught me by surprise. I pitched into Wanda. She reached for the table but grabbed the tablecloth instead. Together with the entire table setting, we crashed to the floor. I landed on top of her amid a debris field of shattered glass and broken china. Her firm breasts pressed against my chest. Our legs lay intertwined.

Mortified, I held my breath.

"Touch me like this ever again," Wanda said, "and I'll put you in my rabbit stew."

EIGHT

ON THE BACK OF AMTRAK'S COAST STARLIGHT, making the fast nighttime run up the East Bay to the Oakland yard, the *Pioneer Mother* pitched and rolled like a carnival ride. I was doubtful anyone could serve drinks under these conditions—being jolted side to side and jounced into walls.

I looked at Wanda with dismay. "Is it always going to be like this?"

"You'll get your sea legs soon enough. Can you tuck in that corner for me?"

The black window mirrored the scene we carried out in Horace's brightly lit stateroom. We tucked in the high-thread-count Egyptian cotton sheets and spread the Nepalese cashmere blanket. We unfurled the French tile bedspread and smoothed it with our hands. Wanda made a mountain of heirloom silk eiderdown pillows. She held up a leopard-print cushion trimmed with gold frill.

"Off or on?" she said.

"Definitely on."

"You don't think it's too tacky?"

"Too tacky?" I said. "For the king's bedchamber at the Palace of Versailles?"

"Good point," Wanda said. The cushion went on as the focal point of the bed.

The wild luxury of Horace's master stateroom was in stark contrast to our double bedroom, three doors down the hall. With the upper and lower berths deployed, it resembled a jail cell.

After the beds were made, after the lavs and the communal shower were fully loaded with bath and facial soaps, hand and body lotions, and clean washcloths and towels, I turned my attention to stocking the bar. Reeling down the narrow hallway from the forward equipment locker, liquor bottles pressed to my chest, I gripped the handrail with my free hand.

We were too far back in the train to hear the engine's horn, and the grade crossings came and went suddenly, streaks of red light flashing in the windows followed by the faint tinkling of warning bells. I had to take a wide stance behind the bar as I filled the wine chiller.

At ten o'clock, coming to rest in the middle of an Oakland street near Jack London Square, we made our last stop before the railroad yard. I took a break from my bar setup duties and went out to the platform to have a look. In the dim light, a handful of people stepped from the long train. A few others boarded. It was a short stop.

Moments later, we rounded a curve and arrived under the white lights of the Amtrak yard. A crew of six trainmen with hard hats and flashlights directed the Amtrak switch engine that took us off the Coast Starlight. The engine drew us perhaps a quarter mile down the track to a series of turnouts, where we switched three tracks over and entered the Union Pacific yard. A long line of boxcars sat parked on an adjacent track. Standing on the open platform, I caught a whiff of salty air off the bay. In a gap between cars I could see the enormous cranes of the Port of Oakland, and across the bay, beneath a thick blanket of fog, the lit skyline of San Francisco.

The rail yard bustled with locomotives pulling long trains of double-stack containers. As the locomotives passed, the low rumble of their power plants shook our windows like tremors from an earthquake. The blasts of their air horns were earsplitting.

By midnight we were finally ready to receive our important passenger. Wanda announced she was going to bed.

"Get some sleep, Majordomo," she said. "You'll need it."

I was too exhilarated to turn in—I kept returning to the open platform to watch the moving trains.

My sister, Libby, was just starting her sophomore year at West Texas

A&M University. I had told her I signed on as bartender aboard a private railcar, but that was before I saw the *Pioneer Mother*. I decided to send her a picture. I knew its archaic implausibility would make her laugh.

I moved like a trespasser, leaping from the open platform's bottom step into darkness, carefully negotiating the rocky ballast of the railroad bed. I traversed the hard dirt trough of the sub-grade and crossed the next track, lurching ever-forward on my bum leg. Two tracks over was enough distance to get a good profile shot of the *Pioneer Mother*. Using my cell phone, I framed the photo. The windows of the railcar radiated butter-colored light, and the misty silver sky threw into relief the horizon of her roof and the comical shape of the kitchen stovepipe that punched through.

I snapped the picture.

Suddenly, I was bathed in a wall of bright light. A train bore down on me, blasting its horn. I froze. The intensity of the headlight and the multiple turnouts in the track made it impossible to discern which track the train was on. It appeared to be heading straight toward me. I found my legs and was ready to bolt, but another blast of the horn shocked me into indecisiveness. The train passed on the track between me and the *Pioneer Mother*. Had I broken for the old Pullman I would have been dead.

Back aboard the railcar, with trembling hands, I texted the picture to Libby with the message, "Stuck aboard this relic, doing my penance…" I nearly sent the same photo to Bianca, to update her on this latest development in my life, but, out of respect for her wishes, I left her alone.

Ready for sleep, I went through the late-night routine Wanda had delineated: I locked the back door, lowered all the window shades, and turned out the lights. In the powder room I changed into running shorts and a T-shirt.

Carrying my clothes under one arm, I opened the door of our double bedroom, letting in a trickle of light. Wanda slept on her stomach on the lower berth, her elbows at sharp angles on either side of her pillow, her hair a wild mass. A rickety ladder bisected both beds. I latched the door behind me, found myself steeped in darkness, and pitched my clothes in the general direction of my duffel.

At the top of the ladder, the trick was to pivot my hips onto the mattress without hitting my head on the ceiling. With two titanium rods in my lower back and a dozen screws holding my pelvis together, it was a difficult maneuver. I swung a leg off the last step, felt a sharp jab, slammed my head against the ceiling, swore, and collapsed painfully onto the narrow bed. The mattress sagged and the springs squeaked.

"Jesus, Majordomo, are you doing calisthenics up there?" Wanda said.

"It's like sleeping in a damn sarcophagus."

"You're here to work, not bellyache."

I lay on my back in the darkness, not knowing how to respond. Her gumption made me smile.

"I wasn't bellyaching," I said.

NINE

Special to *Sunshine Trails*
"Window on the West," by Horace Button
"The Roosevelt-Savoy Grill"

SAN FRANCISCO—Since its early days doing business as Roosevelt's Oyster Bar, on stilted legs above the waterfront, the venerable Roosevelt-Savoy Grill, now found in the heart of San Francisco's financial district, has been the indisputable linchpin of this city's fine-dining establishments.

On occasion this reporter's professional obligations include the necessity to revisit such hallowed grounds of gustatory endeavor as the Roosevelt in order to ensure its historically high standards have been kept in good repair. One recent night, having suffered the ignorant vulgarity of yet another restaurant opening perpetrated on a guileless public by a so-called "celebrity" chef, I rewarded myself with a late-night audit of the Roosevelt Grill.

My glum spirits were immediately buoyed by the low lighting, glossy wood floors and crisp white tablecloths. Tuxedoed waiters delivered bottles of Bollinger extra brut to the dining room in beaded silver ice buckets. King-size martinis were lined up along the celebrated mahogany bar.

Caesar salads are prepared tableside, as they should be, and the Roosevelt's timeless menu includes oysters Rockefeller, seafood cioppino and a steak au poivre guaranteed to unloose in your head a full orchestral version of Gershwin's "Rhapsody in Blue."

Sadly, I have one flaw to report, a crack in the substructure of this iconic institution that can only be attributed to the steady march toward lassitude that comes with the passing of time and, thanks to a bush-league University of California system, a plethora of graduates holding superficial, liberal arts degrees. In the Roosevelt's dining room, gentlemen are no longer required to wear jackets.

Signed,
Your ace reporter,
HB

THE NEXT MORNING THE CALIFORNIA ZEPHYR left the Oakland yard thirty minutes late. Indignant, the train conductor blamed me.

"These horseshit extra switching moves cost us precious time," he said. His thick black beard, navy blue uniform jacket, and boxy black-billed cap gave him the look of an old Trotskyite. I stood with him on the tracks behind the train, where he visually inspected the *Pioneer Mother*'s red marker lights. Until he confirmed they were working, the Zephyr couldn't leave the yard. "You got a manifest for me? How many people on this thing, and where are they getting on?"

Wanda had equipped me with the required form.

"Picking up one passenger," I said, handing the sheet of paper to the conductor. "In Emeryville."

"Tell him I've got two hundred being inconvenienced."

By this time the sun was burning through the fog. The conductor started walking toward the front of the train. He stopped and turned back to me.

"Don't get me wrong," he said. "I like these old railroad cars as much as anyone, but they have no business operating in this day and age."

At Emeryville, Horace stood far removed from the crowd. He wore a derby hat and leaned on his silver-headed stick. He smiled fleetingly at the sight of the old Pullman. An Amtrak Red Cap waited beside a baggage cart overflowing with the same mountain of luggage I'd seen at Mount Hollow.

I watched our arrival from the *Pioneer Mother*'s open platform.

As the train's brakes squealed and we slowed to a stop, I raised the trap-door and let down the steps.

"Morning, Jack," Horace said. "Be with you momentarily."

A sea of passengers streamed for the coach and sleeper cars ahead of us. They dragged their rolling suitcases, backpacks, and picnic coolers behind them.

The Red Cap, a squat Pacific Islander, called me "sir." He lifted Horace's bags up to the open platform, and I stacked them inside the door. Meanwhile, Horace made his way up the full length of the train, stopping to say a few words to each uniformed car attendant along the way. At the forward-most locomotive Horace called something up to the engineer's cab. The engineer stuck his head out the window and said something back. Horace gave a hearty laugh and rapped his walking stick twice on the side of the towering locomotive. He turned and started back toward the *Pioneer Mother*.

I paid the Red Cap to bring me a copy of the morning newspaper. Horace had already tipped him liberally for the bags.

Inside the Pullman, I ferried Horace's luggage up the narrow hall-way to his stateroom. I put the suitcases on the bed, which Wanda had covered with a protective woolen blanket.

"Underwear, socks, and handkerchiefs go in the top drawer," she said from the doorway behind me. "Undershirts and pajamas in the second drawer, shoes and sweaters in the closet. Ties, suits, shirts—everything else hangs."

"What do I do with the briefcases?" I said.

"You can leave them on the floor by the desk. And be careful. One probably has a loaded gun."

"A gun?" I said. "What kind of a gun?"

"I don't know. A little one."

"A pistol?"

"Teeny-weeny. Like what a poker player keeps in his pocket."

"A derringer?"

"That's it."

"Why would he carry a loaded derringer?"

"He says it's in case anyone ever tries to make him drink milk."

I was standing at the master stateroom closet, hanging the last of Horace's shirts, when the train jolted forward and began to move. I parted the window curtains above the writing desk and looked out.

We were skirting the shoreline of San Francisco Bay. A stiff breeze propelled waves across the turquoise water, and seabirds darted above the whitecaps. We passed half-submerged knots of pilings—remnants of abandoned piers. I stepped into the hallway and looked out at the lee side of the tracks. I saw the patchy lawns, rusty swing sets, and concrete slabs of residential backyards. At crossings, behind lowered gates, grim-faced drivers sat in idling cars.

Soon the train was moving too fast to process the particulars of any one house. And then suddenly the scenery turned industrial: junkyards with their heaping piles of scrap; warehouses with broken windows and rusty corrugated roofs; self-storage facilities with dumpsters overflowing; and everywhere fleets of forklifts, delivery vans, and semi-trailers parked in dry dirt lots surrounded by razor wire fences. Occasionally someone stopped working and stared at the passing train.

I found Horace in the sun-drenched observation lounge. He occupied the parlor chair nearest the door. His walking stick had been deposited in an umbrella stand, his derby hat relegated to a rosewood side table. He stared at the passing bay, his eyes glazed, his face tinged with floating patches of red.

"Good walk?" I said.

"Let's set the ball rolling, Jack. What's on the champagne card?" With an embroidered handkerchief he dabbed at beads of sweat on his forehead.

I had a bottle of Taittinger on ice. I served the champagne in a cut crystal flute, which I delivered to Horace on a tray. To keep the champagne flute from toppling over, I pressed my thumb hard against the foot of the glass.

Horace downed the champagne in two quick swallows.

As suddenly as the train had started, it began to slow.

"Richmond," Horace said. "Keep your head down."

Thirty minutes later the California Zephyr was making the sweeping curve onto the Benicia-Martinez railroad bridge. On such broad curves

I could look out and see the head-end of our train: two silver-and-blue locomotives belching smoke; a windowless baggage car; eight double-deck Superliner cars behind it. The railroad bridge ran parallel to the highway bridge, which soared high above the waters of Carquinez Strait.

By this time, Horace sat eating breakfast at the dining table while Beethoven's Symphony No. 5 played on the satellite radio.

The smoked Scottish salmon, eggs Sardou, and hot french bread were the warm-up act. In the galley Wanda drizzled *béarnaise* sauce over baby lamb chops. She topped the plate with an enormous pile of matchstick fries.

"French fries?" I said. "For breakfast?"

"Not french fries. *Pommes allumettes.*"

"Are you trying to kill him?"

"My job isn't to keep him alive. It's to keep him happy." Wanda handed me the plate. "Here, take this out."

I managed to serve Horace his lamb chops and *pommes allumettes* without dumping them in his lap.

From my post behind the bar I kept a close eye on my charge. For the lamb chop course, Horace went to a ten-year-old Châteauneuf-du-Pape. I refilled his wine glass whenever it got below half full, and I brought new fluted ramekins of *béarnaise* sauce and more bread when he ran low.

"Would you like to see this morning's *Chronicle*, Mr. Button?"

Horace looked at me and frowned. He blotted a hunk of bread over a yellow splash of *béarnaise* on his plate.

"Sure. Why not?" he said. "Let's see what the society ladies are up to with their leaf blowers and garden parties."

He opened the newspaper and studied it for a moment.

"I see the redistributionist bureaucracy is at it again," he said. "They take us for a nation of sheep." Then: "The final straw, Jack. The cheeky bastards have banned cigar smoking in public places—now they want to take away our *foie gras.*"

The next thing I knew a section of newspaper came flying across the lounge. It hit the wall with a loud splat and fluttered like a wounded bird to the floor.

"I can't stand it!" Horace said. "These liars should be lined up and shot!"

"Did I miss something?" I said. I'd just scanned the front page of that same paper.

"Don't show me another newspaper the rest of this trip," Horace said. "Not one more word about those imbeciles in Washington!"

I tried offering him other sections of the newspaper, but he waived them off.

There was nothing for me to do but to keep pouring Châteauneuf-du-Pape.

ELEVEN

ON A LONG, STRAIGHT STRETCH OF CAUSEWAY approaching Sacramento, California, the railroad runs parallel to Interstate 80. For drivers on the highway that Tuesday morning in August, the old Pullman hitching a ride on the back of the California Zephyr must have seemed an oddity—an antique running at breakneck speed, hanging on for dear life, looking frilly and absurd as if some time-traveler's experiment had gone horribly wrong.

The *Pioneer Mother* was no more anachronistic or improbable than its demanding passenger, but tending bar aboard this vintage railcar suited me. For once, I was free to reflect on ground covered without guilt or self-rebuke. I relished seeing the endless thread of receding, creosote-stained track, the golden rolling foothills and heavily forested canyons east of Sacramento, the tunnels that plunged us into blackness and then yielded us, just as suddenly, into bright sunlight. With each passing mile, I was shedding my incriminatory past as a snake sheds its skin.

In the serpentine curves of the Sierra Nevada Mountains, hugging sheer granite cliffs, the train slowed to a crawl. Then, on Donner Pass, we cleared a long snow shed and came to a dead stop. We sat for nearly an hour under a chairlift at the deserted Sugar Bowl Ski Resort, where high weeds and blue lupine flowers overgrew the detached chairs that were scattered haphazardly around the bottom terminal of a lift. Frequent stops for no apparent reason, slowdowns on extended stretches of track, long-drawn-out delays on sidings while waiting for an oncoming train to pass—these things did not bother me, but they drove Wanda mad.

"Who the hell's operating this thing?" she said. "A stoned sloth?"

Working behind the stoves in the cramped galley, Wanda's trains always ran on time. She could flawlessly choreograph a four-course meal without seeming to think about it, but you wouldn't know it by the way she trash-talked her work.

"Dog vomit," she said, poking at the sauce *béarnaise*. "Monkey piss," she said, dipping a finger into a pot of consommé Julienne. "Regurgitated hog maw," she said, taking a tray of potatoes au gratin from the oven. "Flush hard, ladies and gentlemen of the Zephyr," she said. "It's a long way to *Mother's* galley." She held her nose, she fanned the air with kitchen towels, she sneered at the plates of food as they went out.

From the other side of the pass-through, I watched her closely. I listened for her voice. In my former world, the world of pampered, Division 1 college athletes, humility was a rare trait. If I was moderately attracted to this woman, I dismissed it as early onset of Stockholm syndrome—the hostage falling for his captor.

I threw myself into my bartending duties without regard to where we were headed or when we would get there. My future was squarely in the hands of my eccentric employer, a quirky chef, and the crew of the train to which we were yoked.

The Zephyr left Reno nearly two hours late.

That night, after dinner, Horace retreated to his parlor chair in the observation lounge, where he drank cognac and smoked a cigar. As our train left Winnemucca, Nevada, I stood with Wanda in the dimly lit galley. We ate extra helpings of the petrale sole and boiled potatoes that Horace had dined on. Wanda garnished the fish simply with lemon wedges and parsley. The next stop, around midnight, would be Elko, Nevada.

"So what's his bugaboo about Washington, D.C.?" I said.

"Keep your voice down," Wanda said.

I looked at her questioningly.

"Touchy subject," she said.

"What's so touchy about it?"

"I think it's politics in general. He covered Washington as a journalist. Back in the day. He got so disgusted, he quit."

"Escaped to the world of food and wine and the finer things in life?"

"Exactly."

I told Wanda about Horace's scuffle with Senator Rawlins at Mount Hollow.

"I'm not surprised," she said. "He gets around politicians and it's like fire and gasoline."

"I swear the senator wanted to kill him."

Wanda covered her mouth with the back of a hand and laughed. "That's Mr. Button for you. He can really get under a guy's skin."

I continued eating in silence.

Wanda glanced at me. "The fight with the senator. Was it on account of Mr. Button's sister?"

"His sister?"

"She's a pretty hot ticket these days, you know."

I swallowed hard and wiped my mouth with a paper towel. "Who's his sister?"

"Ruth Pepper. You didn't know that?"

"Hurricane Ruth?" This stunned me. A Nevada cattle baroness, Ruth Pepper had arrived on the national political scene, seemingly out of nowhere. In an upset win that shocked the nation, she'd been elected the junior U.S. senator from Nevada. Blunt. Outspoken. Conservative. Love her or hate her, you couldn't open a newspaper or turn on a TV without seeing her face. When Senator Rawlins had taunted Horace about his sister, I pictured some low-level office holder. I had no idea she was Ruth Pepper.

"Mr. Button hates that she's gone into politics," Wanda said. "It makes him throw a lot of newspapers."

"I can see that." I took another bite. "Have you ever met her?"

"Never. It's my impression she doesn't come around that much. He's a lot older than she is, obviously."

"Wow. Hurricane Ruth."

"By the way, Mr. Button hates talking about her. I wouldn't bring her up if I were you." Wanda took another bite. Again, she covered her mouth with a hand. "God, this fish is nasty. I hope your tetanus shots are up to date."

"Are you kidding? It's amazing."

A bell chimed in the galley. This meant Horace wanted me. I set down my plate and went to the observation lounge to check on him.

Horace had a pen in one hand, a yellow legal pad in the other. He glanced at the empty snifter on the side table and gave me a withering stare.

"You mustn't allow these lapses in service, Jack, and I'll tell you why," he said. "The city editor who dwells in my head is a strict grammarian, a nitpicking perfectionist, but he's also an incorrigible drunk. Liquor gives him the vapors. As long as you and I keep him stiff as a goat, I can get my work done."

I quickly refilled the snifter, telling him I envied anyone who could turn off the demons in his head simply by having a few drinks.

"Same approach gets me through this literary festival every year," Horace said. "You'll see what I mean, Jack. The entire event is a concession to logical thought. There's a reason they hold this thing in the summer. The same program under gloomier skies would make a sensible man go shopping for rope."

"Is this exclusively food and wine writers?"

"Once upon a time it was. Now they've opened it up to every kind of lout and swindler: celebrity chefs hawking their dreary cookbooks, bartenders peddling their harebrained drinks, travel writers telling you what to do when your transmission goes kaput in Great Falls, Montana. So many pages of uninspired drivel…"

"You've written a lot of things," I said. "Ever a novel?"

Horace eyed me dubiously. "No. A decidedly miserable lot, fiction writers. I liken them to greyhounds chasing a mechanical rabbit. Few ever catch what they're after, and the ones who do, need to be shot. Why do you ask?"

"It's something I've recently pictured myself doing," I said. "It's why I became a bartender—to free up my days to write."

"I've noticed you jotting things down here and there behind the bar," Horace said. "Wanda says you're keeping a journal."

"When I was fourteen I bought a cheap notebook. What started out as a record of weight training and conditioning goals turned into a daily journal I've kept ever since."

"And how's it going, being a writer? Making any progress?"

"To be honest, it's frustrating. No matter what I start, I get about fifty pages into it and then throw it in the trash. I think the muse must have a thing for older men."

Horace chuckled. "Well, it's persistence more than anything…"

Sometime after we'd left Elko, and Horace had retired to his stateroom, I was restocking the wine chiller, shuttling bottles between the equipment locker and the bar, when I ran into Wanda in the hallway. She was wrapped in a towel. Ringlets of wet hair fell past her bare shoulders. Squeezing around a nearly naked woman on a moving train is an unusually erotic experience.

"What's with the gawking, number fifty-five?" she said. "You've never seen a woman coming out of a shower?"

"I'm sorry," I said. "It… it isn't that." I turned and stumbled away.

Mortified, I finished stocking the bar. I moved to the observation lounge, took up the manual carpet sweeper, and worked it around the dining table.

My mind churned.

How had she known my number? What else did she know? Who had told her? What did she really think of me? Wanda was no sports fan—that much I could tell. It proved that physical distance was inconsequential, that running from my past was impossible. Even this cloistered chef knew who I was.

I unloaded glasses from the dishwasher, I emptied ashtrays, I straightened stacks of magazines: *Sunshine Trails*, *Bon Appétit*, *Saveur*, *Cigar Aficionado*, *Southern Living*.

Around 1:30 a.m., the train slowed. We inched along, and then came to a stop. I went out to the open platform. Overhead, the canvas awning snapped in the wind. The sky was full of stars. We were somewhere in the badlands of the Great Salt Lake Desert, parked on a siding. A thin layer of dust covered the railing that penned me in on three sides. On the distant horizon a brilliant white light burned.

The light grew closer.

I stayed out on the open platform and waited for the train to pass.

About a hundred yards out, the engineer of the overtaking train throttled up. I waved to the darkened cab and got a friendly blast of the air horn. Six yellow locomotives rumbled past. Blankets of smoke spewed from their rooftop exhausts, shrouding the stars. In a storm of whipping wind and dust, a long succession of double-stacked containers flashed by, the flanges of metal wheels shrieking against the steel track. Discharges of pressurized air assaulted my eardrums. The piercing notes were like bloodcurdling human screams. The hair on the back of my neck stood on end.

And then the train was gone.

The desert fell silent. The moment saddened me. *Life is passing me by. I am Quasimodo, dwelling in the obscure shadows of my master's holy place.*

A few minutes later, I climbed into my bunk in our pitch-dark bedroom.

Wanda rustled in her lower berth. "What time is it?"

"Nearly two."

She groaned.

I rolled onto my side and peered over the edge.

"Hey," I said.

"Hey what?"

"How'd you know that was my number—fifty-five?"

"I don't know. Lucky guess."

"I'm serious, Wanda. How'd you know that?"

"I Googled you."

"Oh." I lay on my back and stared up at darkness. We must have been coming up on civilization. The engine's horn was faint but persistent.

"For the record, Wanda, I'm not the sleazebag you think I am," I said.

"Far from it, Majordomo," Wanda said. "Actually, I'm impressed. I take it you play football a lot better than you drive a motorcycle."

TWELVE

Special to *Sunshine Trails*
"Window on the West," by Horace Button
"The Grand Harvey Hotel"

DENVER—The trained ear of this reporter can invariably pick out the bona fide seasoned traveler among the provincial idiots and mournful dolts who fancy themselves cosmopolitan wanderers, for in any discussion of the great hotels of North America the sophisticated traveler will cite the Grand Harvey, in Denver, as one of the top five.

Picture her on a midwinter's eve, resplendent against a muted backdrop of snow-capped mountains, looking majestic as any Bavarian castle, her white stone façade brightly lit, her arched and turreted foyer bustling with arriving guests, her spotlighted flags too haughty to salute even the stiffest of winds.

Now, make the acquaintance of the obliging cast of players who sweep in from stage right: the parking valet who promptly opens the door of your limousine, which was dispatched to meet your arriving train; the handsome bellmen in woolen plus fours and cable-knit ski sweaters who wield their luggage carts in ballet sequences worthy of Nureyev; the gracious doormen, big as oxen, who are formidably decked out in eighteenth-century greatcoats and beaver-fur top hats. They hold open the heavy brass doors, and as you pass by, they snap a smart two-finger salute and greet you by name.

Behold the spacious, glittering lobby! The polished marble floors echo the din of the guests. A string quartet plays Haydn. You're struck by the collection of eye-popping oil paintings, each an original, each rendered in the misty, romantic aesthete of the Hudson River School. The scenes depict the taming of the American West: Lewis and Clark crossing the Rockies; Leland Stanford hammering home the golden spike; a pastoral sunrise over Yosemite Valley. Why, just over there is a Bierstadt! And a Church! And a Durand!

And that good-looking fellow riding herd on all this heroic splendor—that's no Hollywood leading man, that's Herr Fritz, general manager of the Grand Harvey, just back from a skiing holiday in St. Moritz, in his native Switzerland.

Herr Fritz welcomes you and assures you the details of your room are handled. Your bags will be delivered to your suite, and the front desk has your key whenever you're ready. At the base of the marble staircase he bids you a good stay. Upstairs is that celebrated bastion of masculinity, the Pony Room. It is the distinguishing feature of this exalted hotel. The French horns are calling.

The Pony Room is packed. That's Frank the Barman—anticipating your arrival, he's saved you a coveted seat at the long mahogany bar, which is staffed by a brigade of bartenders and bar-backs.

The Pony Room, in its entirety, is in fact a succession of connecting smaller rooms off the main lounge, a labyrinth of dens of varying shapes and sizes, some intimate and some more formal, a few with working fireplaces. The layout induces a nightly cavalcade of high-spirited, ad hoc parties—at least that is what I am told. I would never leave the front bar of the Pony Room. I know I would regret it if I did.

Signed,
Your ace reporter,
HB

THIRTEEN

THE NEXT AFTERNOON, between Grand Junction, Colorado, and the west portal of the Moffat Tunnel, ascending the western slope of the Rockies, we passed through some of the most dramatic mountain scenery I'd ever laid eyes on. Much of the way, we followed the Colorado River through a massive gorge. Walls of red rock rose dramatically above the meandering, sometimes roiling waters of the river, filled with pods of young rafters who mooned our train. On the flat tops of the mountains around us, sections of the forest were aglow with bright golden clusters of Aspen trees.

Somewhere in this stretch, Horace emerged from his stateroom after a long nap. He sat on the open platform and took tea: petite sandwiches of watercress on lightly buttered, thinly sliced white bread, diced pineapple, and red grapes with Stilton cheese. Horace lifted his teacup to me in a sort of salute.

"Earl Gray," he said. "What the Queen drinks."

"Is that so?" I said. The sun felt good on my face as I stood on the platform attending to my employer's needs.

"Look around you, Jack," he said. "Do you think, for one minute, that the jet traveler experiences this beauty from thirty thousand feet? Why, most people could go a lifetime..."

After nightfall, as our train made its way down the Front Range of the Rockies, I feared Horace might give himself a heart attack. Up and down from his seat at the bar, pacing, looking out the darkened windows for familiar landmarks, he kept checking his watch. The Zephyr was running more than three hours late.

"Jack, we've utterly missed the opening-night dinner," he said. "But, if I'm reading the tea leaves right, we can still make the after-party."

An hour later the Zephyr came to a stop in the railroad yard at Denver. We waited a good fifteen minutes for the Trotskyite train conductor to board the *Pioneer Mother*'s open platform, and the delay compounded Horace's distress. The conductor used his radio to guide the train as it backed its way to Union Station. We passed a number of modern apartment buildings and the imposing grandstands of Coors Field, which were lit by high clusters of stadium lights. At the station platform we finally ground to a noisy halt. After the long, steep descent from the Continental Divide, the old Pullman's brakes smelled like burning rubber. A girl with shaggy brown hair and big round glasses, who couldn't have been more than eighteen, approached the *Pioneer Mother*. She asked in a quiet voice if she could come aboard.

"Sorry," I said. "We don't take visitors."

"I'm Cassidy," she said. "The intern? I've been waiting since seven o'clock."

I apologized. I invited her onto the open platform and ushered her inside. With wide eyes she took in the interior of the railcar. Horace glared at her from his seat at the bar. He already had his suit coat on.

"Well, Jack, has she got the rental car or hasn't she?" Horace bellowed. "We haven't got all goddamned night!"

I turned to Cassidy. She nodded vigorously.

"It's the black Escalade right outside the Terminal Bar," she said, handing me a set of car keys. She also gave me an envelope. "This is for Wanda from Mr. Whitehead's secretary. It's your finalized schedule for the week."

"God help us!" Horace said. "What pretentious parties has that pain in the ass dreamed up now?"

Cassidy stared at Horace. She quickly backed out the door.

In our double bedroom Wanda helped me swap my white waiter's jacket for my blue blazer. She smoothed the jacket's padded shoulders.

"I like it, Majordomo," she said. "You make a convincing bodyguard."

She was staying behind to oversee the old Pullman's move to a

siding. She had prep work to do for the next night, when we were hosting Billy Whitehead and his mother, Poppy, for a late dinner.

"I still don't get what I'm supposed to do," I said.

"Just bring him back alive," she said. "Whatever it takes."

I had never seen Horace interact with the general public and was
unfamiliar with the world of culinary celebrity.

"Why do I get the feeling I'm about to experience some form of
mayhem?" I said.

I walked side by side with Horace through the busy bars and restaurants of Union Station. The night was warm. At the front of the train
station, in a thriving urban district of red-brick buildings, people
streamed past the open door of the Escalade as I stretched a seatbelt
across Horace's ample midsection. His breath smelled of mouthwash,
and his clothes bore the woody scent of sandalwood—I couldn't tell if
this was from his cedar-lined closet or his cologne.

"Something about a day spent riding the Iron Horse," Horace said.
"Scaling the Rockies, fighting off Indians. It gives the weary traveler a
keen thirst for tanglefoot. To the Pony Room, Jack, and step on it!"

At the entrance to the Grand Harvey Hotel, a swarm of bellmen met
our car. Horace began peeling off twenty dollar bills. The hotel doorman, a burly black man, held open one of the heavy brass doors.

"Welcome back to the Harvey, Mr. Button," the doorman said. He
touched the brim of his top hat with one hand while palming a twenty
with the other.

Horace and I made our way through the vast white-columned lobby.
A string quartet played something classical and stirring. Well-dressed
couples congregated around stylish settees. A middle-aged man in a
blue suit walked briskly toward Horace.

"Mr. Button!" he called. "You have arrived!"

Horace met the man in the center of the lobby. They shook hands
affectionately. The man had a suntanned face and blindingly white
teeth.

"Jack, meet Herr Fritz," Horace said. "The world's greatest hotelier."

"Mr. Button, you are too kind. Hello, Jack. Welcome to the Harvey."
Herr Fritz spoke with a slight German accent. He shook my hand

warmly. "Your boss is a wonderful friend to this distinguished property." He turned to Horace. "How was your trip?"

"I'm afraid I've missed my cherished leg of lamb served from the trolley with boiled greens on the side," Horace said. "But we still have the Pony Room."

Herr Fritz gestured toward a massive marble staircase. "Please. Be my guest."

I followed Horace and Herr Fritz up the stairs. The soles of their black leather shoes left imprints in the red carpet.

At the top of the staircase, near the entrance to the Pony Room, Herr Fritz bade us adieu. "If there is anything I can do to assist during your time here," he said, "please let me know."

"I think you'd better put the rescue squad on standby, Herr Fritz," Horace said. "I am about to fall into a great glass of gin."

Horace entered the Pony Room, and the crush of people inside cheered. A man with a flattop haircut stepped out from behind the maître d's lectern and greeted Horace by name. Horace pumped the man's hand enthusiastically and shouted into my ear, "Frank the Barman!" Frank led Horace through the crowd to a reserved barstool midway down the bar.

Horace said something into Frank's ear, and from the way Frank nodded I knew Horace was ordering his favorite cocktail: a Tanqueray martini. Frank pointed to me and mouthed something about a drink. "Thanks, I'm driving!" I shouted. Frank gave me a thumbs-up and disappeared behind the bar. A press of people quickly formed around Horace. Men shook his hand and clapped him on the back; women bussed him on both cheeks. I was pushed farther and farther from the bar, until I found myself standing in the middle of a parquet dance floor. I went to the back of the room and stood against a wall. What could I do but wait?

There was the sound of a champagne cork popping from an adjacent room. A throng cheered. I decided to have a look.

I found Billy Whitehead holding court in front of a roaring fire. A buffalo head hung above the fireplace mantel. The buffalo wore a red fez. Near the fireplace, a magnum of Dom Pérignon sat cooling in an ice bucket.

"So here I am without a stitch on, mind you," Billy was saying, "and I'm carrying this shower curtain full of all these bees, carrying it like a football—" He stopped to wink at a red-haired man who sat on a long sofa among a gaggle of tittering women. "So I haul these bees over to Lost Paradise—that's the camp next door—and I heave this damn thing over the transom of the bathhouse, where a lot of showers are going." As he said this a woman cackled drunkenly. "The next thing you know there's six or seven guys, all naked as jaybirds, running full tilt up this road. Those bees are madder than hell and chasing them. The guys in the next camp see them coming. They all start screaming. They think they're being overrun by a horde of African bushmen!"

The alcove erupted with laughter.

"I don't know who that slowest runner was," Billy said, "but he ended up with a patootie full of stingers!"

Oh, how the men and women around the fireplace loved this. Billy Whitehead in the flesh—the bees-in-the-bathhouse story straight from the horse's mouth! They laughed as if they were drugged.

Billy said to the red-haired man, "Zeke, you really must be my guest at Mount Hollow one of these summers. Russ Rawlins... the senator... you know who he is. He was there just last week. Gave us a highly classified talk. Really fascinating. The world's connected in ways your average Joe can't imagine. Flush a toilet in San Francisco and it drains some Swahili's swamp in Nairobi, that sort of thing."

If Billy saw me, he didn't acknowledge me. I moved on.

I came upon a large, low-ceilinged salon where *Sunshine Trails* and Perrier-Jouët were cohosting a champagne reception. The event was well attended. Young women poured wine at a long, glistening bar. I stood back and studied the crowd, trying to pick out the celebrity chefs from the paying customers. In the center of the room two fat, showy men in bowling shirts traded quips, each trying to one-up the other. I pegged them as celebrity chefs—what other sort of jackass would presume to put himself on TV and school the rest of us on how to grill a piece of meat? The paying guests were easy to spot: open-mouthed stares, clothes a little too casual for the setting, humongous conference badges hanging from lanyards around their doughy necks.

I made eye contact with a petite, attractive woman across the room. Her dark hair flowed from a prominent widow's peak, and her lips were a deep red. She wore a tiny black cocktail dress. Taking short, choppy steps on stiletto heels, she hurried toward me.

"Don't say a thing," she said, ducking behind me. She grabbed my arms and urged me to the left. Her fingernails were sharp as hawk's talons.

I chose to play her game. I looked straight ahead. "And you are?"

"You know who I am."

"I think I'd remember—"

"Don't talk. Act natural." She had strong hands.

"Are you in some kind of trouble?"

"The entire mob is after me."

"The mob," I said. "That's interesting."

"There they are! Don't look!"

I looked. The person I saw coming our way was Billy Whitehead.

"Jack! How's life on the train?"

"Good, Mr. Whitehead. I'm enjoying it."

"This must mean Horace has arrived." He saw the fingernails digging into my arms and craned his neck. "Who's that behind you? Is that Wanda?"

"Shut up, Billy," said the voice behind me. "I'm not here."

Billy listed hard to his right. "Why, Giselle! Giselle Lebeau! Your cookbook! Fantastic! Number one on the *New York Times*!"

I turned around and marveled at this stunning woman. She had piercing turquoise eyes. An enormous diamond pendant hung from her sculpted neck.

"It's Giselle!" A woman with the rangy physique of an active senior was making a beeline toward us. She carried an over-the-shoulder canvas conference bag and took long strides in her white cross-trainer shoes. A man followed, a camera jouncing from his neck. He was Silicon Valley Orvis: a blue blazer over designer jeans and a red Stanford baseball cap—no mistaking that S.

The woman came up to Giselle and pawed at her. "Honey, you're such a delight!"

The man with the cap pushed in. "Giselle, your duck with olives—"

"And look how tiny you are!" said the woman. "Such a doll!"

The man glanced at me for a moment, but my broken face was no match for Giselle Lebeau's intoxicating presence. He turned back to her.

"That grilled hanger steak you do with the anchovy butter," he said, kissing his fingers. *"Merveilleux!"*

The woman pulled a conference program from her tote. "Would you sign this for me? I want to frame it and hang it in our kitchen."

Giselle hesitated. "Sorry, I don't have a pen."

The woman dug through her bag. "I'm sure there's one in here somewhere."

"We have the greatest remodeled Tuscan kitchen," the man was saying to Giselle. "All your cookbooks… Angie and I signed up for your cooking demonstration the minute they opened registration. We'll be there. Wouldn't miss it!"

Giselle watched Angie fish in her bag.

"Victory!" Angie handed pen and program to Giselle, who stared back blankly.

"Make it to Ed and Angie," Angie said, smiling quickly. "If you would."

Giselle wrote something across a corner of the program. She signed her name with a flourish.

"I'm gonna tell all my friends," Angie said. "You really are as sweet in person as you are on TV." Tilting her head, she tried to make sense of Giselle's indecipherable scrawl. "Wow. This is such a treasure."

"Hey, can we get a picture?" Ed said.

"Would you mind?" Angie said.

Giselle put on a brave face. "Sure."

"Here, do us a favor." Ed showed me which button to press. He and Angie closed in on Giselle, hugging her delicate shoulders. On three, Giselle flashed her magnificent smile.

"Perfect," Ed said, double-checking my work in the camera's view-finder. He looked at me again, started to say something, then grasped Angie. "Hey, we still have those drink coupons and they're about to close the bar."

They thanked Giselle for the picture and backed away.

Billy turned to Giselle. "You and I need to talk."

"Not tonight, Billy. I have an excruciating headache." Her fingertips went to her temples.

"You should consider doing your next book with us."

"Do you know how many times I've heard that?" Giselle said. "Just today I—"

"I can show you research," Billy said. "The astonishing impact of putting our two brands together."

"Brands are for cattle." Giselle looked at me. "Who's your friend?"

"Jack? Jack's just a temp."

"Maybe your temp can walk me to my room."

"I wouldn't get my hopes up," Billy said. "He's with Horace."

Giselle stared at me. "That's a shame."

I glared at Billy. He concentrated on Giselle.

"Let's discuss it over dinner soon," Billy said. "What you and our publishing arm could do working together."

"Only if it's on the train," Giselle said.

"I'm sorry, the train?"

"This railroad car I've heard so much about—"

"Oh, the *Pioneer Mother*!" Billy's face lit up. "It's short notice, but why don't you join Mother and me for dinner tomorrow night? We're dining with Horace. On the train. Right after the Rocky Mountain Burger Bash. Mother's an acclaimed food snob, you know. She won't eat hamburger."

Giselle studied the swarm of people at the bar. I had the bad habit of comparing every woman I met to Bianca. I decided this tight little number had her beat. She had a clean, strong jawline and skin the color of milk. She looked to be in her early thirties. That she had Billy Whitehead eating out of her hand impressed me.

"I've never actually met Horace," Giselle said, turning back to Billy, "but I'd love to dine with him. I hear his chef does fabulous retro."

"Wanda? She's fantastic. Horace raves about her. He's her biggest fan."

"He probably thinks I'm a twit."

"What makes you say that?"

"Simple dishes, everything healthy, done in thirty minutes. He must be appalled."

"Who cares what Horace thinks? He's a relic. You're a culinary diva with an Emmy award–winning TV show and a string of best-selling cookbooks. The important thing is Mother and I would love to have you as our guest tomorrow night."

"I'll have to move some things around," Giselle said. "But for the chance to dine with Horace Button I'll do it."

"Good, then it's a date. We'll see you after the Burger Bash."

At midnight I was sitting at the bar in the Pony Room, waiting for Horace, who continued to regale his audience with stories.

A man came and sat next to me. He had a white goat beard and a string tie. His conference badge said he was a food and wine writer. He ordered an eighteen-year-old scotch.

"Excuse me," I said, "but do you follow the industry?"

"I like to think I know a little something about it," he said.

"What can you tell me about a woman named Giselle Lebeau?"

FOURTEEN

AT NINE THIRTY THE NEXT NIGHT I stood behind the *Pioneer Mother*'s bar, watching Horace quaff straight bourbon from a heavy rocks glass. The dining table was set for four. Piano music played softly on the satellite radio. A bottle of Dom Pérignon chilled in an ice bucket. In the galley, Wanda put the finishing touches on dinner. The aroma of warm beurre blanc sauce wafted through the railcar.

Horace was explaining to me the subtle difference between bourbon and Tennessee whiskey — Tennessee whiskey is filtered through sugar-maple charcoal before being cast into an oak barrel for aging — when Billy Whitehead appeared on the back platform. He held open the heavy door for his mother, Poppy, who swept flamboyantly through the observation lounge, heading straight for the bar.

"Horace, lamb, it's been positively ages!" she said. "Give Mother a kiss!"

With her white hair and gruesome mask of makeup, and with her skeletal hands reaching for Horace's face, she might have been a corpse that had just jumped from a coffin. She formed a bony vice, flattened Horace's ruddy cheeks, and planted a kiss on his mouth.

Defenseless, Horace's eyes rolled back in his head. He took a breath and regarded the old woman with affection.

"Poppy," he said. "Still doing spectacularly well, I see."

"Nonsense. I haven't got a pot. The estate lawyers have positively scalped me. They've given it all to Billy." She set her purse on the floor and settled on the barstool next to Horace. "What about you, lamb?

How are you these days?"

"How do you think I am?" Horace said. "Your idiot son is intent on ruining our magazine. As publisher emeritus, you can't possibly support him."

Poppy laughed in Horace's face. "Of course I support him. You and Lincoln had your fun. Now it's Billy's turn."

By this time, Billy had stalked angrily up to the bar. He took a handful of nuts and began flicking them into his mouth, glaring at Horace.

"You could at least have called," Billy said.

"It's against my constitution," Horace said.

"You should learn to use a cell phone. You stood up some very important people."

"The world's greatest thinkers and the Sultan of Brunei," Horace said. "They never miss a Rocky Mountain Burger Bash."

"You can't be a no-show at your own event," Billy said. "The paying guests were looking for you—and so were members of the press."

"Grown men pounding ground round into patties in a hotel parking lot," Horace said. "It struck me as undignified."

"You're such a pigheaded snoot. The consultants say—"

Horace slammed his whiskey glass onto the bar. "I know what the consultants say! You remind me every waking minute!"

Poppy snapped her fingers at the two men.

"Boys, boys," she said. "Were you born in a barn? Mother needs a drink."

Billy cut me an impatient glance. "A Gibson for Mother." He looked at Poppy and then back to me. "Make it a double. And I'll have a champagne cocktail."

Horace winced.

"What?" Billy said. "You don't approve of a champagne cocktail?"

"You've a genius for trash, Billy. You should package it and sell it to your hamburger crowd. That you'd do that to Pérignon Cuvée is unconscionable."

"I pay for it, I'll drink it any way I please. Spare me the raised eyebrows."

I filled a silver shaker with ice, poured a double shot of gin, gave it a dash of dry vermouth, and stirred the drink with a long spoon.

After pouring the Gibson into a martini glass, I added a cocktail onion, and slid the drink in front of Poppy. She gave the glass a swirl. She wore a blinding diamond necklace and immense rings.

"It's no wonder our circulation is plummeting," Billy was saying. "Droning on and on about the piety of the martini, about tuxedoed waiters making tableside Caesars. It's fit for a museum, not a magazine. And speaking of museums, this old railroad car has outlived its usefulness."

"As if you'd know anything about usefulness," Horace said. "Your entire life, you haven't done a stroke—"

"We should sell this hoary gin parlor," Billy said. "Before the Amtrak inspectors ban it as a public hazard."

"You're a traitor to your father's legacy. This railcar has a rich history."

"Oh, nobody gives a damn that Nixon slept here!"

"Look behind you. Judas and Benedict Arnold just walked across the tracks."

Billy turned around and shrieked. Giselle Lebeau stood on the open platform, looking in the window. She knocked tentatively on the glass.

"We'll pick this up later," Billy said, marching through the observation lounge. "But mark my words. This magazine needs a new direction." He pulled open the door and affected a broad smile. "Giselle! You made it! Come in, come in!"

Billy helped Giselle out of her designer black leather jacket. Beneath it she wore a tight blue dress and black spiky heels. Adorning her neck was a large sapphire and diamond pendant.

"Can you believe it?" Poppy said to Horace. "That cute little thing has her own television show."

Behind me, a silver platter hit the pass-through window with a clang.

"Sarcoptic deer mange," Wanda said.

Startled, Billy and Giselle looked over. I set the platter on the bar in front of Poppy.

"Care to try some venison tartare?" I said.

"Are you kidding?" Poppy said. "If Wanda boiled a dirty sock,

I'd try it." She took a sterling silver hors d'oeuvre fork and began picking at the meat.

Billy led his guest to the bar.

"Giselle Lebeau, meet Poppy Whitehead," he said.

Poppy swiveled around on her barstool. The two women shook hands.

"I've heard so much about you," Giselle said. "My God, that's a stunning necklace!"

"I'm jealous of my jewels," Poppy said, pretending to pout. "People look at them more than me."

"And Giselle, meet Horace Button," Billy said.

"Ah! The short-order superlative has arrived!" Horace climbed off his barstool, face flushed, and clasped both of Giselle's hands. "Welcome to my hoary little gin parlor."

"What fun!" Giselle said, looking around. "Do I get a tour?"

"That depends. Are you an Amtrak inspector?"

"I'm a big fan, Mr. Button. I grew up on your books."

"Billy tells me they belong in a museum."

"If anything belongs in a museum, it's you."

Poppy burst out laughing. "Caw! Caw! Horace, you old museum piece!"

Giselle blushed. "I'm sorry, that came out wrong. What I meant to say is I consider your body of work to be a national treasure."

Billy said to Horace, "You'll be glad to know Giselle has agreed to serve as honorary chef at your tribute dinner. She'll be making her signature *boeuf en croûte*."

Horace beamed. "Why, that's wonderful news!"

"Maybe I shouldn't be telling you this," Giselle said, "but my father was a huge fan. He once put on a white tie and tails and went as you to a Halloween party. He'd be amazed if he knew I'm actually standing here with you now. This is such a great honor." She took in the eclectic furnishings of the observation lounge. Her eyes shimmered. "And talk about going in style! Those Venetian baroque wall consoles—are they original pieces?"

Horace put an arm around Giselle's waist and pulled her close.

"Kid, you're on the level in my book. Let's get you a drink and I'll give you the full tour. What will it be?"

"Gin and tonic," she said. "But a light one. I'm working in the morning."

"A light one, hell!" Horace said, feigning offense, making lighthearted fun. "You'll get it any damn way Jack makes it—and that's final."

Giselle turned to me. "All right, Jack. Any way you want to make it."

I started on a light gin and tonic.

"Now what's this banana oil about working in the morning?" Horace said.

"I'm cooking French," Giselle said. "On live network TV."

Horace's eyes gleamed. "French! *Ça c'est la vraie cuisine!*"

I put the gin and tonic on the bar. Giselle took it without a glance at me. She clutched Horace's arm.

"All right," she said. "Now I'm ready for the tour."

Horace held out his tumbler. "Fill 'er up, Jack. The exquisite and I are going on a reconnaissance mission."

I topped off Horace's glass with bourbon.

"Don't take too long," Billy said. "Mother hasn't eaten all day. With her vasculitis, she might faint."

"Black out from this ocean of gin, is more like it." Poppy pursed her red lips. She chomped down on another bite of venison.

"Come on, kitten," Horace said to Giselle. "We'll start with the galley."

Still chewing, Poppy watched them go around the corner. "He always was a pushover for pretty girls."

Through the pass-through window I caught the scene playing out in the galley.

"Hi, I'm Giselle."

"Wanda."

"Wow. This place is tiny. You really cook in here?"

"I try."

"How many on your staff?"

"Just me."

"That doesn't seem possible."

"Ha."

"Where did you learn to cook?"

"Culinary Institute of America."

"Hyde Park. Nice pedigree."

"Yeah, I saw 'CIA' and thought I was signing up to kill people."

"Funny."

"True, though."

"Where else have you worked?"

"The Roosevelt Grill, in San Francisco. Then I moved over to the Dorsey-Palace Hotel."

"Impressive kitchens."

"The Dorsey-Palace was where I found her," Horace interjected. "A kitchen deaconess of the highest order, studying under the world-famous Oscar Pagenpopp. One bite of her pheasant *en casserole* and I knew I had to hire her."

"And the rest is history," Giselle said.

"Weird, huh?" Wanda said.

"What's on tonight's menu?"

"A few random things. Frogs' legs in a garlic beurre blanc. Lobster Newburg."

Billy looked at his mother and shook his head. "Like a broken record," he said. "The man is hopelessly stuck in the past."

"Yum," Giselle said. "Your lobster Newburg—are you serving it with cornbread or toast points?"

"Cornbread."

"Toast points would be easier."

"Mr. Button insists on cornbread. Made from scratch."

"From scratch?"

"Why tempt the gods or risk the black mark of scandal?" Horace said.

"What else are you making?" Giselle asked.

"Turtle soup," Wanda said. "Haricots verts and hazelnut salad, an assortment of cheeses. It's late so we're eating kind of light."

"Light?" Giselle said. "I might explode."

"We're showing you the ropes, kid," Horace said. "It's how we did it in the Paleozoic era. We routinely went until the sun came up."

"That's probably a stretch for me," Giselle said. "Will I have any trouble getting a cab out here?"

"Don't worry about a cab," Horace said. "Jack can take you back to the hotel. The rail yard toughs won't dare mess with a brute like him."

To my knowledge, not a single word of business was spoken the entire night.

The Dom Pérignon and Château Lafite-Rothschild flowed like two Babylonian rivers. By one o'clock in the morning, the party had degenerated into bedlam. Giselle had spilled turtle soup on the front of her dress, Poppy was puffing on a Dominican cigar, and Billy stood on a parlor chair, singing "Hello, Dolly" into a dessert spoon. Horace drank port and smoked a cigar. Giselle perched on the arm of his chair.

"I like you, kid," Horace said, squinting at her through a haze of blue smoke. "You're a fine little moccasin."

"I think they enjoyed your meal," I said to Wanda as she looked over my shoulder at the riotous scene in the observation lounge.

"They're wasted," Wanda said.

"My fault," I said. "Apparently, I over-served."

"Trust me, the word isn't in their vocabulary." Wanda put a hand on my shoulder. "Make sure they get to the hotel in one piece. I'm gonna hit the rack."

The party went on into the night. Horace called loudly for a round of Pousse-Cafés—the bane of any bartender. He had to come behind the bar to teach me this fussy drink: grenadine, yellow Chartreuse, Crème de Menthe, sloe gin, green Chartreuse, and brandy. He showed me how to pour the liqueurs over the back of a spoon, creating multicolored layers in the glass. I finally got the technique down, but my charges were calling for more Pousse-Cafés faster than I could make them, so I came up with a shorthand version of the drink. Mine had half the ingredients and I skipped the whole spoon business, so they came out looking more like swamp water, but no one seemed to notice or care.

Poppy finally announced she was ready to return to the hotel, and the party sputtered. This led to a series of minor catastrophes: Poppy couldn't find her purse; Horace discovered an unexplained patch of blood on his elbow; Billy had a violent case of the hiccups, and Giselle insisted on going barefoot back to the hotel. She carried her high heels in her hand. On the open platform I forced her to strap on the shoes as protection against the broken glass, bodily fluids, and other pathogen-infested debris that littered the tracks. She relented, but not before kicking me in the shin and calling me a Nazi.

It was a slow, arduous trek down the gravel frontage road to the parked Escalade. Poppy carried a gin Rickey and a lit torpedo cigar. She leaned on Billy, who howled like a coyote at the moon. At one point we approached an encampment of homeless people bedded down in sleeping bags along a cyclone fence. I worried about the glittering display of jewels in our party, but the occupants of the encampment simply raised their heads and watched us pass.

A wobbly Giselle clung tightly to my arm. The rich leather smell of her jacket mingled with her floral perfume, and when she bumped against me I caught the musky scent of her scalp. The lights of the Denver skyline blazed before us as a long freight train made its way through the yard, sounding its horn.

"What time is it, anyway?" Giselle said.

"Past two," I said.

"That's a hideous lie—I have to be on set in four hours!"

I had to help her into the backseat of the Escalade; she kept falling over like a child trying to mount the stirrups of a tall horse. Using two hands against her rump, I finally got her inside. Getting Poppy into the backseat with Giselle required a similar—albeit far less pleasurable—maneuver. Poppy wanted to take the half-smoked Romeo y Julieta *Edicion Limitada* No. 2 into the Escalade with her.

"Let's leave this behind," I said, reaching for the cigar. "The rental agency charges a hundred dollars for smoking."

"Screw the rental agency," Poppy said, holding the cigar out of my reach. "I'll buy the goddamned truck and donate it to the Humane Society. They can use it to drive dogs to daycare."

"Have you ever eaten dog?" Giselle said to her.

"God, no, honey. I don't even eat pot roast."

Billy sat in the passenger seat. As I started the Escalade, his eyes were shut and his head bobbed. By the first intersection his chin balanced on his breastbone. A trail of drool seeped from the corner of his mouth. He hiccupped in his sleep.

The impressive Billy Whitehead.

Behind me Poppy and Giselle were talking yachts.

"Billy is building me a big one," Poppy said. "A thousand feet long."

"No, Mother," Billy said. "A hundred feet." He spoke with his eyes closed.

"He's calling it *Euthanasia*," Poppy said.

"*Utopia*," Billy said.

"I don't care what anyone says or how much they post about it on the blasted Internet," Poppy said. "A boy can build his mother a yacht if that's what he wants to do. What business is it of anyone else's, including laid-off employees? Lincoln, my husband, taught me that. 'Screw the ingrates,' he'd say."

"How long were you two married?" Giselle asked.

"Long enough," Poppy said. "I was his second wife, and I'll tell you why it worked: I was his Madonna *and* his whore."

"Mother!" Billy said.

"Well it's the God's truth! That's what a good wife is. There wasn't a thing I wouldn't do for that man—and I mean *anything*. He and Horace, they went through brick walls in those days. And they didn't give a damn what anybody said or thought. 'To hell with the dumb clucks,' they'd say. 'Let them eat bird seed and crap plover's eggs!'"

"Mother..." Billy said again.

"Oh, don't be such a bluenose. I'm trying to teach this girl something about life. It takes balls to make it in this cutthroat world—especially if you're a woman."

"Has Horace ever been married?" Giselle said.

"My heavens no, darling. He's always been *that way*, you know. I'll tell you something about Horace. He's a horse of another color. Sex means nothing to him. *Sunshine Trails* is his Madonna. Gluttony is his whore."

At the Grand Harvey Hotel, I brought the Escalade to a stop under the bright lights of the porte cochere. The lone valet on duty pulled open the front passenger door, rousing Billy.

"Welcome back to the Harvey, Mr. Whitehead."

"Heave ho," Billy said. "Watch the old man blow." He stepped out of the Escalade and nearly stumbled into the valet's podium. The valet caught him.

"Tricky pavement, sir," the valet said. "Watch your step."

In the backseat Poppy blew Giselle an air kiss. "Bonsoir, my dear. You've been a delight."

"Ma'am." The valet helped Poppy from the Escalade. She stepped out holding the gin Rickey and the smoldering cigar. She followed after Billy, who was wandering off toward the parked cars.

"My Lord in heaven, boy," Poppy said. "Where are you going?"

The valet corralled them and steered them toward the lobby doors.

I persuaded Giselle to let me walk her to her room. At this time of night even the finest hotels had their stalkers, rapists, and autograph hounds.

We entered through a revolving brass door and crossed the deserted lobby to a bank of elevators. Giselle walked barefoot on the marble floor, carrying her high heels. She looked straight ahead, walking with great purpose, putting one foot in front of the other.

"You okay?" I said.

"Fine."

We stepped into a waiting elevator.

"Floor?" I asked.

"Twenty-eight."

I looked at her. The Harvey had only eighteen floors.

"Eighteen," Giselle said.

As the elevator began to rise Giselle slumped to the deck and buried her head in her hands.

"Goddamned Pousse-Cafés."

"We'll get you some water."

"I'm supposed to cook in five hours. Pot-au-fucking-feu with fried zucchini and eggplant. How am I gonna pull that off?"

"You'll manage."

"I feel like crap. I'll probably chuck on live TV."

"You won't chuck."

We were nearing the eighteenth floor.

"Maybe you should get up," I said.

"In a minute."

"How about now?"

"How about never?"

"Come on. Our stop."

I helped her up. The elevator doors opened.

"Which way?" I said.

"This way."

I followed Giselle down the long corridor, watching her carom off walls. At the end of the hall, she stopped and leaned against a set of imposing double doors.

"The Presidential Suite?" I said.

"I think Horace liked me," Giselle said. "He isn't the monster people make him out to be. Billy's a dimwit, partying and building yachts while *Sunshine Trails* burns. And the mother's a horror show, but I respect her for it. I wouldn't mind being like her one day when I'm old."

"A room key?" I said.

"In here. Somewhere." Giselle handed me her small white evening clutch.

I rummaged through the contents of the purse: a cell phone, a hairbrush, a silver compact mirror, some loose credit cards.

"I envy Horace," Giselle was saying. "At least he has his little *Pioneer Mother* family to go home to."

"And you don't?"

"An ex-husband and a cat. Let me tell you something, Mr. Pousse-Café. Being famous isn't everything it's cracked up to be. Life on the road can be tough—very, very tough."

"You travel a lot?"

"Nonstop. Every corner of the globe. In search of kitchen essentials and the origins of the five mother sauces."

I came across Giselle's driver's license. I held it up to the light. *Nice picture.* I did the math. She was thirty-two. She lived in Marina del Rey.

"Hey, snoop," she said. "Put that down!"

I found the room key and we entered the suite. The mirrored foyer had a chandelier and a wet bar. To the left was a formal dining room. Piles of mail and stacks of magazines covered the dining table. The corner living room was teeming with floral arrangements. Draped over every sofa and chair were articles of women's clothing, many still sporting price tags. The open boxes on the floor said Bergdorf's, Nordstrom, and Bloomingdale's.

"Celebrating something?" I asked. "Or did somebody die?"

"I can't explain it," Giselle said, shrugging off her jacket, tossing it over a Queen Anne chair. "These things just appear. All day long."

She went to the wet bar and twisted the top off a bottle of Fiji water.

"I'll just check the place out before I go," I said. "Make sure it's safe."

"You don't have to do that," Giselle said. "Check the place out, I mean."

I smiled. "People have passkeys."

Giselle followed me as I systematically went through the suite, looking behind drapes, checking behind doors. The lights were on in the bedroom and the sheets on the king bed had been turned down. She laughed at my cumbersome technique of dropping onto my stomach to look under the bed.

"No boogeyman?" she said.

"All clear," I said.

Getting back on my feet left me feeling slightly winded.

"I suppose a goodnight kiss would be out of the question," Giselle said.

"I have to go," I said.

"Stay," she said.

I studied her eyes, now glazed over from alcohol. I wanted to tell her that I had walked her here in my capacity as her protector, as a proxy to Horace Button and *Sunshine Trails*, and that no honorable man would take advantage of a woman in her condition, but I knew that might upset her.

"It's late," I said. "You need sleep."

She set the water bottle on the nightstand. She reached behind her and unzipped her dress, letting it fall to the floor. She wore a black push-up bra and lace-trimmed panties, which rode low on her slender hips.

I quickly went to the window and pulled the drapes.

"All of Denver doesn't need to see this," I said.

She cornered me and wrapped her arms around my neck.

"I can still feel that biker chick's turtle soup on me," she said. "I need a shower." She kissed me on the side of my face. Once. Twice. When she went for my mouth I pulled away.

"Giselle, I can't do this—"

"You've been undressing me with your eyes the whole night." She took hold of my necktie.

"I need to go—"

"Shh. Don't talk." She slid the knot down the length of the tie, then slipped the tie free from my collar. She began dancing, working the tie as if it were a stripper's boa.

I picked up the phone and dialed the hotel operator.

"I'd like a wake-up call," I said, "for the Presidential Suite…" I held the receiver against a shoulder and said to Giselle, "What time?"

"Pousse boy." She tried looping the tie around my neck.

"Come on, Giselle. This is the hotel operator—"

"Jack." She lunged at me and pecked me on the cheek. "Jack Sprat. Jack Sprat could eat no fat."

"I said what time?"

"Maybe I want to sleep all day."

"Stop playing around."

"I'll show you playing around—" She lunged for my belt buckle.

"Giselle, no!" I pushed her hand away. When she made another try I grabbed her wrist and held it firmly.

She frowned. "Why are you being so mean?"

"I'm asking you a simple question. What time for your wake-up call?"

"How should I know?"

I released her wrist. "Think. What time do you need to be on the set?"

"Six o'clock."

"And you need what, an hour to get ready? Hour and a half?"

"Hour."

"So five o'clock. You want a wake-up call for five o'clock?"

Giselle looked puzzled. "I don't know, I guess so."

I relayed this to the operator. By the time I hung up, Giselle was sitting on the edge of the bed, looking dejected. She had my tie draped loosely around her neck. One end was lost in her cleavage.

"May I please have my tie back?" I said.

She looked up at me coquettishly. "Only if you come and get it."

"It's late, Giselle. I'm not playing this game."

Her eyes welled suddenly and she brought her hands to her face. "Okay, tell me the truth, Mr. Pousse-Café. What's wrong with me?"

"Nothing's wrong with you. It's just… there's someone else."

She stared glumly at the carpet. Suddenly she perked up.

"Oh, but didn't you know?" she said. "Chefs make terrible wives. They only care about making their soufflés rise"

"Not Wanda," I said. "Somebody else."

Giselle sprang to her feet and put her arms around my neck. "Then she'll never know."

"But I'll know," I said.

"Are you serious?"

"You need sleep."

"Aren't you fucking thoughtful, telling me what I need." She kissed me hard on the mouth.

I just looked at her. "What was that?"

"A down payment. Future wages. I want you to work for me. Come be my bodyguard."

I forced a smile. "I'll get back to you on that."

"I'll ask Billy. He'll give me anything I want, including you."

"You've had too much to drink," I said, peeling her arms off my neck. "Take some aspirin and go to bed."

She sat down forcefully.

"Don't talk to me like that," she said. "I'm not a child."

"May I please have the tie?"

"No." Giselle curled into a ball with her back to me. "I'm going to sleep with it. I have to sleep with something tonight."

"Fine," I said. "I'll show myself out."

As I was passing through the living room, turning out lights, she called to me.

"Hey, Pousse boy!"

I peeked inside the bedroom. She remained in a ball.

"What?" I said.

"That girl who cooks for Horace," she said without looking at me. "She has people helping her, right?"

"Good night, Giselle. Don't forget to take some aspirin."

I drove back to the railroad yard with the windows down. The Escalade's leather interior reeked of cigar smoke.

I boarded the *Pioneer Mother* and faced a floodtide of dirty dishes. Wanda was in the darkened galley, sitting on a barstool in her terrycloth robe, working at her computer. The screen cast a glow over her face.

She looked up. "Where the hell have you been?"

"The party went late."

She snorted with contempt.

"I walked her to her suite, Wanda. Nothing happened."

"Her *suite*?"

"She has the Presidential Suite."

"Isn't that a little gauche? When people in the world are starving?"

"None of these people are starving," I said.

"Where's your tie?"

"I don't know, I must've left it in the car."

Wanda glowered. "You slept with her."

"I told you, Wanda. I walked her to her room. That's all."

"That is so predictable—"

"Wanda, nothing happened."

"Bullshit. I don't believe you."

"Jesus. What am I supposed to say to that?"

Wanda powered off her computer. "This place is a pigsty. Get it cleaned up before you come to bed." Clutching the laptop under one arm, she left the galley and stormed up the hallway.

I forced myself to turn and go the other way. In the bar, I splashed cold water on my face.

What business was it of hers if I *had* slept with Giselle? No way was I going back to our double bedroom. How could I spend another minute in the presence of this bossy bitch?

My adrenaline running high, I attacked the cleaning of the Pullman's chaotic interior with a newfound mania. I loaded the dishwasher, hand-washed the wine goblets and crystal champagne flutes, emptied the ashtrays, and ran the carpet sweeper under the dining table and around the observation lounge. I feather-dusted every flat surface and vacuumed every drape. I wiped down the mahogany walls with a mixture of vinegar and hot water, and I polished the brass. The entire time, I toyed with the idea of becoming Giselle's bodyguard. I pictured her standing in the bedroom of the Presidential Suite, imploring me to stay. I saw myself working for this accomplished woman by day and sharing her bed at night. Traveling the world, staying in iconic hotels, dining at five-star restaurants—the pampered life of celebrity awaited me after all.

Before I knew it the light in the windows was turning blue and Wanda was in the galley, starting breakfast.

FIFTEEN

Special to *Sunshine Trails*
"Window on the West," by Horace Button
"First Call: Musings on the Morning Cocktail"

SAN FRANCISCO—I had occasion the other day to bury an acquaintance who dropped dead of a heart attack while exercising at a gym. His eulogizers vouched for his clean Christian living. He was ever-watchful of his diet, punctilious about his daily exercise regimen and unswerving in his avoidance of alcohol.

I am ashamed to say this last assertion was taken as a laugh line by a number of us tosspots in the doubting Thomas section of the church.

Before the service, we had stopped for an a.m. elbow bender at a temple of the hangover called Gil's, in North Beach. At Gil's a gentleman can get a Manhattan with his bacon and eggs, and a forenoon martini gracing a table is as commonplace as an open newspaper.

Pallbearers and mourners often appear en masse at Gil's for an early line of bracers, as we did. There's something comforting, almost spiritual, in Gil's whiskey sours and sloe gin fizzes—ask the well-lubricated parish priest in the next booth.

Of course, one cannot credibly discuss going on a morning toot without mentioning the exalted Essex Fox Tavern, in South San Francisco. Enlightened air travelers consider it a mandatory stop. Whether your destination is Burbank or Baluchistan, the Fox can deliver the belt of squareface that will render you sufficiently stiff to board the pestilential hell-cartridge of death that will take you there.

For me, any memorial service enkindles the desire to engage in personal reflection. Even before the tenant in the casket made his final getaway down the center aisle, two musings entered my besotted mind:

First, what is it about taking a midmorning slug that the self-appointed morality police find so deplorable?

In this modern age, when delusional, overreaching elected officials regulate away the simple pleasures of our daily lives—from smoking a cigar at AT&T Park to sipping a Pouilly-Fumé on Marina Green at sunset—morning drinking, like obesity, has suffered an unwarranted and excessive degree of bad press.

Unlike indolent housewives and demented grannies who pass out and sleep it off when they get stinko, serious morning drinkers tend to be professionals in their métier and exemplary in their comportment. As the sun crosses the yardarm you'll seldom see a patron exit Olaf's Tearoom, on Union Square, and go staggering down the sidewalk with his shirt collar amiss and his umbrella turned inside out, though he may have quaffed five or six of Mr. O's signature daiquiris since ten o'clock that morning.

Chances are this dapper gentleman is on his way to the courthouse to preside over an important trial or to a glass tower to consolidate the nation's railroads.

My second thought: The sanctimonious and self-righteous eulogizers, pouring it on thick in the name of God, asserted that our fallen hero of the hour was a good Christian and a teetotaler, and for these reasons alone he will spend eternity in Heaven.

In my head I pictured a dinner party full of dutiful Christians where not a single drop of alcohol was served, and I multiplied that by an eternity.

I can categorically state that when the Old Man with the Scythe taps me on the shoulder, I shall be calling for the "down" elevator.

Signed,
Your ace reporter,
HB

SIXTEEN

"COFFEE'S MADE IF YOU WANT SOME." I buttoned my white waiter's jacket.

Wanda pulled a stainless steel mixing bowl from a lower cabinet and banged it on the counter. She began angrily cracking eggs. She did it with one hand, breaking each egg hard against the rim of the mixing bowl and using a thumb to separate the contents of the egg from its shell, which she threw in a wastebasket at her feet.

"What's your problem?" I said.

"You didn't come to bed."

"You sound like we're married."

"You can't do this job without sleep."

"I don't know what you're in such a stink about. I was concerned for a guest. She had an important—"

"And I'm just the stupid cook, is that it?" Wanda took a sauté pan from a lower cabinet and kicked the door shut.

"Would it surprise you to know that you intimidate her?"

Wanda glanced at me skeptically.

"She didn't believe you made last night's dinner by yourself," I said. "Apparently she has an army of employees who prep for her."

Wanda whisked the eggs into a yellow froth.

"She invited me to come work for her," I said. "As her bodyguard."

The whisking turned furious.

Two hours later I was placing silver trays of scrambled eggs, boiled shrimp, diced potatoes, and duck sausage frittata over a line of chafing dishes. The dining table was set for six. The *Sunshine Trails* senior editors were smoking cigarettes on the open platform. One of them finally peeked inside the door.

"Ready for us?" Clive Grant, the magazine's lanky executive editor, was dressed in a rumpled tan suit that looked as if he'd slept in it. A conference badge hung from his neck. His curly blond hair tumbled past his shirt collar.

I hurried to hold open the door. "By all means," I said. "Come in."

Clive stepped confidently over the threshold and into the observation lounge. Behind him was Nigel Coffey, *Sunshine Trails*'s managing editor.

"Morning," Nigel said. He wore a tight-fitting Italian suit and carried a black leather shoulder bag. The dark circles under his eyes made him appear ghoulish.

Allison Kirschbaum, the magazine's creative director, came in next. She sported a fierce pixie haircut and lugged a large designer purse. She gave me a tight smile.

"Right," she said. "This must be the place."

I held the door, waiting on a willowy young woman who stood with her back to me, finishing a cigarette. Her red and green dyed hair — alternating strands like crazy parrot feathers—belied her tailored blue business suit. Fabiana MacPhee served as the magazine's executive food editor. She took a final drag of her cigarette, flicked the butt onto the tracks below, exhaled a stream of smoke from her nostrils, and entered the railcar without saying a word.

I went around the observation lounge, soliciting drink orders. Fabiana asked for hot green tea. The others declined anything from the bar and took turns at the silver coffee urn.

Waiting for Billy to arrive, the four editors acted like soldiers under siege. They stared gloomily out the windows, didn't speak to one another, and jumped at every little sound from the galley. They turned up their noses at Wanda's food. At the unmistakable sound of a man vomiting violently outside the railcar, they traded horrified glances and turned to me expectantly.

"Sorry," I said. "A lot of homeless around here."

I went out to shoo away this trackside bum and found Billy

Whitehead standing hands on knees beside the *Pioneer Mother*'s silver trucks. At his feet, receding into the riprap beneath the crossties, was the previous night's party.

His face was ashen and his lips quivered.

"Fucking Horace," he said, wiping his mouth with the back of a hand.

I took him inside, sat him at the dining table, and gave him a wet bar towel.

Allison leaned in. "Do you think it's flu?"

"I think I got some bad Tex-Mex at the Burger Bash," Billy said. He pressed the towel to his face. I brought him aspirin and a tall glass of club soda.

The others took this as a cue for the meeting to start. They staked out places around the table, pulling laptops from bags and arranging thick file folders in stacks.

I poured coffee. Sunlight streamed through the windows. The sleepless night was catching up to me—my head felt heavy and my eyes stung.

Allison took a typewritten manuscript from a folder and showed it to Clive. "Have you seen this?"

"Yes."

"We can't possibly print it."

"I know." Clive covered his face with his hands, making a mask of his long, tobacco-stained fingers.

"It's outrageous," Allison said.

"Yes."

"Irresponsible."

"Yes."

"Not to mention embarrassing."

"Allison, I agree. I've already brought it up with Billy."

Fabiana scrutinized her cell phone. "We said nine o'clock, right?"

"Waiting on Horace," Nigel snorted. "What's new?"

"I won't mention the irony of sitting in an antique train car, talking about ways to modernize the magazine." Fabiana peered at her laptop. "Has this thing got Wi-Fi?"

"Are you kidding?" Nigel said.

Horace arrived seven minutes later. Billy looked at him with reproach.

"Brushing my teeth in a light Moselle," Horace said.

Clive managed to produce a low-throated chuckle. No one else even smiled.

Getting Horace situated for a breakfast meeting required perseverance. First there was the matter of locating a particular pillow to support his back—I found it in his stateroom. He insisted on having certain pens at hand, as well as a favorite leather writing portfolio that was embossed with an image of the *Queen Mary*. These things I also eventually found in his stateroom.

I brought him a Manhattan from the bar.

"Breakfast this morning?" I said.

"A synthesis of everything the kitchen has to offer," Horace said. "Just to be certain God still dwells in His abundant Heaven."

I made Horace a heaping plate of food.

Billy refused to eat. The others put food on their plates to be polite.

"All right," Billy said, "let's talk about how we're going to right this listing ship. Start with you, Clive. Tell Horace everything you told me."

Clive shifted uncomfortably. "Yes, well, sure," he said. "The thing of it is, Horace, we're in a bad spot here. I can't keep my staff and circulation's off the cliff."

Horace took a sip of his cocktail. "We have a dearth of paying customers, and you're blaming me?"

"Not blaming you," Clive said. "Just sounding the alarm. We've gone from a high of 1.6 million subscribers to fewer than 500,000 today. It's our lowest level in twenty years. We need to make some changes."

"You're bent on taking me round and round this same mulberry bush," Horace said. "My answer won't change. If you want to follow the whims and vagaries of paid consultants, go find yourself another magazine."

The editors exchanged nervous glances.

"I'm simply stating fact, Horace," Clive said. "Editorial drives circulation, circulation drives advertising. The fish rots from the head."

"Our book is down 60 percent," Nigel said, jumping in. "We need a fresh look, a new direction."

"What you mean is somebody needs a new yacht," Horace said.

Billy didn't react. He stared out the window.

"Come on, Horace," Clive said. "That isn't fair. The point is, the world has changed and *Sunshine Trails* hasn't."

"A magazine can't be all things to all people," Horace said.

"We're frozen in time, completely out of touch."

"Backpedaling to the last century, more like it," Fabiana said.

"And what of it?" Horace said. "It beats the deplorable here and now."

"Look, Horace," Clive said. "We can't keep writing about gala after-theater suppers and the mink-and-monocle crowd sailing for England at midnight. It makes us irrelevant. Our readers don't even know what it means."

"Instructing the hoi polloi in worldliness," Horace said, "is hardly trivial."

"It's this: as a magazine, we're missing the mark. We've failed to evolve."

"We can't turn our backs on our readers," Horace said. "They have certain expectations."

"This isn't about turning our backs," Clive said. "It's about softening our historical fixation on conspicuous consumption and regal excess, about realigning with public sensibilities. Look, our biggest poles in the tent will always be food, wine, and travel. But we need to weave some modern touchstones into our fabric: conservation, sustainability, social responsibility—"

"You forgot to mention clinical insanity," Horace said.

"Listen, Horace," Clive said. "Research shows we're falling way behind in the new-households, college-educated demographic. The guide rails for our brand need to be environmental advocacy on the one hand and a healthy lifestyle consciousness on the other."

"I don't understand a word you said," Horace huffed.

"I'll give you an example," Clive said. "We've made an editorial decision. We won't be using your piece on morning drinking. It's inappropriate."

Horace stared with disbelief at the hard faces around the table.

"Who are you people, the Anti-Saloon League?" he said. "I'll remind you Prohibition has been repealed."

"There's nothing funny about alcoholism," Clive said. "It ruins lives. The piece will alienate readers. It'll drive away advertisers."

"You think I give a hoot about public opinion?"

Allison pushed in. "We're a food and lifestyle magazine. We can't possibly be perceived as defending obesity."

"And *pestilential hell-cartridges of death*?" Nigel said, looking around. "That should go over really well with our airline partners."

"Your piece insults a lot of key readership constituencies all at once," Allison said. "Catholics, women, extended families…"

"Not to mention the grossly offensive phrasing *belting squareface* and *going on a toot*," Fabiana said.

"Grossly offensive?" Across the table, Horace blinked at her.

"My cousin was killed by a drunk driver," Fabiana said. "There's nothing funny about that." Her voice quavered with rage.

"Where, dear girl, does the column say anything about driving an automobile?"

Fabiana nearly jumped out of her chair. "I am *not* a girl!"

Horace stared at her with bulging eyes.

"Oh, Horace, get off it," Billy said. "We've been talking about this for more than a year—abandoning the carriage trade and debutante stuff, recasting *Sunshine Trails* as more of a contemporary lifestyle magazine."

"A contemporary lifestyle magazine!" Horace thundered. He gestured with a hand, encompassing everyone at the table. "These rogue opportunists will have us touting tabloid trash like hot dogs and circus mustard."

"Not tabloid trash," Clive said. "Perfect weekend getaways, fun bicycle trails…"

"Dream kitchens, saving the forests…" Nigel said.

"And healthier relationships with food," Allison said. "Ingredients treated with respect. The two-hour Provençal lunch. The ethically responsible meatball."

"It's Halloween in the madhouse," Horace said. "You're all certifiable."

"It's where we need to go," Clive said. "The decision has been made."

"I beg your pardon, Clive, but *what* decision has been made?" Horace said.

"Ask Billy."

Horace glowered at Billy. "Dammit, Billy, we're supposed to be partners."

"Jesus God, Horace," Billy said. "We're talking survival here."

"Reckless groupthink. You're all drinking from the same contaminated well!" Horace threw his napkin on the table. With some effort he began to stand up.

"Hold on, Horace," Billy said. "Where are you going?"

"Back to my stateroom to lick my wounds."

Clive looked anxiously at Billy.

"Wait," Billy said. "There's one other thing. You'd better sit down."

Horace eyed Billy warily and lowered himself back into his chair.

"From now on, you're relieved of day-to-day editorial responsibilities," Billy said. "You'll be editor-at-large. You'll report to Nigel."

Horace's jaw dropped. "Nigel? Nigel's your number two."

"I am perfectly aware of Nigel's position on the organization chart," Billy said. "Hereafter, everything you submit to the magazine goes through him."

Horace's face reddened. He looked contemptuously at Nigel and then back to Billy. "Your father and I didn't build this magazine only to have it scuttled by an ignorant freeloader—"

"I've made my decision," Billy said. "Mother supports me one hundred percent."

"That's the understatement of the year—"

"Nigel has a good feel for where we need to go. I'm optimistic that the two of you can forge a productive working relationship."

Horace scowled at Billy. He jabbed a finger into the table. "I've never been more rightfully appalled than I am at this instant! I'm a founder and a stockholder in this company—"

"You might as well be an employee, for the good that'll do you," Billy said.

"—and now you're giving me a hatchet between the eyes—and on the day before my tribute dinner, no less!"

The editors all stared at a spot on the table. The railcar was silent. Even Wanda had stopped working in the galley. I caught a glimpse of her face in the pass-through.

"Not so much a hatchet, Horace," Billy said. "Let's call it a passing of the torch. It'll sound better in the press release. You're excused from the rest of this meeting." He turned to Clive. "Next item on the agenda…"

A few minutes later, the bell summoned me to the master stateroom. On a hunch, I took a fresh Manhattan with me. I knocked on the door.

"Come," Horace said. He sat on the edge of the bed looking shell-shocked. His necktie was off and his shirt was unbuttoned. His silver cuff links lay scattered like dice on the writing desk next to the type-writer. At the sight of the Manhattan he whimpered weakly, licked his lips, and reached for the drink.

He took a long sip, and then he rested the cocktail on a knee and gazed vacantly at the floor.

"Well, Jack, don't we make a sorry pair?" he said. "Our pockets picked by our respective teammates and our hats thrown into the street after us."

SEVENTEEN

BAM BAM. BAM BAM BAM.

The persistent knocking startled me awake.

I had fallen asleep in the sunlit observation lounge, seated on a barstool.

A young man dressed in the woolen plus fours and argyle knit vest of a Grand Harvey bellman stood on the open platform. He held an enormous bunch of red roses.

I let him in. A hotel limousine sat idling on the frontage road beside the tracks.

"You can put the flowers on the table," I said.

The bellman set the glass vase on the dining table and handed me a small, flat box.

"This goes with the flowers," he said.

The box had a card tucked beneath its silver ribbon. The card had my name on it.

I searched the pockets of my waiter's jacket and found a tip for the bellman. He took the money without looking.

"Cool digs," he said. "But what's that awful smell?"

"Lunch. The chef's cooking liver."

The bellman made a frightful face and left.

I slipped a finger beneath the flap of the envelope and opened the card.

Dear Jack,
Please forgive my atrocious behavior last night. My memory is dim, but I recall you were a perfect gentleman. I am most grateful for your chivalry. You are a rare and noble man. Though we've only just met, you hold a

very special place in my heart. Let me know if there is ever anything I can do for you.

Yours,
Giselle Lebeau

P.S. I made it through the morning, thanks to you!

The limousine pulled away, a white cloud of dust rising in its wake. I popped open the gift box and found my necktie wrapped in tissue and neatly folded. I laid the tie on the table and reread the card, which smelled faintly of perfume.

Wanda stood at the edge of the bar counter. "Who are the flowers for?"

"For me," I said. "From Giselle Lebeau."

Wanda's gaze shifted to the necktie on the table. Her eyes darkened. "You *did* sleep with her!"

"I told you, Wanda, I helped her to her room."

"And she sends you flowers."

"Apparently."

Wanda scowled. She crossed the short distance to the dining table and snatched up the roses. "We should get rid of these before Mr. Button sees them."

She carried the flowers out to the open platform. I watched dumbfounded as she tossed them over the railing. The vase shattered on the tracks below.

Wanda stepped back inside the railcar. I stared in disbelief.

"What?" she said.

"Jesus, Wanda. What was that all about?"

"She was a guest. It's crossing a line."

"I can't believe you—"

"It's almost lunchtime," she said. "Open the Brunello. Set the table. And put some music on."

I set the table to Tchaikovsky's 1812 Overture. The punch of cannon fire coming from the speakers underscored my feeling that my life was under siege, that my days aboard this old Pullman were numbered.

Horace declined to take lunch at the dining table. I delivered the meal to his stateroom, where he remained the rest of the day. For much of that time he lay in bed, weeping into a Brooks Brothers handkerchief. At Horace's directive, Cassidy the intern cancelled his scheduled appearances for the day, including a dinner party for the magazine's major advertisers that was to be held aboard the *Pioneer Mother* that night.

At one point Wanda caught me in the hallway, just as I was coming out of Horace's stateroom. We conferred in low voices. In deference to our employer's anguish we'd settled into a working truce.

"How's he doing?" Wanda said.

"If you're keeping score he's gone from Manhattans to gin and tonics to vodka martinis. I think he intends to run the table."

"Just what I was afraid of."

That evening a violent thunderstorm descended on Denver. Horace couldn't resist the allure of a good storm. He went out to the open platform and sat on a folding chair, under the protective cover of the old Pullman's roof and awning. He looked over the railroad yard and to the skyline beyond.

I went to check on him. The air was charged with electricity and smelled like rain.

"Mr. Button—"

A bolt of lightning flashed overhead, followed by a deafening clap of thunder.

"The rebuking finger of God," Horace said, his eyes turned skyward. "I'm encircled by vicious little eunuchs."

"Can I get you something to drink?"

"How about a cloudburst of Hennessy and soda to rival this downpour."

I brought the Hennessy and soda in a highball glass.

"You really ought to sit and watch this storm, Jack," Horace said. "It's quite magnificent."

I pulled up a second folding chair and joined him.

In the distance, brilliant streaks of lightning cleaved the black sky. Booming thunder echoed off the buildings. Rain came sideways.

When the turbulent weather finally began to dissipate, Horace pulled a cigar from his pocket. He carefully clipped the tip using a gold cutter.

"Living well and reporting on life's better vintages," he said, "that's where I've always made my good name. That mission requires the highest degree of professionalism in my own camp. You sympathize with that, Jack. I see it in the way you tend bar. You discharge your obligations with the utmost professionalism."

There was a flash of lightning. I braced for the ensuing clap of thunder, which came several seconds later. Horace waited patiently for it to pass. He licked the head of his cigar, preparing to light it.

"As for me, I am no fan of mankind," he said. "I choose to serve *humanity*. What these mush-heads don't understand is that by sharing these experiences with my readers, I'm elevating the human condition. I won't apologize for a word of it."

He used a jet torch lighter to light the cigar. He got it going with a series of quick puffs.

"Then again, maybe Billy's done me a favor, making me editor-at-large," Horace said. "No responsibilities. I might enjoy the freedom, once the initial shock wears off."

The leather-scented cigar smoke drifted slowly away from the open platform. The night air remained humid. Horace's cocktail was getting low.

"Top that off for you, Mr. Button?"

"Oh, right you are." He handed me his glass.

"Thank you, Jack," he said, when I returned with the freshened drink. He invited me to continue sitting with him.

"I don't know how much you know about me," he said, smoking the cigar, pausing for an occasional sip of his drink, "but I grew up a hotel child in Nevada. We lived on the top floor of the old Silver Horseshoe in Reno. My father owned a number of newspapers. At an early age he packed me off to boarding school in the East, where I became a holy terror. By the time I got to college I was an unabashed anarchist. They kicked me out of Harvard for it. My writing skills and a little luck were the only things that saved me from the penitentiary. By then my father had sold off his newspaper holdings for cattle land in northern Nevada. But the newspaper business was in my blood. I got on with the *New York Herald Tribune*. I worked my way up to politics. I hated every minute of it, shuttling between New York and Washington, covering the halls of

Congress. You'd find more virtue in a Nevada brothel."

"So you made a change?"

"I switched gears. Took an honest look at myself. Painting the town red at Manhattan's best hotels and nightclubs—that was my true calling. I left the political beat, started writing a society column. The column developed a following, primarily among Midwestern housewives. Those poor ragamuffins still lived like they were in the Great Depression. They were smitten with the glamour of nightlife in New York, which in itself was little more than an illusion. The column eventually evolved into *Sunshine Trails* magazine. My father staked our purchase of an old travel magazine out of bankruptcy. Lincoln, my business partner, was even more reckless than I. That's how we got Billy."

"You managed to build an impressive brand," I said.

"It wasn't easy," Horace said. "At the time I started in New York, the good life wasn't anything I could afford. I was a shill for the hotel industry. Most of us society columnists were, in those days. We had every luxury at our beck and call. Decked out by the finest tailors, dining on the cuff in the best hotels, being chauffeured around town in Rolls-Royce limousines. The only condition was we had to consent to being photographed for the society pages of *Town & Country*. It was a free pass. I camped out at all the swank dinner clubs: the Waldorf, the Plaza, Sherman Billingsley's Stork Club. It was Sherman who first chartered a plane to fly fresh pompano up from Florida's Gulf Coast. The pompano was broiled."

"Pompano?" I said.

"Think of it as not unlike a mackerel." Horace brought the cigar to his mouth and puffed on it thoughtfully for a few moments. Finally he turned to me. "I don't mean to pry, Jack, but I sense in you a young man who's somewhat down at the mouth."

"I'm sorry. I haven't had a lot of sleep."

"I'm talking about life in general. Charting a course. Dr. Rose told me of your accident."

"It was my own doing. I'm not looking for sympathy."

I'd said it too sharply. I searched Horace's face for forgiveness, but he was gazing at the skyline.

"I find athletics distasteful," he said. "The crowds are uncivil. Their cheers are undignified." He took another sip of his drink. "There's a reason I wanted to tell you my story, Jack. It wasn't until *Sunshine Trails* that my life truly came together. The second act often proves much more rewarding than the first—it did for me, in any event. You may think at age twenty-five your life is over, but the first quarter-century is nothing more than the low woodwind noise before the main curtain. The trick is to keep moving forward, to keep pursuing the things you love."

My hand went instinctively to the pocket where I kept Bianca's letter. "And if those things don't love you back?" I said.

Horace looked at me and raised an eyebrow. He returned his gaze to the city lights in the distance.

"Tell me," he said. "The roses that came today. Were they for you?"

I nodded. "From Ms. Lebeau."

"Christ, Jack." Horace turned to me with dismay. "We don't fraternize with the guests. It's bad practice."

I managed a smile. "Wanda made that abundantly clear."

"Billy's pursuing a business relationship with Ms. Lebeau. Your liaison could complicate things."

"Mr. Button, I was concerned for her well-being. I walked her to her room. Nothing happened."

Horace eyed me intently. "I'd like your word on that as a gentleman."

I met his penetrating stare. "You have my word."

Horace studied my face for several seconds, then went back to puffing his cigar.

"Mousse of Sole Washington," he said. "Do you know it?"

"Another seafood dish?"

"I'll ask Wanda to prepare it for you one of these nights. It's the test of a truly outstanding chef. It can be problematic, trying to retain in concentration the flavor of so delicate a fish."

"I don't think Wanda likes me well enough to fix me a problematic fish."

"Don't judge her too harshly. She's been through some difficult times."

"I really don't know anything about her."

"Well, you might make the effort."

"It takes two."

Horace turned to me, looking testy. "I suggest you patch up your differences, Jack. We're a family. The storm clouds have gathered. We need to circle the wagons."

EIGHTEEN

Special to *Sunshine Trails*
"Window on the West," by Horace Button
"Energy Diet"

SAN FRANCISCO—It isn't enough that the environmental gangsters have forced us to install smart meters on our homes so they can monitor personal energy use and impose rolling blackouts at will. Now we can hardly turn on the radio and not hear some self-important fathead exhorting us to go on a so-called energy diet.

Never has a greater fraud been perpetrated on the American public than the trumped-up hand-wringing of a universal calamity just around the corner in the form of an energy crisis.

In its perpetual states of crises, the government's knee-jerk reaction is always to insist that the citizenry cuts back. But why, for the richest nation on a planet of material plenty, is the answer never simply to *increase* supply? If you wear the hat of a businessman, which this reporter does on a fairly regular basis, the fatuousness of our elected leaders in this regard defies logic.

California's self-induced water shortage is instructional. Under the fiction of saving a three-inch fish called the delta smelt, and citing the Endangered Species Act, a handful of unelected, delusional lawyers in Washington managed to compound the state's water problems by redirecting more than 150 billion gallons a year from the Central Valley into the ocean. That's *150 billion gallons*—kaput, gone, flushed forever down Davey Jones's locker.

The economic consequences to the Valley have been dire: farmland going fallow, unemployment rates spiking, farmworkers standing in lines at the local food bank, the state forfeiting millions in tax revenues. And everywhere, food prices are skyrocketing.

Has it occurred to California's political brain trust that a substantial portion of their state borders a wet, aqueous thing called the *Pacific Ocean*? Do they realize the worldwide market demand for water treatment technologies, which includes the ability to desalinate seawater, is projected to reach north of $50 billion in the coming year, much of that demand supplied and serviced by California-based companies? Australia, China and Spain are actively making freshwater from seawater, and so are the more civilized (sic) countries in the Middle East. Yet in California, when it comes to water, we can't seem to find our backside with both hands.

So when I hear it's time to go on an energy diet, I'm justifiably suspicious—and actively resistant.

Aren't these the same jack-booted mandarins who've shuttered California's nuclear power plants? Who've slapped cease-and-desist orders on productive coal mining operations in West Virginia? Who've scotched drilling in Alaska's ANWR? And aren't these the same enviro-swindlers who want to put the brakes on tapping California's Monterey Shale oil reserves, estimated at 15 billion barrels of crude, citing preposterous lies about fracking and how it poisons our drinking water?

Instead of finding ways to increase our energy supply, these pious public-office frauds have prosecuted the cynical flimflam of artificially limiting supply while imposing ever-increasing consumption taxes on commodities that should be, for generations to come, cheaper than the lip service paid by politicians and more abundant than human stupidity. Masking their endgame of fleecing the taxpayers, they paint for us a bleak future of sacrifice, belt-tightening, and ever-dwindling resources.

In the words of Ronald Reagan: "My fellow citizens, I utterly reject that view."

And to think these boobs have the audacity to bombard us with radio ads about going on an energy diet.

Signed,
Your ace reporter,
HB

NINETEEN

"You must admit, Mr. Button, your personal politics have certainly raised some eyebrows."

"Of course."

"You call the energy crisis a hoax on the public."

"Yes."

"You believe welfare should come with drug testing and a work requirement."

"I do."

"You refuse to board a commercial airliner, the sight of tattoos makes you actively ill, and you blame the decline of dress standards in restaurants on the regents of the University of California."

Horace smiled aloofly, but his eyes danced. Being the center of controversy suited him.

A clutter of cameras and pole-mounted lights, anchored by sandbags, filled the observation lounge. Horace sat in his favorite parlor chair. Heavy makeup gave his face a doll-like, plastic sheen. Beads of perspiration glistened in his hairline.

The interviewer was an aging broadcast journalist who hosted a popular national television newsmagazine program. Stuart Tuttle had a craggy face and wispy tufts of hair the color of brown shoe polish. He wore a shawl-collared knit cardigan. A pair of reading glasses balanced on the bridge of his nose.

"The list of outrageous statements goes on and on," Tuttle said, glancing at his reporter's notepad. "You've called for the elimination of the

United Nations. You've condemned the European Union as Germany's third attempt to take over Europe. And with respect to Africa, you've said American partisans of democracy—our State Department—ought to take a lesson from the missionaries and simply get out, before they end up—and I quote—'*cooking in pots as the chef's blue plate special.*'" Tuttle looked up. "Hardly examples of enlightened, progressive thinking."

"The truth is, I don't give much credence to enlightened, progressive thinking," Horace said. "Why should I? What's it ever done for us?" He raised his martini glass and took a sip. The diamonds in his pinkie ring glittered under the glare of the lights.

I watched from my post behind the bar. My gaze kept shifting to the copy of the *North American Food and Wine Literary Festival Media Guide* that sat a few feet in front of me. A mug of coffee and a thick binder of notes sat on top of the guide. The coffee, notes, and book belonged to the TV producer, who was using the granite bar top as his desk. He sat with his back to me, concentrating on the interview. He was going bald in that way that looks as if someone had taken a lawnmower to the top of his head, leaving the long hair on the sides for another day.

"I look around at this luxurious bubble you live in," Tuttle said, waving a skinny arm. A yellow plastic Livestrong band hung limply from his wrist. "You travel by private train. A staff caters to your every whim. Compared to most people, Horace Button, you are a *very* rich man. So, when it comes to politics, why don't you simply shut up?"

Horace shook his head, his eyes narrowing.

"My commentary extends to every aspect of living," he said. "I believe in American exceptionalism. And that translates to everyday life—what we eat, what we drink, how we interact with one another—"

"How we dress in restaurants?"

"Indeed."

"You don't believe women should wear trousers?"

"Not in a five-star restaurant, no."

"And it embarrasses you when grown men wear shorts and T-shirts?"

"Like little boys at summer camp—"

"But why should it matter to you how people dress? What do you care?"

"It doesn't take a genius to see that this country is going to hell in a handbasket. We're spiraling into bankruptcy—morally, politically, financially. Slovenly attire is one symptom of a failing society. It demonstrates ignorance on a mass scale."

"And who do you blame for that?"

"*Whom* do I blame?" Horace said. "I blame the politicians, I blame the media, and I blame the universities."

Tuttle's face registered confusion. "Help me out here. What's the gain? What's in it for them?"

"Ignorance makes people easier to manipulate. It's an insult to every thinking American."

"You sound like—excuse the phrase—you sound like some rich, unapologetic, Republican snob. Is Horace Button all about money?"

"Money is fleeting, a thing to be thrown off the back of trains," Horace said. "But good taste and dignified living must be defended—to the death."

I was about to lift the mug off the media guide and sneak a peek when the producer, eyes still fastened on the interview, reached for his coffee.

"You have a famously conservative sister," Tuttle said.

The producer's hand froze.

"Yes." Horace eyed his questioner intently.

"Does she share your extreme political views?" Tuttle said.

"You'd have to ask her."

"Will Ruth Pepper ever run for president?"

"I wouldn't know."

"She hasn't talked to you about it?"

"Never."

"But she's your sister—"

Horace waved a hand. "I'm busy, she's busy."

"When was the last time you spoke with her?"

Horace shrugged. "How should I know? A while back."

"Did she say anything about the election?"

"She called to thank me for some books."

"Some books?"

"I sent her some signed books. My niece attends private school. They auctioned them off for a fundraiser."

"Tell me honestly, what kind of a president do you think your sister would make?"

"I have no idea."

"She doesn't have a lot of experience."

"She doesn't derive a freakish pleasure from feeding at the public trough, or steering billions of taxpayer dollars to her capitalist cronies, if that's experience."

"Would she be in favor of pulling our embassy officials out of Africa…" He looked down at his notes. "… Before they find themselves *cooking in pots*?"

Horace glared at Stuart Tuttle. Seconds ticked by.

"You aren't going to answer my question?" Tuttle said.

Horace made a circular motion with a hand. "Move along."

"Does Ruth Pepper favor pulling out of the U.N.?"

Horace stared stone-faced at his interviewer.

"Does she believe in man-made global warming?" Tuttle said.

Horace looked at me and raised his glass slightly, my signal to shake another martini.

"Mr. Button, why won't you answer my questions?" Tuttle said.

"Because I find them disingenuous." Horace stood up. "I know a thing or two about honest journalism, Mr. Tuttle. This is unabashed seek-and-destroy. This interview is over."

"But we've only just started," Tuttle said.

Horace unhooked the small microphone from his lapel and let it fall to the floor. "If you're intent on doing a hit piece on my sister, I suggest you call her office and make an appointment. At least give her the opportunity to defend herself."

"What did you think we were going to talk about?" Tuttle said. "Stuffing a turkey?"

"Stuffing a turkey would be preferable to your morbid goat bleats." Horace negotiated around the light poles and sandbags.

"Why are you walking out?" Tuttle said. "No one set any ground rules here." He wheeled around and asked the producer, "Are you getting this?"

"Still rolling," said the producer.

"For the record, Mr. Tuttle, I refuse to be photographed with you," Horace called over his shoulder. "That hideous sweater makes you look like a monkey."

A few minutes later, I delivered the fresh martini to the master stateroom.

"Never again, Jack," Horace said. "I don't know how I get talked into these things. They're malicious witch burners, bending the truth to serve their partisan pabulum." He stood over the sink in the lav, using a washcloth to wipe the makeup from his face. "You can set the drink on the desk. And let me know when the bastards have gone. What time do we leave for the hotel?"

"Ten should be very comfortable."

"The books are already there?"

"Cassidy has them in the ballroom."

"Ah, good."

Horace was scheduled to talk about his newly released book, *Speakeasy: A Collection of Essays on the Nation's Most Colorful Clubs, Taverns, and Saloons in the Time of Prohibition.* The lecture started at eleven.

In the observation lounge the members of the television crew were busy packing up equipment.

Stuart Tuttle and his producer stood near the door, arguing.

"Jesus Christ, Stu, did you have to go after him with a flamethrower?"

"What choice did I have? I couldn't just sit there and let him spew that crap."

"And your segue to Hurricane Ruth—that was way too soon. What happened to a little foreplay, first?"

"Fuck him," Tuttle said curtly, turning away from the producer. "I'm gonna go get a scotch."

Tuttle left the railroad car. The producer returned to the bar, exasperated.

I put a finger on the media guide.

"Mind if I take a look?" I said.

"Help yourself," the producer responded.

I opened the book to the Saturday calendar, scanning the schedule quickly.

"Find what you're looking for?" the producer asked.

"Right here. Giselle Lebeau's in the Grand Pavilion, doing a live cooking demonstration."

"You like to cook?"

"No, I need to see her. She's something of a friend."

"Sexy chick."

I handed the guide back. "Thanks."

"No problem." He began gathering up his notes. "Hey, be honest. This guy you work for—is he for real?"

"Mr. Button? Absolutely."

"You know, in Europe they'd throw him in jail for that kind of hate speech."

"Well, luckily for my boss, Amtrak doesn't go to Europe."

The producer laughed.

TWENTY

HALFWAY THROUGH HORACE'S LECTURE, I slipped out of the Trinidad Ballroom, left the conference center, and followed a meandering path through a forest of pine and aspen trees. My brisk pace wasn't entirely due to the downhill slope.

I came around a bend. Billy Whitehead was coming down a converging path. I tried turning away, but he called out to me.

"Jack!" Billy said. "You've come from Horace's talk. How's it going?"

"Great," I said. "He has them rolling in the aisles."

"It's a gift," Billy said. "He's a remarkable speaker. On your way to see Giselle?"

We fell in walking together.

I said, "I thought I'd have a look—"

"That makes two of us."

The Grand Pavilion was a high-peaked white tent located in the hotel's overflow parking lot. Through the plastic cathedral windows I could see a large, lighted stage, and on the stage a modern demonstration kitchen.

Festival volunteers checked credentials at the door. A woman stopped me.

"This is a closed event," she said.

"Giselle Lebeau's a personal friend," I said.

"Sorry," she said. "No one gets in without a ticket."

Billy stepped in. "It's all right, he's with me." His badge said *Major Sponsor—All Access.*

The woman looked at Billy. "Of course, Mr. Whitehead." She smiled and let me through. "Enjoy."

The tent smelled of braised beef and sun-warmed plastic. The cooking demonstration was over. A crowd gathered at the front of the stage. Cameras flashed. Across the way, a woman in a Peter Pan hat played shepherd to a long line for autographed books. Banners touted Giselle's latest cookbook, *French Made Easy*—on the cover, Giselle stood in a rustic kitchen, smiling warmly, offering forth a pot of stew.

I followed Billy up the wide center aisle. He came to an abrupt halt.

"Look at her," he said. "Can you imagine having that hot little bird on your masthead?"

At the apron of the stage, in a flood of bright light, Giselle sat behind a draped table amid stacks of books. Her hair was pulled back and she wore a white double-breasted chef's coat.

"Hey," said a man's voice behind me. "You're Jack Marshall!"

I turned. Who could forget Ed in the Stanford baseball cap and his wife, Angie, Giselle's autograph collectors from the champagne reception?

"I knew it was you!" Ed said. "See, Angie, didn't I tell you that was Jack Marshall? I recognized the scars—"

"Ed!" The woman swatted his arm.

Ed looked sheepish. "Okay, so I'm no diplomat. But I'm alumni." He shook my hand. "Ed Gable, class of seventy-seven. You've already met Angie. Boy, nobody ran the double-A-gap blitz like you guys did."

"Sounds like you know your football," I said.

"Season ticket holder," Ed said. "We were heartbroken over your accident."

"Awful," Angie said.

"You dropped some pounds." Ed scrutinized me. "The face turned out pretty good, though."

"Face looks great," Angie agreed. "Really great."

"So what are you up to these days?" Ed said.

I glanced at Billy. Agog over Giselle, he'd tuned us out.

"I work for *Sunshine Trails*," I said.

"You're a writer?"

"Bartender. Private parties, mostly."

Ed cast his eyes down. He licked his lips and put a fatherly hand on my shoulder. "Well, don't get discouraged. Something better will come along. Always does. Hey, can I get your autograph?"

The pity on his face, the way his voice brightened suddenly—he seemed to be throwing me a bone.

"You don't want my autograph," I said.

"Are you kidding? You were Jack Marshall! Come on, Angie. Find something he can sign."

Angie dug through her tote bag.

"There's this." She pulled out the conference program Giselle had signed.

"Perfect," Ed said. He handed me the program.

"Here's a pen," Angie said.

I glanced at the program and offered it back to Ed. "I can't sign this."

"'Course you can!" Ed said. "You're a legend!"

"Not this."

"Please. We insist."

I took the pen and scrawled my name in the lower right corner, opposite Giselle's. I added my number: 55.

"Thank you," I said, handing the pen and program back to Ed. "It's been a long time since anyone's asked for my autograph."

"Hey, you were a playmaker," Ed said. "Size, speed, grit—you had it all. No telling how far you could've gone. But listen to me ramble." He glanced toward the stage. "Better hurry if you want books. She's only here until twelve thirty, you know."

Billy and I lingered in the aisle, watching Giselle from a distance. At twelve thirty sharp the woman in the Peter Pan hat announced the session was over. Stagehands were already stripping cooking utensils from the demonstration kitchen and loading in new supplies for the next celebrity chef.

Giselle left the autograph table, pushing through a cluster of fans.

"Whew," she said to Billy. "Glad that's over." She gave me a quick smile. "Jack. What a nice surprise."

"Celebrity suits you, Giselle," Billy said. "You have these people eating out of your hand."

Giselle looked at him. "Do you always get what you want?"

"I don't know what you mean."

"I could use some air." Giselle started up the aisle.

"I learned something extraordinary about you the other day," Billy said, following. "From a consultant. Why you're an overnight success."

"Five years of public television and a ruined marriage," Giselle said. "I'd hardly call that overnight."

"You're all about sex."

Giselle glanced skeptically at Billy. She kept walking. "I cook for a camera."

"Men see you as the perfect wife. They fantasize about making love to you five ways to Sunday, and then imagine you hopping out of the sack to fix them a foot-long sandwich."

"Tell your consultants I don't do sandwiches."

"You're missing my point."

Giselle stopped. "What's your point, Billy?"

"The wives sense it. They feel compelled to compete with you. That's why they watch your show, why they buy your books. They want to be like Giselle Lebeau."

Giselle resumed walking. "That's why you want me for *Sunshine Trails*?"

"I can't win with Horace. He still thinks it's about the food."

"Isn't it?"

"It's about sex," Billy said. "And it can be all about you, Giselle. We can extend your brand, cut deals with our advertisers, place dishware and bath products in all the big-box stores. You can help us take *Sunshine Trails* back to its glory days—a status symbol for the middle class. I've outlined a deal structure that I think you'll agree is pretty compelling—"

"I'm supposed to be making *boeuf en croûte* for three hundred," Giselle said. "Can we talk about this later?"

"Anytime," Billy said. "Just name it."

Giselle took me by the hand and turned to Billy. "Do me a favor and give us some space, would you?"

"Space?"

"I want to take your employee for a little walk."

"Jack? Whatever for?"

"He did me a favor," she said, drawing me up the aisle. "Maybe I want to make him a big sandwich."

We left the tent. The morning sessions were letting out. Conference participants gathered on the main path, animated in their conversations, blocking our route to the hotel.

"This way." Giselle led me across a soft lawn. In the harsh midday sun her false eyelashes, heavy black eyeliner, and pancake stage makeup seemed more plausible on a high-class hooker than the sweetheart of America's kitchen.

"Should I know who you are?" Giselle said. "Because that guy back there seemed pretty impressed."

"You saw that?"

"I see everything. Why did he want your autograph?"

"Doesn't matter. It's an old story."

"What if you're an ax murderer?"

"Then you'd be holding hands with a desperate killer," I said. "Which is why you need a bodyguard."

"I need a lot of things," Giselle said. "But a bodyguard isn't one of them. Hold up a sec." She put a hand on my shoulder and slipped out of her high heels. The pleated black skirt she wore came to just above her knees. Her legs were bare. "Okay, better."

She took my hand again and led me behind the conference annex, carrying her stiletto heels by their straps. We ventured off the grass and onto manicured hardpan, the dirt having been raked clean of rocks and leaves. We walked among the groomed trunks of tall pines. In the shadow of the old hotel, the air was cool.

"Can you fly a jet?" Giselle said.

"A jet?" I gazed curiously at this bewitching woman.

"I'm in the market for a Gulfstream. I need pilots."

"Sounds expensive," I said. "Gulfstream pilots."

She took me down a narrow pathway that followed a pitted concrete wall. "My business manager tells me I can afford it."

"What else does your business manager say?"

"That I should be wary of strangers."

"And here you are shanghaiing one."

"I'm not worried. A little bird tells me you're safe."

We came to a quiet garden. Under the shade of horse chestnut trees, Rocky Mountain columbine grew in raised planter beds. At a burbling fountain Giselle stopped and faced me.

"I thought I'd never see you again," she said. "Is everything good between us?"

"Everything's fine," I said. "You didn't have to send the flowers."

"It was the least I could do." Giselle interlocked her fingers with mine. She swung our joined hands coyly. "May I confess something?"

"Of course."

"The other night, at the champagne reception, I couldn't get your attention. I had to resort to extraordinary measures."

"You were trying to pick me up."

Giselle smiled. "Finally. The bartender catches on." She brought my hand close to her face and gave my knuckles a soft kiss. "My knight in shining armor. I can't stop thinking about you."

"I can't stop thinking about you, either," I said. "Look, Giselle, there's something I need to ask you. You barely know me and I barely know you. But I'd like a job."

Giselle's smile disappeared and the color drained from her face. "You have a job."

"The *Pioneer Mother* is headed for the scrap heap," I said. "Mr. Whitehead all but said so. And here you are, traveling alone, constantly mobbed by people. I wanted to follow up on something you said the other night. I'd like to be your bodyguard."

"Sorry, Jack. I don't take charity cases." She looked stung.

"I'm not asking for charity. I'm asking for work."

"You think you can say 'pretty please' and land between my legs?"

"I don't think that at all—"

"God! Do you have any idea how many people hit me up for jobs? Believe me, make the kind of money I do, and they come out of the woodwork. Jobs, cash, cars, they want it all. And they keep coming—not just the people you know, but family and friends and the friends of friends—"

"Giselle—"

"I thought you were someone I could trust."

"I *am* someone you can trust—"

"I mean, whoever asks what I need or want?"

"You don't understand what I'm saying—"

"Hold on," Giselle said. "Hear me out. Do you want to know what my business manager really says? He warns me about nice guys like you—guys who sweet talk their way in and take me for a fat paycheck and anything else they can get their hands on. You want a job? Fine. But don't come to me. I'm not a fucking employment agency. Why are you smiling?"

"Because I seem to have a talent for pissing off beautiful, accomplished women."

"Please don't say that. I'm none of those things."

"Yes, Giselle, yes you are. You're an incredible person. And I'm saying trust me. Make an exception. I'll carry your bags, I'll draw your hot baths, I'll do anything to make you happy. Just let me into your world. Please. My life is going nowhere."

Giselle's eyes welled. She glanced away.

"You're very sweet," she said. "I'm sorry. This has been the greatest year of my life and also the worst. The whole world loves Giselle Lebeau, but nobody loves me."

"That's crazy."

"And then I meet this gorgeous man who doesn't even know who I am. You have no idea how appealing that is to a woman in my position. And he's a complete gentleman, the kind of man a girl dreams about. He walks me to my room and makes sure no one's hiding under the bed. He doesn't want anything for himself, just to make sure I'm safe. And that blew me away. I thought, *Finally, Giselle, here's a man you can really count on.*" As she spoke she began to cry. She quickly brushed away her tears. "You know what I imagined about you? I imagined you were the kind of guy who'd never let me open a door or carry a suitcase, that you'd read me funny things from the newspaper in the morning and join me for long walks on the beach in the afternoon, that you'd be happy just sharing my life. God. Listen to me. It all sounds so stupid. How can I always be so wrong?"

"It doesn't sound stupid, and you aren't wrong."

"It seems pointless. I do all this work and I'm on TV and selling all these books, and still I'm always alone—it's like a curse—I'm forced to put up these walls."

I gathered her in my arms and pulled her close. "You don't have to be alone." I kissed her forehead, I kissed her hair. She turned her face up to me. As I went to kiss her mouth she gave me a nudge. Two women were coming around the corner, admiring the garden. Both wore badges for the literary festival. Giselle buried her head in my chest.

A few minutes later, after the women were gone:

"Can we give it a try?" Giselle said. "See where this goes?"

"Of course we can," I said.

She looked at me intently. "No job, okay? My man doesn't work."

"But I've always worked."

"You pour gin on a train. That doesn't count. It's mindless busy-work." Giselle leaned up against me, toying with the buttons on my shirt. She smiled coyly. "How does Hawaii sound?"

"Hawaii?"

"We're filming next week on Kauai. A Kalua pig at a chef's luau before a live audience. Come with me."

"Are you serious?"

"Completely serious." She stared up at me. "Come on, Jack. What do you say?"

"Count me in. Definitely."

She stood on tiptoe and wrapped her arms around my neck.

"Here's a crazy thought," she said. "Fly back with me to L.A. tomorrow."

"Tomorrow?"

Giselle studied my eyes. "What's wrong?"

"I can't do that to Mr. Button," I said. "I can't leave him in the lurch."

She released her hold on my neck. "Are you kidding? This town has a thousand bartenders. I could pick up the phone and have fifty at my door in an hour. You don't think Horace Button could do the same?"

"I'm sorry, Giselle. I can't just walk out on him. Not after all he's done for me."

"So when are you available?"

"I finish this trip Monday afternoon in Emeryville. That's the end of my contract. Then I need to get my truck in San Jose."

"Fine. Fly to Los Angeles on Monday night, or early Tuesday morning. We can head to Hawaii together on Tuesday afternoon. My office will get the tickets."

"I can pay my own way," I said.

"Don't be stupid." Giselle smiled and squeezed my hand. "And don't be late."

"Late." I checked my watch. "My God, the time!"

I was twenty minutes late to pick up Horace.

TWENTY-ONE

CHAOS REIGNED. A throng of eager fans had Horace pinned down at the front of the ballroom. On the mob's fringe, several people holding autographed books told me Horace's *Speakeasy* talk was their favorite of the conference.

I had to interrupt Horace and remind him of the luncheon in his honor. I finally pulled him out of the ballroom and whisked him through the lobby and out the door to our waiting Escalade for the trip across town.

La Cheminée du Roi was one of Denver's top restaurants. Michel Ricard ran La Cheminée with such attention to detail that he was known affectionately as *le bijoutier*—the jeweler. For Horace, a great friend of Ricard's, the intimate lunch was a rare opportunity to reflect with old and dear friends on his sunsetting career. These were not the pop-icon, culinary celebrities who dominated the scene at the North American Food and Wine Literary Festival, but true gastronomes and oenophiles whose writings appeared mostly in obscure trade organs. Some arrived using walkers.

Ricard's special menu included fresh beluga caviar, terrines of *foie gras*, and roasted guinea fowl. He poured a Château Margaux that left the diners rapturous. To commemorate the meal, paper printouts of the menu were passed around the big table. Each guest signed his name. I watched from the shadows of Ricard's closed bar, where I sat alone eating onion soup from a wide-mouthed earthenware bowl.

Back at the railcar, preparations were underway for the late-night reception that was to follow the tribute dinner and the after-party at the Pony Room. Wanda worked fastidiously in the galley, turning out serving pans of picture-perfect hors d'oeuvres. A FedEx truck delivered a case of 1961 La Tâche grand cru Burgundy and so many cases of Dom Pérignon Cuvée, we had to stack them in the guest stateroom.

Cassidy showed up with a man who took my measurements. She returned an hour later with a full tuxedo—shoes, shirt, and all the accoutrements—that fit me perfectly, except for the jacket, which was tight in the shoulders. I was to accompany Horace to the gala while Wanda supervised the *Pioneer Mother's* move to the boarding platform at Union Station.

The westbound Zephyr was scheduled to leave Denver at 8:05 the next morning, leaving little time for sleep.

At six o'clock that evening Horace and I arrived at the Grand Harvey Hotel. Striding through the lobby in his black tuxedo, Horace looked splendid. I caught my reflection in a mirror: scarred face, jacket bursting at the seams—a trademark Hollywood villain.

Our first stop was the conference annex. Horace wanted to inspect the lavishly decorated Grand Ballroom—the Trinidad, Aspen, and Denver rooms had been opened up to form one great banquet hall, adorned with thirty round tables. Members of the banquet staff were scattered throughout the ballroom, putting finishing touches on the table settings. Along the back wall, elaborate temporary scaffolding held video cameras and spotlights. The focal point of the room was an elevated dais with a long, draped table. At the center of the table was a hotel lectern. Horace sprang up the few steps to the dais. He examined the table and the lectern, looked over the room, and declared it all acceptable.

We left the ballroom and boarded an elevator for the seventeenth floor.

At Poppy Whitehead's suite, people spilled from the foyer into the hallway. The men wore black tie, the women formal gowns. Everyone drank champagne. The white hair, the jewels—I had never seen so many diamonds in one place. The partygoers quickly swallowed Horace up. I pressed my way through the suite, looking for Giselle. Near a portable bar, Poppy greeted guests. She wore a long, pink gown and a rock that could have passed for the Hope Diamond. I saw Allison and Fabiana, the *Sunshine Trails* editors. They were engaged in a serious conversation with an extremely fat man. At one point I came face-to-face with Nigel Coffey, ostensibly Horace's new supervisor. He pushed past, acting as if he didn't know me. "Good luck, asshole," I said under my breath.

In the living room, Billy Whitehead buttonholed me.

"So, Jack, what's going on between you and Giselle?" he said.

"Nothing very interesting, Mr. Whitehead. Just comparing notes."

"Notes?"

"She had something she wanted to run past me."

"Giselle Lebeau going to you for advice? I find that hard to believe."

"Is she here?"

"I don't think so. I haven't seen her." Billy put a hand on my shoulder. "You know, Jack, she's a tough nut to crack. This deal we're proposing —if you have any advice for me, I'll certainly make it worth your while."

"I'll keep that in mind, Mr. Whitehead."

"Please," he said. "It's Billy." He smiled at me. "You and I are buddies, right?"

As showtime approached, I joined the crowd at the elevators, waiting for a car down. The elevators in the Harvey were small and slow, and it was a long wait. We streamed as a pack to the conference annex lobby and got our table assignments for dinner.

Table thirty was farthest from the dais and closest to the kitchen's swinging doors. Seated to my left was a young nanny with a baby carriage stashed against the wall. Her two charges, a boy about five and a girl about three, sat on their knees and drew with crayons on the white linen tablecloth. Meanwhile, the nanny texted on her cell phone and left the children to fend for themselves. I attempted to introduce myself to the elderly woman sitting to my right. Her hearing aids squawked, and she gave me a thousand-yard stare. The purpose for table thirty, I realized, was to quarter the oddballs.

I nodded pleasantly at the people across the table, and we made attempts at conversation, but the ballroom grew louder by the minute, and we settled into a comfortable rhythm passing around a basket of rolls. We smiled at the children as they defaced Herr Fritz's tablecloth.

The lights finally dimmed and the show started.

To the beat of timpani drums, spotlights swept the ballroom. The unseen announcer had a booming, Godlike voice.

"Ladies and gentlemen," he began. "Welcome to the forty-third meeting of the North American Food and Wine Literary Festival, where tonight we pay tribute to one of the world's legendary food and wine writers. A gourmet and gastronome of the highest order... renowned member of the Confrérie des Chevaliers du Tastevin... bon vivant, boulevardier, founder and editor-in-chief for *Sunshine Trails* magazine... author of more than a dozen definitive works ranging from contemporary dining to travel and entertainment... "

At this point the eight chairs on the dais stood empty. Then, like boxers coming to the ring in a championship prizefight, each celebrity chef was introduced: "A powerful force in the food world, this culinary superstar and national television personality is a best-selling author and chef-proprietor of fourteen restaurants in ten major American cities, including New York, New Orleans, and Las Vegas—" To rousing applause the celebrity chef of the moment came bursting through the doors. The spotlights followed as he strode triumphantly up the aisle, pumping his fists, giving high fives, and eventually taking a seat on the dais. The introductions went on ad nauseam until most of the chairs on the dais were filled.

In private, Horace referred to these showboat chefs as the cocktail wieners of the industry, but in the end the literary festival was a business, and it took having these famous names on the program to sell the dinner tickets, which cost about what you'd pay for a night in a deluxe room at the Grand Harvey.

When Giselle was introduced ("This global media icon is a household name...") the crowd went wild. Walking up the aisle, waving, smiling her famous smile, blowing kisses, she looked stunning in a shoulder-baring blue chiffon dress with a high split up the side. Amid the raucous applause were catcalls and wolf whistles.

After Giselle took her seat on the dais, Billy and Poppy were introduced. Billy strolled arm in arm with his mother up the aisle, the royal prince escorting the Queen Mother.

It was finally Horace's turn to enter the ballroom. To a standing ovation, he made his way—red-faced and somewhat unsteadily—up the aisle, casting a critical eye at the audience.

Billy made for a witty master of ceremonies as he led the first toast. Three hundred of us raised glasses of Veuve Clicquot's La Grande Dame.

Then Billy called Giselle up as the honorary dinner chef. To warm applause, carrying a champagne flute, Giselle glided to the lectern. Billy opened his arms theatrically and said something that made her laugh. He kissed her on both cheeks.

"Billy, thank you so much," Giselle said, stepping up to the microphone. "And how nice it is to be here on this special occasion."

"We love you, Giselle!" someone called from the back of the room.

Giselle looked in the direction of the voice and laughed. Her blue eyes sparkled.

"I love you, too," she said. She drew a breath and squared her shoulders to the lectern. "All right. Serious business. There's an old San Francisco expression: to see the elephant. Do you know it? The French equivalent is *faire la bombe*. It means you've gone out and done everything you could possibly do. You've painted the town, you've drunk the best wine. You've experienced every hedonistic pleasure life has to offer. In sum, you've seen the elephant. That's what I think of when I think of Horace Button."

Unnoticed by Giselle, Herr Fritz quietly ascended the side steps of the dais and discreetly made his way across the stage. He leaned over and whispered into Horace's ear. Horace blanched.

"Horace Button has seen the elephant," Giselle was saying. "He's..." She sensed the activity on the stage and turned. "Is everything all right?"

At that moment a disturbance rippled through the ballroom—a gasp, a low murmur, a cry of disbelief. Isolated cells of blue light were being cast around the darkened room as people turned instinctively to their phones.

"Oh, my freaking gosh," said the nanny next to me, staring at her phone. "Hurricane Ruth is dead!"

Just then a banquet server—a young woman with her hair tied severely back—charged out of the kitchen doors and said to a cluster of servers, "They killed Ruth Pepper!"

Across the room a woman wailed.

Giselle stepped back from the lectern. She looked from Horace to Billy. Herr Fritz was helping Horace to his feet. Horace took a few wobbly steps, then stopped and scanned the audience, using a hand to shield his eyes from the bright lights.

"Jack? Where are you, Jack? Please, I need you!"

The noise level in the ballroom rose sharply. People left their chairs. The servers stood in groups of six or seven, looking around hopelessly. No one seemed to be in charge.

I pushed my way to the front of the room, where Herr Fritz and Giselle were helping Horace from the dais.

"I don't understand," Horace was saying. "What have they done?"

I grasped Horace's arm, taking over for Herr Fritz, who urged us to a side door.

"You must come this way," he said.

Giselle looked at me, hesitating, but Herr Fritz was firm.

"*Schnell!*" he barked.

TWENTY-TWO

HERR FRITZ GUIDED US DOWN an austere service hallway behind the ballroom. Giselle and I had Horace propped between us, and we labored to keep up with the general manager's aggressive strides.

"What's going on?" Horace kept saying. "I don't understand. What's happened to Ruth?"

People stared as we emerged from the hallway into a public room. Herr Fritz led us around a corner, past the hotel lobby, and through the double-glass doors of the hotel's administrative offices. The long corridor was vacant, the lighting dim.

Herr Fritz unlocked the door at the end of the hallway.

"Do they know what happened?" Giselle said.

"My guess is assassination," Herr Fritz said. "Her political enemies are known to be insidious and cunning."

His spacious office was brightly lit, and a fire burned in the fireplace. Above the mantle a television streamed a 24-hour cable news channel. We deposited Horace on the long upright sofa that faced the fireplace. Our eyes turned to the TV. "US SENATOR RUTH PEPPER KILLED OUTSIDE HER DC HOME," said the bright graphic across the bottom of the screen.

Horace whimpered.

"My God," Giselle said. She telegraphed a look of despair.

Herr Fritz used a remote to urge the volume louder. "I saw this and thought I must notify you immediately," he said. "I must help you to escape the banquet room."

"You did the right thing, Herr Fritz," I said. Giselle joined me behind the sofa. She put a hand on Horace's shoulder.

Raul Page, the news anchor, was a familiar face. Young and slender with a sly manner and a flair for the melodramatic, he spoke without a script.

"A gas leak, a car bomb, a missile," he said. "It's simply too early to tell what caused the blast in this upscale neighborhood. But, keep in mind that Ruth Pepper is—*was*—certainly no stranger to controversy. If this turns out to have been a targeted killing, there will be no shortage of suspects. And no telling what kind of group or individual might take credit for this murderous act." Raul touched his earpiece. He looked down and off to the side. "Things are unfolding rather quickly, as you might imagine. We go now to our reporter Tabitha Tregor, on the ground in Washington."

A self-important blonde stood on a darkened residential street.

"Raul," she said, "I'm actually about a mile from Ruth Pepper's home. It's been quite chaotic around here, with all the first responders rushing to the scene. They're not letting anyone past this security perimeter, and probably won't for some time."

"Tabitha, what's the word on other victims?"

"We don't know anything yet about other victims. There are reports Ruth Pepper was with her husband at the time of the blast, but that hasn't been confirmed. We're checking with emergency rooms at local hospitals to see if anyone's been admitted. You'd have to expect that in an explosion of this magnitude, anyone nearby would have certainly been affected by the blast. So no one has ruled out finding more victims, either injured or dead."

"But so far Senator Pepper is the only confirmed fatality?"

"It's an extremely fluid situation but yes, so far Senator Pepper is the only fatality positively confirmed."

"Listen to these louts," Horace said, slumping on the sofa, thundering over this shoulder. "They're practically celebrating!"

"The media has been infiltrated by traitors," Herr Fritz said. "I can turn the TV off if it makes you sick to your stomach."

"No, Herr Fritz," Horace said. "Leave it on. We can only hope there's been some mistake."

"There has been no mistake," Herr Fritz said. "We're a nation at war. The pacifist politicians are the only ones who do not understand this. May I offer you a drink?"

"Do you have brandy?" Horace said.

"I have kirsch. It would be my pleasure to share it with you—"

"God, no!" Horace said. "Please. Keep that for yourself."

"Shall I summon room service?" Herr Fritz reached for the house phone.

"No offense, Herr Fritz," Horace said, "but room service is a lousy way to get a drink."

"Mr. Button," I said, "I can run upstairs to the bar."

"Good of you, Jack." Horace wiped his face with a monogrammed white linen handkerchief. "Get me a sidecar to start. And a string of martinis to follow. Keep the bar on full alert. It's going to be a long night."

"I'm on my way," I said.

"I'll go with you," Giselle said.

As we reached the door, Horace called out.

"Jack! The sidecar—have them pour a vintage cognac. A common man's brandy at a time like this is unthinkable."

In the hallway, Giselle slipped her hand into mine. She stopped me at the double doors to the lobby.

"Wait, I can't go out there yet." She looked frightened. "It's like the whole world's falling apart. Am I crazy to be scared?"

I gathered her in my arms. I stroked her raven-black hair, which was stiff with hairspray.

"You're not crazy," I said. "It scares me, too."

She looked up at me with seductive eyes. "Can't we please just go to Hawaii?"

The adrenaline pumping through my veins, the formal attire, Giselle's powerful sensuality—I felt reckless, perverse, unstoppable. I took her by the shoulders and pushed her against a wall. When I leaned down to kiss her, her mouth surged against mine. We knocked into a framed travel poster, pitching it askew. My hands frantically explored the curves of her back. In the formal gown's loose bodice, her breasts seemed unbridled. I brought a hand to the front of her gown.

Giselle ducked her face and pushed away my hand. "Not here."

Breathless, I stared wild-eyed.

"I can't risk it," she said. "It's too public."

This brought me to my senses.

The Pony Room was thronged with guests in tuxedos and formal gowns. I pushed through the crowd. Frank spotted us and took my drink orders.

"It's for Mr. Button," I said.

Two television screens streamed the same cable news broadcast.

We withstood the jostling crush at the bar, Giselle tethered to my hand. I couldn't take my eyes off her. When the men and women realized it was Giselle Lebeau they were bumping against, they gawked, too.

"Do you think we're really on the verge of war?" Giselle asked me.

"Who knows?"

"Why now, of all times?"

People in front of the television screens called urgently for everyone to quiet down. The on-screen graphics heralded breaking news. Raul came on, grim-faced.

"...and it has now been confirmed that Ruth Pepper's husband, David, was found deceased at the scene," he said. "This formally takes the death toll to two. Furthermore, sources close to the investigation say the blast was caused by an improvised explosive device, or I.E.D. Whether this was the first of a series of planned attacks on high-ranking government officials is unknown, but authorities are taking no chances—Washington has gone into total lockdown. Airports and government buildings are at their highest levels of alert. And members of Congress, we understand, are getting around-the-clock protection from the Secret Service and other federal law enforcement agencies.

"This is a dark night for our nation," he continued. "And we can't help but ask, who was behind this? And can they be found—and stopped—before they strike again?"

In the Pony Room, a feverish energy coursed through the crowd. The noise level swelled.

Frank set a large serving tray on the bar in front of me. The tray brimmed with supplies: a sidecar, a martini glass, a cocktail shaker, a full liter of gin, a bottle of dry vermouth, paper cocktail napkins, a jar of queen olives, a chilled bottle of Veuve Clicquot.

"It's heavy," Frank said.

Giselle reached for the bottle of champagne. "I can carry this."

I lifted the tray.

"It's fine, Frank," I said. "Thank you."

In Herr Fritz's office, Billy and Poppy had joined the vigil. They stood with Herr Fritz, staring at the television. Horace reclined on the sofa, pressing the handkerchief to his eyes. When I set the tray on the coffee table in front of him, he managed to sit up. I handed him the sidecar and a napkin.

"Thank you, Jack," he said.

"Ah, the train steward," Poppy said. "Just the person I want to talk to!"

She pulled me aside. With a long silver cigarette holder—but no cigarette—she indicated Horace. She spoke quietly but firmly. "He couldn't roll a hoop right now. I need you to take charge. Get him to Washington."

"Washington?"

Giselle looked over.

"There's a funeral to plan," Poppy said. "And no doubt a mountain of family business to attend to. We'll fly you out tomorrow. My office will make the arrangements. Your job is to get him there sober."

"I don't think he'll do it," I said. "Fly, I mean."

"Silly child, of course he'll fly," she said. "This is his sister we're talking about. We can't have him dawdling on a milk train."

TWENTY-THREE

WANDA PICKED UP ON THE THIRD RING. The news of Ruth Pepper's death stunned her.

"What do we do now?" Wanda asked.

"Cancel tonight's railcar move, for one," I said.

"This is Amtrak. You can't change things on a dime."

"Wanda, there's no way we're leaving for California in the morning. Mr. Button's headed to Washington. He and I fly out tomorrow." I paced the vacant corridor of the hotel's administrative offices.

"Where is he now?" Wanda said. "How's he taking it?"

"He's distraught but not hysterical. He's drinking a lot of martinis. We're watching the news."

Wanda went silent a moment. "So I assume tonight's reception is off?"

"Believe it or not, Mr. Whitehead insists we go through with it."

"You can't be serious."

"I'm completely serious. Brace yourself. It's going to be gruesome. I'll call when we're on our way."

The scent of a familiar perfume signaled that Giselle was behind me. She wrapped her arms around my waist and pressed her head against my back. As I ended the call, she gave me a squeeze.

"You don't have any obligation to these people, you know," she said.

"I know."

"You don't have to go to Washington, D.C., either."

"No."

"Just tell them you quit."

"Sure, easy as that." I turned and took her in my arms.

"I can't change Hawaii," she said. "They schedule these things way in advance."

"I understand."

"I need to be in L.A. tomorrow night. I'm having dinner with my producer and director. We're going over scripts."

"Giselle, I get it."

"Look, Jack. Loyalty impresses me as much as anyone. But it doesn't mean you have to put your life on hold."

"Washington, D.C., and a hotel room. That's it. I'll get him settled and I'll be on the first plane to Los Angeles."

"You promise?"

I kissed her lightly on the forehead. "I promise."

By ten o'clock Horace was on his feet, pacing in front of the fireplace, adamant about joining the party in the Pony Room.

"Keep me within eyesight at all times, Jack," he said. "Watch my back. I'd hate to think one of these scoundrels with a bomb could catch me unawares."

"What about you, Mother?" Billy said. "Coming with us?"

"Are you both out of your minds?" Poppy said. "How can you possibly party on a night like this?"

"You should listen to your mother, Billy," Giselle said. "Are you insensitive or just stupid?"

"Don't condemn me, Giselle," Billy said. "Some of our biggest advertisers are up there. We've already cancelled on them once. Herr Fritz, will you join us?"

Herr Fritz sat tensely behind his desk.

"No," he said, "I shall remain here, keeping an eye on operations." He lit a cigarette and dropped the spent match into an ashtray. "An innkeeper has a certain—how do you say, *dutifulness* not to fraternize with his guests. It would be highly improper."

"All this duty-and-propriety stuff, Herr Fritz," Horace said. "You risk giving the Krauts a bad name."

"I trust you can defend my position to your admirers," Herr Fritz said.

In the lobby we put Poppy on an elevator to the seventeenth floor. Giselle reluctantly agreed to go with us to the Pony Room. She held onto my arm as we followed Horace and Billy up the marble staircase.

"I can't believe we're actually doing this," she said to me. "We should have taken that elevator upstairs to my suite."

The crowd in the Pony Room quickly parted for Horace as he made his way to the bar. A man jumped up from his barstool.

"Please, take this one," he said to Horace.

"Would you mind?" Horace said. "I'm dizzy with shock, you see."

Behind the bar, Frank worked shoulder to shoulder with the bartenders. He had his suit jacket off and was sweating.

"She was a good lady, Mr. Button," he said. "You could just tell."

The revelers quickly gathered around Horace. They offered condolences and bought him drinks. Some leaned in and snapped selfies with their phones. Giselle and I looked on from a quiet corner.

"They're like rubberneckers at an accident," she said. "Why don't they go home?"

Billy came up next to us. "Because they paid good money and they want their party."

"Don't they know two people are dead?" Giselle said.

"Death is a turn-on," Billy said. "It makes you do things you wouldn't normally do. I say, Jack, is that lipstick on your collar?"

"I'm about to steal your bartender," Giselle said.

Billy took a step back and blinked. "Congratulations. Congratulations to you both."

"Unless you want to try and stop me," Giselle said.

"Don't be silly, Giselle. I wouldn't stop you from doing anything."

By midnight, the crowd at the bar had diminished to perhaps twenty people. The men stood or sat with their backs to us. They looked priestly in their black tuxedos but were vulgar in their drunkenness—the backslapping, the roars of laughter.

I turned to Giselle. "So tell me about Hawaii."

"You've never been?"

I shook my head.

"It's an amazing place," she said. "The balmy air, the way it grows fragrant at night. The food is incredible. Fresh local catch fused with Asian spices and European sauces. I like to end my nights with a piece of Kona mud pie and a full-bodied cabernet, preferably in a crisp, cool bed. I sleep with the shutters open and drift off to the cadence of the pounding surf."

Billy was heading our way. He had an arm around the shoulders of a moonfaced man with a white Quaker beard. The man's massive belly strained the buttons of his tuxedo shirt. His drink slopped and left puddles across the dance floor.

Billy hauled the man in front of Giselle.

"Victor, meet Giselle Lebeau." Billy winked. "Victor's been dying to meet you."

Giselle put out a hand and flashed her smile. "Hello, Victor. I'm Giselle."

Too drunk to take her hand, Victor teetered in his shiny black opera shoes and peered at Giselle with one eye.

"I've a bone to pick with you," he said.

"A bone?" Giselle said.

"Your olive oil. It's crap."

Giselle shot Billy a wrathful look.

"I can't believe you put your name on it," Victor was saying. "Like cat piss and rancid walnuts."

Giselle's face flushed. She glared at the man. "And you're the world's expert in olive oil?"

"Might be. Now you mention it."

"Victor owns the Siena Ranch brand," Billy said. "He's one of our major advertisers."

Victor leered at Giselle. "You're a beautiful lady. But putting your name on that shitty olive oil makes you look like an ignorant housewife."

"Thanks for the opinion, Victor," Giselle said. "I'll get right on it."

Victor reached into his pocket and produced a business card.

"Classy dame like you should be using Siena Ranch," he said. "My olive oil and your pretty face. We'd make a great team."

"Keep your fucking card," Giselle said. "I'm not interested."

"Oh, Giselle—" Billy said.

"No!" Giselle said quickly. "People are setting off bombs, and this asshole's trying to sell me olive oil!"

"I think what Victor's trying to say is there may be a partnership worth exploring here," Billy said. "It doesn't have to be tonight. Certainly not tonight. Let's just table the thought for now. Besides, we came to tell you that the bus is out front. We're ready to move the party. I hope you'll join us."

"Not on your life," Giselle said. "I'm going to bed."

Victor swayed. "See that, Billy? Snooty bitch won't even take my card!"

"Hey," I said. "Watch your mouth."

Victor jutted his jaw. "What're you gonna do, tough guy? Punch me?"

Billy steered the man away. "Come on, Victor. Let's get you on the bus."

"Wouldn't even take my card!" Victor said to Billy. He looked over his shoulder and gave Giselle the stink eye. "Ignorant housewife!"

"What was that about?" I asked.

"Extra virgin olive oil. I came out with my own brand last year."

"Is there really something wrong with it?"

"Of course not." She gave me that same wrathful look, but the storm in her eyes quickly blew over. "It's brought me nothing but headaches, if you want to know the truth. I'm sick of hearing about it."

Victor skidded on a wet spot on the dance floor and fell on his back. Billy struggled to get him on his feet. The two men looked as though they were wrestling.

"I can't believe you're actually going off with this bunch," Giselle said to me.

"You should come with us," I said. "You could be our celebrity bartender."

"I'd probably crack a bottle over Victor's head."

"Might do him good."

People were settling their bar tabs and moving toward the door.

Billy called out, "Let's go, folks. The bus is leaving!"

I looked at Giselle. "You really won't come?"

"That old railroad car is nothing but trouble, as far as I'm concerned.

Sorry. Guess I'm more fun when I'm drunk."

We made our way across the room, holding hands, delaying the inevitable. We slowed for a knot of people converging on the doorway. Ahead of us, Horace saw Giselle and stopped.

"The short-order superlative!" Horace took Giselle by the hand. "I ruined your lovely dinner." He spoke with a thick tongue.

"Not at all," Giselle said. "I'm so sorry for your loss."

"It was an enormous bomb, you know. Poor thing didn't stand a chance."

"Horrible."

"Killed her husband, too."

"We can only hope they're in a better place."

"You know, I'm not one for God and all that business, but in this case I hope you're right. 'Onward, Christian Soldiers' and all that…" Horace put his mouth close to Giselle's ear. "I'll tell you something about David. He had a keen mind. He collected fire hose nozzles."

"I'm sure he was a wonderful person."

Horace gave Giselle's hand an appreciative wag. "You're really first-class. I hope you're coming with us?"

"I'm afraid not. Too many late nights this week already."

"That's a shame. That's really a shame."

We followed the crowd through the door. At the top of the stairway Herr Fritz stood waiting for Horace.

"Mr. Button, Godspeed on your journey—" he said.

"A good old fashioned Irish wake, Herr Fritz. Come with us."

"I'm afraid I have a hotel to run."

Horace embraced Herr Fritz drunkenly. He kissed the hotelier's cheek.

"Your friendship means the world to me," Horace said. "I hope you know that."

"May justice prevail. May their souls rest in peace."

"Thank you, Herr Fritz."

I interjected. "Herr Fritz, may I ask a favor?"

"Anything, Jack."

"Would you see Ms. Lebeau safely to her room?"

Herr Fritz looked at Giselle. "But of course. It would be my distinct honor." He bowed slightly.

I turned to Giselle. "Sure you won't change your mind?"

She gave me a wistful smile. "I'm sure," she said. "Go do your job. Get your boss to Washington."

TWENTY-FOUR

Special to *Sunshine Trails*
"Window on the West," by Horace Button
"A Healthy Aversion to Flying"

SAN FRANCISCO—The sociopathic scoundrels of the airline industry should be pilloried in the town square, if not introduced personally to Madame Guillotine. In an indefensible scheme with epic ramifications they have condemned generations of future travelers to universal steerage.

The early years of air travel looked promising. The airlines sought to imitate the tone of the exalted passenger trains of the 1940s—trains like the Twentieth Century Limited, which pampered its patrons with the best of everything. But as time ticked by, the tactic of imitating luxury travel turned out to be nothing more than a disingenuous bait and switch.

Having hooked the traveling public on speed and a wicked efficiency, the airline industry cut luxuries to the bone.

Nowadays any trip by air hits the skids early and quickly degenerates into an appalling experience that will have you doing math at 30,000 feet, calculating how long it would have taken you to drive.

Airports are maggot bins of humanity, the terminal gates like stock-yard pens. For the privilege of entering these gulag-like waiting rooms, a gang of grunting TSA agents subjects you to perverse indignities for which you'd fire your own doctor.

The genius of airline marketing is they have elevated a class of customer that would otherwise be traveling by long-distance bus: screaming infants, hillbillies in shorts and backwards baseball caps, the cast from the Ringling Bros. and Barnum & Bailey Circus who fill the cramped seats of every cut-rate flight: the circus fat lady, the tattooed woman, the runt shot out from the cannon, the chattering apes and monkeys. And over there, the two rows of clowns in matching T-shirts, all on their way to the same dirt-cheap, plague-ridden cruise on the Mexican Riviera.

The mental and emotional torment visited upon the public by a conscienceless airline industry is a national disgrace. The so-called meals are just enough to forestall a riot. Toilets are filthy. The slightest weather delay forces connections to be missed, luggage to be lost and decorous citizens to camp out in airport corridors like pestilential refugees. Is it any wonder airport police are little more than white-coated orderlies who board planes with nets and taser guns, to haul away those driven mad by the ordeal? Here's a guaranteed profitable concession for any airport property: open a loony bin. You'll have standing room only in a matter of days.

And forget flying first class. It's an illusion. You're still breathing the same disease-infected air and enduring the same howling infants. The contents of your first-class meal would garner a horse laugh in any third-tier steak house. Worse, when traveling in the front cabin, your seatmate is likely to be intolerable—a pompous, empty-headed Hollywood actor, a swarthy, supercilious South American, or a puffed-up, loudmouthed Eastern European—and after the plane lands you'll invariably suffer the dolt from the last row in coach who smugly points out that he "arrived at the same time you did, but at one-third the cost."

I get few questions more than "Button, what's your aversion to flying?"

Aboard my private railcar, the *Pioneer Mother*, I have Wanda's cooking, a bartender at my beck and call, my own bed and bathroom, and a hot shower when I want one. In the spacious observation lounge I read, write and watch the world go by. For fresh air I can take a stroll on the open platform. Once there, I often light up a cigar.

I say, "Why fly when you can take the train?"

Signed,
Your ace reporter,
HB

TWENTY-FIVE

I WAS IN HAWAII, dozing in a comfortable bed on the upper floor of a plantation-style hotel, the shutters thrown open to the balmy breeze. Giselle lay next to me, her hair mussed, her naked body partially hidden by a tangled sheet. Outside, waves crashed on the beach.

The air horn of a diesel locomotive blew sharply. The rumbling train shook our bed.

I fought to stay in Hawaii, but the train had awakened me and brought me back to this railroad yard in Denver and my coffin-like berth. The late-night reception had gone long. By the time Billy and his advertisers finally boarded the bus for their trip back to the hotel, dawn was breaking and Wanda and I were ready to drop. Insubordinate, neither of us had set an alarm. The blackout shade made it impossible to distinguish night from day. I reached blindly for my cell phone, which I kept on a small shelf above my head when I slept, and I checked the time: 10:14 a.m. As the one with front-of-house responsibilities—and therefore point man on cleaning up—sleeping late was not among my assigned duties. To shooting pain, I rolled out of bed, found the rickety ladder with one bare foot, and descended. I missed a rung and stepped on Wanda, who howled.

"Sorry," I said. "Can't see a thing."

"Don't tell me it's morning."

"Past ten."

"Holy Mother of God. I need sleep." Wanda pounded her pillow. "Come get me when Mr. Button's awake."

"That won't be for a while," I said. "Sleep as long as you can."

I probed the darkness, feeling for the door. In the hallway, the glaring sunlight hurt my eyes.

Dirty dishes were piled high in the galley. Empty wine bottles and plates of half-eaten food were scattered throughout the railcar. Lamp shades were knocked askew. Under a window, on a silver platter, a lone wedge of roast duckling quesadilla sat curled and hardened in the sunlight. I heard the faint sound of sobbing. Sitting in a parlor chair with her hands over her eyes was Cassidy. My first thought was that she had been raped by one of our drunken guests, and I immediately suspected Victor. I don't know why I thought this—Cassidy looked perfectly put together in her gray skirt and cardigan. She balanced a white letter-sized envelope on her lap.

"Cassidy," I said, "what's wrong?"

She wiped her eyes with the heels of her hands.

"Did somebody hurt you?" I asked.

"No." Her voice was soft.

"Why are you crying?"

"It's Mrs. Whitehead. She's going to kill me."

"I doubt that."

"I've never been fired before."

"Why would she fire you?"

"Because I was supposed to get you and Mr. Button on a flight this morning. It leaves in twenty-two minutes."

"That obviously isn't going to happen."

"I got here at eight o'clock like Mrs. Whitehead said, but all the doors were closed and I could hear people snoring. I didn't dare wake anyone up."

"Please, Cassidy. You did nothing wrong."

"But I promised to get you on that plane!"

"Listen to me. After the night we just had, we'll be lucky to get Mr. Button on a plane before dark. There's no way we'd have made a flight this morning."

"Will you tell that to Mrs. Whitehead?"

"Of course I'll tell her."

An unopened bottle of the '61 La Tâche sat on the bar.

"Do you have a boyfriend back home?" I said.

"Yes."

"Do you ever drink wine?"

"Sometimes."

"Good." I handed her the bottle. "Take this home and drink it with your boyfriend. Mr. Button would want you to have it."

She handed me the envelope, which contained two first-class boarding passes.

"Hey," I said to her. "Before you go, can I ask a favor? Would you mind finding us a Sunday paper?"

"It's so horrible what happened," Cassidy said. "How's Mr. Button doing?"

"He has his own way of coping," I said. "I'll leave it at that."

Twenty minutes later she returned with a special Sunday morning edition of the *Denver Post*. "BOMB KILLS RUTH PEPPER" exclaimed the headline. The entire front page was devoted to the double murder. I set the paper on the bar and assured Cassidy that Horace and I would go out on the earliest possible flight.

"But today, right?" she said. "Because Mrs. Whitehead's really been on me about this—ever since it happened last night."

"Believe me, today's my goal, too."

The newspaper contained mostly wire-service copy—the predictable, knee-jerk stories that often appear in the early hours of a major incident that will take weeks, if not months, to fully comprehend. The president of the United States vowed to bring the perpetrators to justice. Russell Rawlins expressed sadness and shock over Ruth Pepper's death. The slain senator's offices in Reno, Carson City, Las Vegas, and Washington, D.C., had all been sites of spontaneous candlelight vigils.

I was reading the paper when Wanda came down the hallway, looking somewhat disheveled in her chef's whites.

"I asked you to get me when Mr. Button was awake." Her voice had an edge.

I looked up from the newspaper. "He's still asleep."

"Then who were you talking to?"

I told her about Cassidy and the missed flight. Wanda shrugged. She tilted her head and joined me at the newspaper.

"What's it say?"

"Not much," I said.

We were soon hard at work cleaning the railcar. After I finished vacuuming the observation lounge and straightening up the bar, I took a break and went out to the open platform. I called my sister.

"Sorry, Lib, sounds like I woke you up."

"It's all right. Saturday night in a college dorm—you don't exactly get a lot of sleep." There was a sudden ruckus in the background —exuberant voices and rap music blaring. "Y'all quit making a fuss," Libby shouted. "I'm on the phone with my brother." In a moment the commotion passed. "Sorry, Jack. It's a nonstop party around here."

"Listen, Libby, I called to tell you something important. You heard the news about Ruth Pepper?"

"I did. Jeez, that poor lady."

"Get this," I said. "Horace Button—the guy I work for—he's Ruth Pepper's brother."

"The guy with the railroad car?" Libby said. "Are you serious?"

"He and I are flying back to Washington, D.C., today," I said.

"Washington, D.C.? That's crazy, Jack. They may blow up the whole dang place."

"Well, they won't get very far. By now the National Guard's probably posted on every corner."

"Still, be careful."

"There's something else I have to tell you. After D.C. I'm on my way to Hawaii. On Tuesday, I think."

"Hawaii?"

I told her about meeting Giselle and my invitation to join her on Kauai.

"Jack! Are you telling me my brother's having an affair with Giselle Lebeau?"

"Not an all-out affair. It's—there's this spark between us and we want to see where it goes."

"My gosh. So tell me, what's she really like?"

"I think you'd like her a lot. She's real nice but a real pistol, too. You should've seen her last night in this bar. She nearly took some poor guy's head off because she thought he was being disrespectful."

"Well, I'm happy for you but I feel sick about Ruth Pepper."

"So what's going on with you?"

"Not a whole lot, other than being stuck in this cruddy hellhole and signing up for a full load of classes so I can graduate in two more horrible years. Oh, and did I tell you I got a job at the movie theater, selling tickets? It's like I've gone full circle back to the Midland Multiplex, working for Dad all over again."

"Ever hear from him?"

"Not a word."

"No, me neither. I'm sorry I screwed things up so bad for us, Libby—"

"You need to let it go, Jack. Just get on with your life."

"Well, seeing Mr. Button lose his sister like this... I can't imagine what it would be like to lose you."

"It's not like I'm going anywhere," Libby said. "Good ol' Canyon, Texas—I'll probably be here till the cows come home."

"I'll make it up to you, Libby, I promise."

"You always say that, but you've got no obligation to me. I need to make my own way in the world, just like everybody else."

At noon, I heard the shower running—our cue to get cracking. While Wanda made breakfast, I set the table and launched classical music on the satellite radio. Horace arrived at the dining table a few minutes later, his hair neatly combed, his face clean-shaven, his expression impassive. He wore his three-piece herringbone suit—his traveling outfit.

"Morning, Jack," he said.

"Mr. Button." I held a chair for him. He sat heavily. Unfurling his napkin, he affixed it to the top button of his shirt and spread the cloth across his broad middle.

I brought the coffee pot. "Fresh coffee?"

"Most certainly." Horace smiled quickly. He watched as I filled his cup.

"Your breakfast should be ready any minute."

Horace nodded. "Good."

He took a sip of coffee. He glanced at the windows.

"Jack, is there a problem? We're not moving."

"No problem, Mr. Button. It's just a matter of firming up our plan. I thought I'd give you a minute, first."

"Ah. Very kind."

"Would you prefer to discuss it now?"

"It?"

"We can catch a two forty-five to Dulles, but that might be a bit of a scramble. There's a five fifty-four that I think is more makeable. That gets us into Dulles around eleven tonight."

"Dulles?" Horace said. "What's this Dulles you're talking about?"

"The airport, Mr. Button. Just outside Washington, D.C."

Horace looked bewildered.

"It's Sunday," he said. "We're going back to San Francisco."

"Mr. Button... last night—don't you remember?"

He stared at me blankly.

I showed him the newspaper. "You suffered a terrible loss last night. The whole country did."

Horace gaped with revulsion at the bold headline. He plucked the napkin from his shirt and turned to me dolefully.

"I thought it was a bad dream," he said.

"Not a dream, I'm afraid."

Horace stared coldly at the newspaper. "I begged her not go into politics, you know. Absolutely begged her."

His eyes welled, and he brought the napkin to his face. Just then Wanda set a plate of breakfast in the pass-through.

"Food's up," she said.

I left Horace alone in his grief. I returned the plate of bacon, eggs, and hash browns to the galley.

"Can we keep this warm?" I said to Wanda. "It's not a great time."

Wanda ducked her head into the pass-through. At the sight of Horace sobbing into his napkin she quickly turned to the plate of food and began covering it with foil. Before she could finish the task, tears were streaming down her cheeks too.

I touched her on the elbow. "Hey, you okay?"

She reeled into my arms.

"It's so sad." She hid her face in my shoulder.

I held her tightly. "Stay tough. We'll get through this."

A chime rang. By the time I reached the dining table, Horace had regained his composure. He smoothed the napkin on the table in front of him and futzed with a fork.

"Tell me something, Jack. This decision to stay in Denver—who made it?"

"I did, sir."

Horace looked surprised. "You did?"

"Yes, sir. I thought—"

"God dammit, Jack! As long as I'm on this train, *I* make the decisions. Is that clear?"

"Very clear, sir. I just thought—"

"You thought! You thought! You aren't paid to think! You're my goddamned employee!"

I answered in a measured voice. "I understand that you're upset. My rationale was that if you and I had a plane to catch, it didn't make sense to be moving. You can't catch a plane to Washington out of Green River, Utah."

Horace reacted as if he'd been slapped. He recovered by taking the napkin from the table and smoothing it across his lap.

"My gripe isn't with the logic of the decision," he said. "It's that I wasn't consulted."

"Lesson learned," I said.

"You can bring me my breakfast now," Horace said. "And I'll have a Bloody Mary. Make it taste like gasoline."

Horace ate and drank without speaking. He finally finished his meal and summoned me.

"I've thought it over," he said. "Flying is out of the question. In fact, I won't be going east at all." He smiled tersely. "Public funerals and somber speeches… they make me start looking around for the fire exits. We'll head back to San Francisco as soon as it can be arranged—"

"But Mr. Button—"

"No, Jack. I won't change my mind on this. It's nonnegotiable."

TWENTY-SIX

"LAMB, THAT'S PREPOSTEROUS," Poppy said. "You can't skip your own sister's funeral."

She faced Horace across the dining table. She had commandeered a hotel limousine and swooped down on the *Pioneer Mother* the minute I called and told her of Horace's plan. They each gripped a Bloody Mary like a loaded revolver.

"But what if they want to kill me, too?" Horace said.

"Don't be a coward. You've spent a lifetime hectoring people to do the right thing. This is family we're talking about."

"I don't understand. Why is it such a big deal to you?"

"Because, lamb, I care about you. And I'm going to be on your arm the whole time—me and every glittering bauble I own."

"My sister's funeral and you're treating it like a runway show."

"Can you blame me? I missed the last round of inaugural balls. I was at Cedars Sinai getting a new hip. The jewels haven't been out of the vault in a coon's age. I've practically forgotten what they look like."

"The hand-wringing and speechmaking will be insufferable," Horace said.

"Just ignore those Washington phonies. You'll brook the spectacle with maximum graciousness and dignity. Because that's who Horace Button is."

"You think so? You've always known what's best for me."

"You better believe it, mister. Going to Washington is the right thing to do. You have no choice in the matter."

Horace frowned. "All right. You win. But I'm taking the *Pioneer Mother*."

"That's absurd." Poppy turned to me. "Steward, what's the next plane you can catch?"

"There's a five fifty-four to Dulles," I said. "I'm pretty sure we can make that."

"Fine. I'll have my office arrange two seats while you get him packed."

Horace tipped his glass and sucked a green olive into his mouth. "I won't do it. I won't fly."

"You can't be serious," Poppy said. "You have no choice."

I looked at Horace and pictured what I was in for: moving that mountain of luggage to baggage check; negotiating him through airport security; his jaundiced eye and inevitable deep indignation at being treated as steerage. And there was the matter of that derringer, which I still had never seen. What was the penalty for smuggling a loaded firearm aboard an aircraft? Ten years?

I decided the only thing worse than arriving in Hawaii a day or two late was traveling on a commercial airliner with Horace Button.

"Mrs. Whitehead," I said, "Mr. Button's right. We can't fly."

"Why, of course you can fly," Poppy said. "I insist on it."

"Well, leave me out of it," I said. "I don't want any part of it."

Poppy stared in astonishment. "That's defying a direct order. I can have you fired!"

"Fine," I said. "Get yourself another bartender."

Her mouth agape, Poppy turned and looked at Horace. He emptied his Bloody Mary and stared defiantly back at her. Poppy's eyes widened suddenly—in her head she must have pictured the same airport scenes I had.

"All right," she said to Horace. "Have it your way. Take the train."

Horace gave me a nod. "Well played, Jack."

Poppy looked at me and said, "What's it going to take to get this thing to Washington?"

I didn't have a clue. I brought Wanda in from the galley.

"Mrs. Whitehead," Wanda said, "it's Sunday afternoon. Amtrak's private car department is closed. To schedule a move, they need at least twenty-four hours' notice. So best case, assuming we can leave here Tuesday night, that gets us into Washington, D.C., on Thursday afternoon."

"Thursday?" Poppy said. "We can't wait that long. We've got a funeral to plan."

"I don't know what to say," Wanda said. "They're very strict about their rules."

"Then forget those low-level imbeciles!" Poppy said. "I'll call Russ Rawlins myself. He'll get it done."

"He's mentally afflicted," Horace said. "He tried to strangle me."

"I wouldn't know," Poppy said, "but he owes me a favor. I'll call him the second I get back to the hotel. We'll see how inflexible these Amtrak people really are."

Before she left, Poppy ordered me to keep a close eye on Horace.

"Monitor his drinking," she said. "There'll be lots of media coverage in Washington. We don't want a scene."

Whatever Poppy said to Russ Rawlins, it worked.

A few hours later a balding, middle-aged man in charcoal slacks, a white golf shirt, and a blue sports jacket knocked on the door. He introduced himself as Amtrak's regional vice president. He'd already arranged for the *Pioneer Mother* to go out that night on the back of the Zephyr, headed for Chicago. If necessary, he said, they'd hold the train for us. A yard locomotive had been called to transfer us to Union Station.

The man gave me his card and asked me to pass along his condolences to Horace, who by this time was sleeping off the Bloody Marys. The Amtrak executive drew my attention to a white Chevy Tahoe idling alongside the tracks. A uniformed Amtrak police officer sat behind the wheel.

"I've asked him to keep an eye on things," the executive said. "No specific threat, but you know what they say. Discretion is the better part of valor."

The afternoon sun was scorching hot. To the west, over the mountains, thunderheads loomed. I cranked up the air conditioning in the old Pullman and took the policeman a Coke.

Before reboarding, I called Giselle. I caught her as she was arriving at her condo in Marina del Rey. I told her we were taking the *Pioneer Mother* to Washington, not flying after all, and that this would obligate me to Horace until at least Wednesday.

"But I specifically said I wanted you here by Tuesday morning."

"I know, Giselle. You think I like this any more than you do? The man refuses to fly."

"I bought you a plane ticket."

"I'll pay you back."

"Don't be stupid. This isn't about money. You'll just have to catch up to me on Kauai. *God.* This shouldn't be so complicated."

At around six o'clock that evening, a rusty-yellow yard engine delivered us to Union Station. A photojournalist from the *Denver Post* caught the moment: a graffiti-marred locomotive pushing the *Pioneer Mother*, an enormous American flag billowing in the breeze behind the engine. The same photo eventually ran in *Time* magazine.

True to form, the logistics of coupling the *Pioneer Mother* to the rear of the Zephyr caused a delay. The train was scheduled to depart at 7:10 p.m., but forty-five minutes later, as the sun descended behind the Rockies, the conductor—a stout, serious woman—was just getting around to checking the marker lights. She wore a conductor's jacket and a pillbox hat. She kept looking at her watch.

"Sorry to be holding you up," I said.

"Not at all," the conductor replied. She had steely blue eyes. "It's an honor. Let's get you guys to Chicago."

Wanda joined me out on the platform, resting her elbows on the brass railing, watching our departure. We passed Coors Field. The stadium lights were on. We swept along the edge of the railroad yard and followed a series of turnouts to the main line.

The dirty backs of concrete buildings, the fenced industrial yards with their baffling clutter, the dense apartment complexes, their streets and alleyways packed with broken-down cars—all cities look the same when you're leaving them by train.

"East instead of west," Wanda said. "Not exactly what you signed up for."

"I wish I smoked," I said. "I'd have a cigarette."

"I'd join you."

On a long straightaway that ran parallel to a highway, our train picked up speed. Wanda and I gazed at the passing track.

"You don't have much of an accent for being from Texas," Wanda said.

"Got out before it stuck, I guess. My sister wasn't so lucky. She's got a real twang." I looked at Wanda. "You never said where you were from."

"Nowhere, really." She stared numbly at the horizon. "Just … nowhere."

Dust and debris began whipping our faces.

"Well, we aren't paid to stand here." She turned to go inside.

"Listen, Wanda, there's something I need to tell you."

She stopped.

"I'm moving on," I said. "I've got the chance to try something different, and I've decided to take it."

A quizzical expression crossed her face, as though I'd spoken to her in a foreign language. "Another job?"

When I said nothing, Wanda raised an eyebrow. "When?"

"I can stay until we get to Washington, D.C."

"Two days."

"Sorry. Not ideal from your perspective, I know."

Wanda merely shrugged.

"Isn't this where you let me have it with both barrels?" I said.

Wanda gave me a half smile and opened the door. "To tell you the truth, Majordomo, I'm astonished you lasted this long. We're doing a roasted leg of Moroccan lamb for dinner. Can you pull two bottles of the Stag's Leap cab? That should get Mr. Button through the night.

"Provided he doesn't go on a binge," she added.

TWENTY-SEVEN

THE ZEPHYR MADE UP TIME in the night. We reached Osceola, Iowa, at 7:35 a.m., five minutes early. I had time to dash into the gray-brick train station and pick up a copy of the *Des Moines Register*.

As we crossed the rolling hills of southwestern Iowa, I gleaned details of Ruth Pepper's death. She and her husband had attended a political fundraiser and were pulling into their garage when the device detonated. The blast tore off the front of the house and left a crater in the driveway. The Peppers were killed instantly. Jagged scraps of metal—pieces of their GMC Yukon—were found impaled in neighboring yards. Also killed in the blast was the Peppers' family cat. When I read this to Wanda, it brought her out of the galley.

"Wait, they killed the cat?" she said.

"That's what it says."

"Bastards. They should hang for that."

I was studying a related story.

"This is funny," I said. "Listen to this: 'The Peppers' eleven-year-old daughter, Jane, learned of her parents' deaths from an unlikely source. Pizza delivery driver Micah Johns, 25, was attempting to deliver a dozen pies to Ms. Pepper's dormitory room at the Fleetwood Golf and Tennis Camp, in the remote town of Bethlehem, New Hampshire, when he became aware of the girl's identity. Johns had heard early reports of the explosion that took the lives of Senator Pepper and her husband, and broke the news to the senator's daughter. Fleetwood Camp Director Rohan Marsh would not elaborate on a reported financial dispute between Johns and Ms. Pepper over the dozen pies.'"

"What's so funny about that?" Wanda said.

"A financial dispute over a dozen pizzas delivered to an eleven-year-old's dorm room? Doesn't that sound like a prank to you?"

"I don't know. Does it say it was a prank?"

I read on. "'The Peppers' only child was at the camp at the time of the blast, Senator Pepper's office confirmed Sunday.'" I looked up at Wanda. "Nope. That's all it says. But I like this kid already."

"Can you imagine that poor thing?" she said. "One minute you're leading a perfectly normal life and the next, some pizza guy's telling you your parents are dead."

"And demanding payment for a dozen pizzas," I said.

There was a sudden furor outside and the light dimmed for several moments. We were passing a westbound coal train.

"Have you told Mr. Button you're leaving?" Wanda asked.

"Not yet."

"You need to tell him, you know."

"I'm just waiting for a good time."

"Maybe you should reconsider."

"Wanda, I can't afford to put my life on hold. No one can."

I served Horace a breakfast of *escargots à la Bourguignonne*, poached eggs on a bed of crabmeat, and thinly sliced strips of petite tenderloin of beef with asparagus tips. By the time he finished his peach Melba, we were leaving Galesburg, Illinois. It was half past eleven.

"Shall I open another bottle of Bollinger, Mr. Button?"

"Certainly not," he said. "Only show-offs drink more than one bottle of champagne at breakfast. I'll have a martini."

That Monday morning, the *Sunshine Trails* corporate office was inundated with calls and e-mail messages for Horace. Most of the messages were forwarded to Wanda's inbox, but Amtrak Wi-Fi on the Zephyr was nonexistent, and cell phone service was spotty. In any event, Horace failed to respond to a single message. He hated talking on a cell phone and flatly refused to communicate by e-mail. He even ignored the newspaper I set next to his place at breakfast. Around one o'clock, as we approached Chicago, he locked himself in his stateroom and pretended to be working on a think piece. At the rate I took him gin daisies, I knew he was working on getting pie-eyed.

Chicago's skyline was impressive—from a distance the skyscrapers emerge in a cluster from the flat horizon like the Land of Oz. Near the center of the city we drew alongside the Chicago River and then plunged suddenly into darkness. The train inched along, threading a forest of concrete support pillars into Union Station, located in the depths of a riverfront high-rise. We finally came to a stop in a dusky artificial light. It was three o'clock in the afternoon.

On the station platform, camera strobes flashed. A crowd of people gawked at our railcar, many of them reporters and news photographers.

Though we had a three-hour layover and a change of trains, Horace had no intention of talking to the media. He had us pull the window shades.

"Tell them I'm unavailable," he said.

A few minutes after our arrival, a young Amtrak employee wearing a bright red blazer mounted the steps of the open platform and knocked on the door. He carried an urgent message for Horace from a Ms. Rosalind Snodgrass-Smith of Washington, D.C. He handed me a slip of paper with her phone number written on it.

In his stateroom, Horace dismissed the note. "Never heard of the woman. A trap set by an opportunistic reporter, no doubt." He wadded up the paper and threw it away.

On the other hand, Horace eagerly accepted gifts from an array of Chicago's finest hotels and restaurants: iced caviar from the Pump Room; a lobster-claw salad from the Four Seasons Hotel; a magnum of Pérignon Cuvée from Gene & Georgetti.

"Doesn't surprise me one bit," Horace said, looking over the spoils—including a dozen flower arrangements—laid out across the dining table. "The people of the Windy City are uncommonly generous. In normal times, it provides a great excuse for stopping over."

Horace napped in his stateroom while the *Pioneer Mother* was uncoupled from the Zephyr and attached to the back of the Capitol Limited, our train to Washington, D.C. The Limited departed Chicago on time at 6:10 p.m.

Two and a half hours later, in the waning light of dusk, we reached our first stop: South Bend, Indiana.

Horace was in the observation lounge, scribbling on a notepad, drinking his third martini. Wanda had spent the afternoon preparing a turban of fillet of sole and salmon with forcemeat-stuffed crayfish shells. The scent of baking fish permeated the railcar.

"If you look closely you'll see priests moving about on the station platform," Horace said to me, without looking up.

I peered out a window. "I don't see any."

"You don't see any priests?" Horace said.

"No."

"They must be traveling incognito, then."

I chuckled. "Priests traveling incognito in South Bend?"

"On their way to Atlantic City for a protracted gambling vacation, no doubt."

"But Mr. Button, this wouldn't even be the right train."

"Via a little tax lobbying in Washington. Roman Catholic priests are a canny bunch, Jack. They mix business with pleasure as naturally as you and I mix sausage and eggs."

I eyed him dubiously.

"I know for a fact," Horace continued, "that they're professionals. They don't go on binges. They go on in-your-face, two- and three-week screamers, epic routs of debauchery and drunkenness."

Priests on screamers?

"Go into any rectory after five o'clock and you'll find the neighborhood priest with a handful of cards and an open bottle of Jameson's," Horace said. "Meanwhile, the human race careers recklessly down the superhighway to self-annihilation."

I laughed out loud. "The superhighway to self-annihilation?"

"Mark my words, Jack. Overpopulation will do us in long before climate change." He frowned. "I ask you: What has organized religion ever done to keep the human population from breeding like Connecticut river shad? Not a damn thing. And why? Because the Church says birth control is a sin. It interferes with God's mandate for procreation, or some such nonsense. But what's wrong with a little population control?

I'd throw in forced sterilization, a swift death penalty, and legal assisted suicide to boot. I also favor mass famine and a return of the plague, as long as they're confined to certain continents I could name."

That's enough gin for you.

The train began to move.

"I'll take one more perfect martini," Horace said. "It always happens when I'm in the presence of the gilded dome of Notre Dame—I feel like getting stiff as a plank."

I shook him another martini.

"I'd wager the bar car is packed full of them by now," Horace said, lifting his glass, watching me pour the cold gin from a silver shaker. "Priests on their way to Atlantic City, I mean."

At ten that night Horace was back in the observation lounge, having an after-dinner snifter of cognac and a cigar. We had just left Waterloo, Indiana. From behind the bar I studied this xenophobic drunk—his sleepy-eyed head bobbing to the soporific sway of the railroad car, his pink, greedy tongue darting in and out, collecting every last morsel of cognac from his withered lips. An expensive cigar burned in the ashtray. When the tablet on Horace's lap hit the carpet with a *thwack,* I woke him up and put him to bed.

Wanda turned out the lights in the galley and went for a shower.

I emptied ashtrays and ran the carpet sweeper around the parlor chairs, brooding like a caged animal. I'd been living on this railcar for a week, much of that time without sleep or exercise. I was performing the menial tasks of a busboy. It was my own stupid fault. My naïve sense of obligation had kept me aboard this railroad car, foolishly striving to please this pampered, self-indulgent aristocrat. Meanwhile, in Marina del Rey, one of the sexiest women alive waited for me to share her bed.

How many more bad choices can I make?

At five minutes to eleven the train was slowing for a scheduled ten-minute stop in Toledo, Ohio. I went out to the open platform. The train braked to a noisy halt.

The night was black, the air muggy and hot. I leaned over the railing and looked up the length of the train. White spouts of steam arose from beneath the double-decked cars of the Limited. In the dim light of the station platform, people crowded the doors of the coach and sleeper cars.

I plotted a getaway: leave my waiter's jacket on the platform, make my way to Detroit, catch a red-eye to Los Angeles. I'd be there for the trip to Hawaii after all, and Giselle would be amazed and impressed by my resourcefulness. I eyeballed a waiting taxi van in the parking lot.

At that moment a middle-aged couple appeared alongside the train. Walking arm in arm, they stopped to study the lines of the *Pioneer Mother.*

"That's definitely it," the woman said.

"Well, I'll be," said the man.

"Excuse me," the woman called. "But is this Horace Button's private train car?"

"It is," I said.

"We've been following your progress on the news," the woman said. "You've come from Chicago. And Denver before that. Is he inside?"

"Yes, but he's asleep."

"Please give him our condolences," the woman said. "That's such a tragedy about Senator Pepper."

"Thank you, I'll do that."

"We are Edith and Nelson Burhan of Bowling Green, Ohio," the woman said. "We're huge fans of Mr. Button's books and stuff, aren't we, Nelson?"

"Huge," Nelson agreed. "Love the guy. Devour everything he writes. We wish he'd run for public office."

I laughed.

"We're serious," Nelson said. "He'd get both our votes."

"What about his personal chef?" the woman asked. "Is she here too?"

"She is," I said.

"Wilma? Winona?"

"Wanda," I said.

"Wanda," said the woman. "That's it! She's wonderful. We tried her shrimp creole recipe from the magazine. What issue was that, Nelson?"

The man scratched his head. "April or May, I think. It had Lake Tahoe on the cover."

"Anyway, it was divine," the woman said. "Between Mr. Button's great wit and Wanda's cooking, you must be the luckiest man on the planet."

"Oh, I'm lucky all right," I said. "Lucky as a rabbit."

The train lurched without warning and then slowly started rolling forward.

"Please tell Mr. Button we're sorry that we missed him," the woman said. "And give our regards to Wanda."

"Of course," I said. "Nice talking to you both."

The impromptu conversation reeled me back from my self-pity. Giselle was right. Horace was a national treasure. He deserved my loyalty, especially in his time of need. And the little exchange with Edith and Nelson proved that Wanda was a culinary celebrity in her own right.

As the train gained speed, the Burhans waved, and I waved back. At the first bend in the tracks the lights of the station disappeared. I went inside. I pulled a bottle of Pérignon Cuvée from the wine chiller and filled a silver bucket with ice.

I wanted to catch Wanda before she fell asleep.

TWENTY-EIGHT

"ROOM SERVICE." I knocked once and opened the door. The lights were ablaze inside our double bedroom. I had a white linen napkin draped over one arm. "Who ordered the Dom?"

Wanda sat on her bed, in the shadow of the ladder to my upper berth, working on her laptop. She was wrapped in her terrycloth robe. She had one glistening leg crooked beneath her, the other splayed across the top of the covers.

"I think you've got the wrong room," she said.

"Whatever you're working on, save it and log off," I said. "We're overdue for a little revelry around here." I stepped into the bathroom, set the ice bucket in the sink, and lined up two champagne flutes on the narrow counter.

"What's this, Majordomo? Have you lost your mind?"

"Our hotel child went down early tonight. I thought we should take advantage of the situation."

I stripped away the foil from the neck of the bottle and covered the cork with the napkin.

"Are you really going to drink that?" Wanda said.

"You and I together. To commemorate our time on this train." I rotated the bottle in one direction while working the cork. It came out with a muffled pop.

Wanda regarded me skeptically.

"Why are you looking at me like that?" I asked.

"Because I assumed you were a teetotaler."

"I just don't drink on the job." I poured the wine. "Alcohol ruined my life once. It isn't going to ruin it again." I handed the first champagne flute to Wanda.

"I should warn you," Wanda said. "This is company property you're pouring."

"I'll come clean about it to Mr. Button. He can take it out of my pay." I planted the bottle back inside the ice bucket. I carried the second flute and the bucket out to the bedroom.

"There's something I came to say." I nodded at the bed. "May I?"

"Be my guest." Wanda moved her leg to make room for me.

I sat on the foot of the bed and put the ice bucket on the floor.

"First, I want to apologize," I said. "I wouldn't normally do this— leave on such short notice."

"And you're going where, exactly?"

"I'd rather not say. For a lot of reasons."

"Right." Wanda lifted her champagne flute to eye level and studied it.

"I'm just very sorry about the timing," I said. "I know it puts you in a bind."

Wanda glanced at me over her glass. "We'll manage."

"The second thing," I said. "Our lives are about to go in two different directions, and… I think you're an interesting person, Wanda. I consider it my loss that I didn't get to know you better. I hope our paths cross again soon. Cheers."

We touched glasses.

"Cheers," Wanda said grimly.

My first sip of champagne registered strong and sour—it had been more than a month since I'd had a drink. My palate recovered on the second sip.

"No wonder our bosses drink this stuff," I said. "It's amazing."

"You won't get an argument from me." Wanda closed her computer and pushed it aside. She scooted her back against the upholstered wall and sat with her legs straight out in front of her. The old Pullman was rocking.

"Where are we, do you know?" Wanda asked.

"That last stop was Toledo," I said. "Next is Sandusky, around midnight."

"I don't think I'll make that."

"No, me neither."

We drank in silence. Wanda looked pensive.

"So what was Midland like?" she said.

"In a word, desolate," I said. "My dad owned the Midland Sports Multiplex, you know—putt-putt golf, a driving range, some batting cages. He bought it when he quit roughnecking. We kept that place together with bailing wire and tape, but just barely. My little sister ran the snack bar. I painted windmills, kept the books, picked up golf balls, broke up fights, bailed my old man out of jail for his DUIs, you name it, I did it."

"You carried a lot on your shoulders."

"My dad was a carouser and a womanizer. He spent a lot of time in bars."

"Are you a chip off the old block?"

"God, I hope not."

"What about your mom?"

"She ran off with Duane, the Odessa Dairy Queen king. I was twelve. My sister was six. Once my mom started having babies with Duane, that was pretty much it for Libby and me."

"Ouch."

"Yeah, well, Libby and I at least had each other."

"And it was college that finally got you out of Midland?"

"It was football that finally got me out of Midland. College came with the deal."

"What was your major?"

"English Lit."

"As in books."

"That's right, as in books." I indicated the computer. "So what's this classified project you're working on?"

"Funny you should ask that." Wanda cocked her head and scrutinized me. "You have to keep it under your hat. Do you promise?"

"I promise."

"Mr. Button has me working on a cookbook," she said. "*The Pioneer Mother Cookbook*. All the recipes from the railcar."

"Sounds like a great idea."

"We'll see what kind of a market there is for shit on a shingle, which is pretty much the extent of my repertoire. I don't hold out a lot of hope."

"Hey, I just talked to two of your fans back there. They gave your shrimp creole recipe a rave review."

Wanda furrowed her brow. "From the magazine?" she asked.

"Lake Tahoe on the cover?"

"Not enough paprika and too much Tabasco. Amateurs. They clearly don't know what they're talking about." She gulped her champagne.

I refilled her glass and topped off my own. I set the bottle back in the ice bucket and slipped out of my shoes. I turned on my side, getting comfortable. Wanda's glossy legs smelled like coconut oil.

"So how'd you become a chef?" I said.

"Long story."

"I've got until Washington."

Wanda ran a hand through her hair.

"It all started with a benefactor," she said. "A guy I met at a golf course."

"You play golf?" I said, surprised.

"No, but my first chef's job was at a country club. If you call deep-frying beer-battered cod and boiling hot dogs cheffing."

"That's gourmet, where I come from. Where was the golf course?"

"Rhinelander, Wisconsin. Up near the Michigan border. The season is short—the summer months, basically. Anyway, they closed the course for the winter, and this guy offered to take me under his wing. He paid my rent and invited me to travel with him."

I tilted my head suggestively.

"Purely platonic, Majordomo," Wanda said. "He was eighty-one. Between the alcoholism and the cancer surgery, he was pretty destroyed."

"But he had a big heart."

"His name was Max."

"The guy from the old picture," I said. "In your office."

"Right."

"So where'd Max take you?"

"To a lot of dinners and shows, Indian casinos, mostly."

"A gambler?"

"Not at all. But he thought the restaurant fare was a good value proposition. Two people could eat for the price of one and still get a show. He wasn't a total penny-pincher—I don't mean to give that impression. He took me on a seven-day cruise out of Galveston: Jamaica, Grand Cayman, Cozumel. He paid for a veranda suite. We had to share a bed, but I didn't sleep-sleep with him, if you know what I mean. That was never part of the deal."

"Max took you on a cruise."

"Don't laugh. It was a life-changing experience. Three thousand people eating four meals a day, counting the midnight buffet. I took a kitchen tour. I told Max I'd love to be able to cook like that someday. He wouldn't let it go. He insisted I apply to the Culinary Institute in New York. When I got accepted, he offered to pay my way."

"Is Max still in the picture?"

"He died the summer I graduated." Wanda smiled sadly. "Lucky for me, huh? No strings attached."

"I'm sorry to hear that."

"He was sick. We knew it. He wanted me to have something to fall back on."

I plucked the champagne bottle from the ice bucket and filled our glasses again. Beads of cold water dripped from the bottle onto the bed. I brushed the droplets off the blanket.

"So you went home to Wisconsin," I said.

"My home was actually Minnesota. But home wasn't such a great place to be."

"Why was that?"

Wanda drew a deep breath. She glanced at the ceiling and then fixed her bright eyes on me.

"My turn to ask something," she said.

"You're changing the subject—"

"Your accident… what happened?"

"There isn't much to tell. I got drafted in my senior year of college. A lifelong dream, right? Every twenty-two-year-old kid wants to go pro. I went pretty high in the draft, which meant if I was smart about it,

I'd never have to worry about money again. I was arrogant at the time, I thought I was bulletproof. I'd been out at a bar drinking with friends. I had no business getting on a motorcycle. The city of Los Altos sent me a bill for scratching their light pole."

"Are you in a lot of pain?"

"Physical pain? No, nothing I can't deal with. But back to you, Wanda. What was your issue with Minnesota?"

Wanda looked at me gravely. She tucked a wild strand of hair behind an ear.

"I was fifteen when my mother got married for the first time," she said. "My stepfather was abusive..." Her voice trailed off.

I raised myself up on an elbow. "Abusive how?"

"He'd visit me at night. Started feeling under the covers when he thought I was asleep. I was petrified. It progressed from there. By the time I turned sixteen he was out of control."

"Did you tell anyone?"

"I told my mother. She slapped my face and said how dare I say such things about the man who'd given us such a wonderful home." Wanda leaned against the bulkhead and closed her eyes. "Take one for the team, basically."

"And you didn't go to a teacher or the police?"

"I had a better idea. I started sleeping with a knife. One night he came in and I thought I was ready for him. He took the knife away and turned it on me. He went farther than he'd ever gone before. He... did some things that really hurt me. The next morning he went off to work with a kiss from my mother, like nothing happened. That's when I real-ized she'd never stand up to him. So I threw some things in a suitcase and told her I was leaving. She sat there at the kitchen table, watching me clean out her purse. I took a gas card and all the cash. I took her car, too—a puke-yellow Taurus, all rusty and full of dents. She let me go, her only daughter, just like that. I've never spoken to her since."

"Where'd you go?"

"I just drove. Across Minnesota, into Wisconsin. At first I lived out of the car. I stopped wherever I thought was safe—truck stops, gas stations, hospital parking lots. I had run-ins with my share of scum, as you can imagine. Learned some ugly lessons about life, how people can use you and lie. But I survived." Wanda looked at me. "My mother kept paying the gas bill. They never came after the car. I guess that was the price they were willing to pay. Eventually I started working in food service. On my seventeenth birthday I cut up the gas card and threw it away. I didn't need their charity. I mailed the car key to my mother, telling her where she could pick up the Taurus." Wanda eked out a little smile. "She was deathly afraid of ghosts so I left it in a cemetery with the engine running. By then I had my own place, my own life. I was living in Rhinelander, but that was before I met Max."

"I'm sorry," I said.

"Don't be. Lots of kids have terrible lives. It isn't something you can change."

"What about your biological father?"

Wanda shrugged. "Who knows? Never met the man. Out there somewhere."

We sipped quietly a minute.

"So Max sent you to culinary school," I said. "Tell me about that."

"I never worked so hard in my life, but I loved every minute of it. It's creative, you know? The colors and textures and flavors, the way you can bring everything together in a crescendo of lines and shapes and heights. Great food is both spiritual and carnal. It's the chef's job to be the aggressor, to seduce the guest with her food—the way it looks and smells and tastes on your tongue, the way it feels in your mouth. I'm sorry. This must sound pretty stupid."

"Not at all," I said.

"Anyway, I liked everything about school," Wanda said. "Except pastry. Pastry sucks."

"What sucks about it?"

"It's very demanding." She took a gulp of champagne, as if to drown a bad memory.

"You graduated from culinary school," I said. "Then where did you go?"

"I started out in Boston, cooking at some of the big hotels. Moved to San Francisco when I got the job at the Roosevelt Grill. From there I got hired as a sous chef at the Dorsey Palace."

"By the famous chef… Oscar somebody."

Astonished, Wanda looked at me.

"How'd you know that?" she said.

"I overheard you the other night," I said, "when you were giving Giselle the tour."

"Well, anyway," Wanda continued, "the chef's name was Oscar Pagenpopp. He was a despicable pig, a total douche who thought it was his birthright to sleep with every woman who ever worked for him. Word from the female line cooks was that he liked to get naked and smear his gross hairy body with peanut oil, and then he'd chase the poor girls around the hotel room with a bottle of Jack Daniel's and a braided leather riding crop. He whipped the snot out of one poor kid, but more often than not he'd get so drunk he'd pass out before he got the job done—at least that was the story. I was in no hurry to find out. Mr. Button must've had a mole in the kitchen. He knew me from my days at the Roosevelt Grill. The night Oscar set his sights on me was the night Mr. Button offered me the job. Right then and there I packed up my knives and left."

"He rescued you."

Wanda flashed her smile. "He likes to tell people it was my pheasant *en casserole*, but I think he knew exactly what was going on."

"May I?" I offered Wanda more champagne.

"Please." She held out her glass and watched me pour. "Well, hasn't this turned into an uplifting little soiree?"

I filled my glass and set the bottle back in the ice bucket.

"Tell me about the last majordomo," I said. "What happened to him?"

"Fired for stealing."

"What did he take?"

Wanda closed her eyes and sighed.

"You mean what *didn't* he take?" she said. "Wine, liquor, cigars. My heart and soul. I almost married him."

"What?"

"He was South African. His name was Kim. An Adonis with beautiful blue eyes and curly blond hair. He could charm the pants off people. Literally. Played rugby. Claimed to be a martial arts expert."

"One of those."

"He never actually proposed. Thank goodness—because I would've said yes. I could've been married to a felon."

"How did you know he was stealing?"

"The usual red flags. Inventory wasn't matching expenditures. Checks were missing. Cases of wine kept disappearing. We finally caught him red-handed, passing a case of 1970 Château Haut-Brion to emissaries for an Arab sheik. You can imagine his surprise when they turned out to be undercover detectives for the San Jose Police Department. They charged him with embezzlement, grand theft, and felony battery on a police officer. Our thieving martial-arts rugger didn't go down without a fight."

"Sounds like a stand-up guy."

"That was only last month. He's behind bars right now. Ironically, he can't make bail. The arrest was actually pretty entertaining. It went down on the tracks next to the *Pioneer Mother*, right outside the warehouse. We were provisioning for a week in Monterey. Mr. Button serves as an honorary judge every summer at the Pebble Beach *Concours d'Elegance*. Lots of blood and broken bones—on the tracks in San Jose, I mean, not at Pebble Beach, though you can have that there, too."

The train slowed suddenly and our car heeled hard to one side, thrusting me face-first into the soft folds of Wanda's terrycloth robe. She spilled her champagne down the back of my shirt. We laughed.

"Sorry about that," I said.

"It's okay," Wanda said. "I don't bite."

It gave me an excuse to top off our glasses.

I put the bottle back in the ice bucket and settled again into my place on the bed. As the old Pullman moved to and fro, my gaze landed on the V of Wanda's robe and the hint of cleavage behind it.

"All right, Majordomo," Wanda said. "Tell me the truth. Were you ever really engaged?"

"Absolutely."

"And she called it off? Why?"

"I was damaged goods. They cancelled my contract."

"She was a gold digger."

"No, Bianca's a lot more complicated than that," I said. "She was about to start at Stanford Law School. She couldn't see the wisdom in being a successful lawyer married to a notorious drunk driver."

"Notorious?"

"A spokeswoman for Mothers Against Drunk Driving said I was a despicable animal. The sports columnists called me a gutter drunk and a predator, stuff like that."

"Got it." With downcast eyes Wanda ran a fingertip around the rim of her champagne flute. "There's something else I want to ask you."

"What's that?"

"You're not by any chance gay, are you?"

I looked at her, astounded.

"No," I said. "Why would you ask me that?"

"Well, the muscles and the tight shirts—"

"I lift weights—"

"—and the fact you haven't hit on me all week. I'd half expect any guy who's straight to make a pass."

"You're offended that I haven't hit on you?"

"Offended? No, not in the least." Wanda stared cross-eyed at the bubbles in her champagne flute. "Surprised, maybe, but not offended."

"It isn't that I don't find you attractive," I said. "You have a beautiful smile and beautiful eyes—"

"All right," Wanda said. "Stop."

"Truly, Wanda. And you're an amazing chef."

"Don't patronize me, Majordomo."

"It's just… I met someone recently, and we're going to see how it plays out. Does that make sense?"

"Perfectly."

"It isn't a great time to stray."

"Admirable."

"Here. Let's finish this off." I reached for the champagne. I felt drunk. I emptied what was left of the Pérignon Cuvée into our glasses.

Rocking to the sway of the railroad car, listening to the clatter of the wheels and the faint blasts of the train horn, I stole a glance at Wanda. She was looking at me curiously.

"No bullshit, Majordomo," she said. "All this mystery and nonsense. Where are you going, really?"

In my current state I didn't care anymore about keeping Wanda in the dark. *What was the point?* She was trustworthy.

"Hawaii," I said.

"And your mind's made up? You're really leaving us in Washington?"

"I'm supposed to be there tomorrow."

"What's the rush? Last I heard, the volcanoes aren't going anywhere."

"It isn't the volcanoes I'm worried about. It's the person I'm meeting."

There was the shrill sound of metal brakes being applied. The train began to slow.

"Any chance this person needs a cook?" Wanda asked.

"I doubt it," I said. "It's Giselle Lebeau."

Wanda appeared stunned, but her face was quickly obscured by a succession of shadows that moved across our lower berth. As the train came to a stop, the platform lights cast our double bedroom in the garish, overexposed palette of an avant-garde film.

"God, this must be Sandusky," Wanda said, staring out the window. "That means it's midnight."

TWENTY-NINE

HARPERS FERRY, WEST VIRGINIA, and then Rockville, Maryland—these quaint, tree-lined towns were our final stops before reaching Washington, D.C. I watched both stops from the *Pioneer Mother's* open platform, enduring the late-morning heat.

With each mile marker passed, as the metal coupler hitching us to the last double-decked Amtrak Superliner alternately tugged and crashed, as our old Pullman rocked and swayed, I was that much farther from Hawaii but that much closer to freedom.

At 12:40 p.m., as the Capitol Limited closed in on Washington, Wanda was in the galley, carving a whole roasted young duckling. I stood behind the bar, immersing a bottle of red Burgundy in an ice bath. At the dining table, Horace awaited lunch. Tchaikovsky's Violin Concerto in D Major played on the satellite radio. The neighborhoods we glimpsed through the bright green brambles bordering the tracks were wretched—crumbling brick façades black with age, streets strewn with garbage, boxy liquor stores with bars striping their doors and windows.

Our train dipped into the shadows of a freeway cloverleaf loop. We wove through a wilderness of graffiti-covered concrete pillars, where we passed a campsite of brightly colored tarps and tents. We emerged again into sunlight. The metal wheels of our old Pullman clacked sharply as the tracks fanned out into a vast railroad yard filled with out-of-use Amtrak equipment: blue and silver locomotives caked with dust; gray, windowless baggage cars looking funereal and ghostlike in their idleness; endless strings of double-deck passenger cars, some with their doors open, being cleaned. On an adjacent track a garishly wrapped commuter train passed us, outbound from Union Station.

"Oh, look at that," Wanda said with wonder from the galley.

Out my window, vivid against the blue sky, was the white dome of the U.S. Capitol Building.

As we entered the Union Station yard, the train slowed to a sluggish pace. We passed beneath the roof of the train shed and into shadow. People stood shoulder to shoulder on the platform, some pointing and others staring open-mouthed at our arrival. When the train finally came to a stop, a sea of reporters converged on our railcar.

"Ignore the ghouls, Jack," Horace said. "Fodder for their nightly cavalcade of horror—that's all they're after."

I served lunch.

A few minutes later, something on the station platform caught my eye. A lanky man with dreadlocks, wearing the coveralls of an Amtrak baggage handler, drove a luggage cart through the reporters and toward our railroad car. He maneuvered the cart around the rusty iron beams that supported the roof of the train shed and brought it to a stop just beneath my window. The load of luggage on the back of the cart had my attention—all of it neon pink. I poked my head into the galley.

"Did you already hire my replacement?" I asked Wanda.

She looked at me curiously. "No, why?"

"Check it out. On the platform."

She peered out her window.

"Beats me," she said.

There was a determined pounding at the back door. Wanda and I looked at each other. I hurried from the galley. A tall woman stood on the open platform, looking intently in the window. Her reddish-brown hair was pulled back in a tight bun, and she wore a somber blue suit.

Horace had a bite of food in his mouth. He held a fork in one hand and a wine goblet in the other.

"Jack, this is an egregious breach of etiquette," he said, swallowing hard. "Tell that marrow-congealing broad I'm in the middle of a meal."

I walked quickly through the observation lounge and pulled open the door.

"Where is he?" the woman snapped. She had protruding teeth and bright red lips. I judged her to be in her early thirties.

"Where is who?" I said.

"This impossibly ill-mannered human being, Mr. Horace Button."

"I'm sorry, he's unavailable."

The woman glowered. "I don't cotton to being stonewalled. I demand to see him this very instant!" Her accent suggested the Deep South, her voice a seasoned prosecutor.

I glanced over my shoulder at Horace. He shook his head.

I told her, "Mr. Button is having lunch—"

"Is that him?" The woman stretched up on her toes and craned her neck to see past my shoulder. Her perfume had a powdery, floral scent. "You, Mr. Button, are a heel," she said. "Not returning my calls!"

"Please," I said. "The man is grief-stricken. He just lost his sister. This isn't the time—" I tried closing the door, but the woman placed two big hands firmly against it and pushed back with everything she had. Her long fingernails were painted the same high-octane red as her mouth.

We were at an impasse—the door remained ajar. She thrust her head into the opening.

"What about me?" she said, through clenched teeth. "What do you think I've lost?"

The mass whirring of camera shutters in rapid-fire mode sounded like a great flock of birds taking flight. Several shotgun microphones, big as mortar tubes, were aimed in our direction. The woman glanced sideways and lowered her voice.

"Please don't humiliate me in front of the media," she said. "This is a small town. I'm here on family business. I've been trying to contact Mr. Button since Sunday. I'd rather not discuss it in public, but trust me, at this point I'm willing to make a scene if I have to."

I opened the door and stepped aside.

"May I say who's calling?" I said.

The woman handed me her card. On it was the embossed seal of the United States Senate.

"My name is Rosalind Snodgrass-Smith," she said, making her

way to the dining table, raising her voice. She towered over the back of Horace's head. "I am Senator Pepper's chief of staff."

Horace continued eating.

"Mr. Button, do you hear me?" she said. "I am executrix of the senator's estate."

Horace brought his wine goblet to his mouth.

"I am here in regards to your niece, Jane Pepper. As her closest living relative, you've been named her legal guardian—"

Horace spit his mouthful of wine across the white tablecloth.

"Congratulations, Mr. Button," Rosalind said. "You've got a child to raise."

THIRTY

IT WOULD BE AN EXAGGERATION to say we had to pick Horace up off the floor, but not much of one. He labored to breathe. He groaned and clutched his chest.

Rosalind looked at me, panic-stricken.

"Are you having a heart attack?" I said, leaning in. "Should I call 9-1-1?"

Horace shook his head faintly.

Rosalind clasped her silk blouse at the neck and stepped close. She examined the pupils of Horace's eyes, which were dilated. "Are you having a stroke? Can you speak?"

Horace glared at her.

Wanda came out of the galley and stood near the bar, holding a chef's towel.

"Talk for me," Rosalind said. "Say, 'Lookie, lookie, lemon cookie.'"

Horace moaned. He rolled his eyes and turned away. With two hands he seized the wine goblet by its bowl and chugged the rest of its contents. The wine overflowed the corners of his mouth and streamed in bloody rivulets down his jowls and neck, staining the collar of his shirt. He banged the goblet down on the table.

"My goodness." Wide-eyed, Rosalind took a step back.

Horace breathed deeply. The color rose in his cheeks.

"Mr. Button, are you all right?" I said.

"Face-to-face with the Dark Camel at the Black Hole of Calcutta." He spoke as if in a trance.

Wanda looked at me, eyebrows lifted.

"Never mind about camels," Rosalind said. "You've got an eleven-year-old waiting for you in the Grand Concourse, and she's making a holy mess out of a corn dog and fries."

Horace turned defiantly to Rosalind.

"There must be some misunderstanding," he said.

"There's no misunderstanding—"

"I can't raise a child. My appetite doesn't permit me the time."

"Your appetite is immaterial," Rosalind said. "The language in the trust agreement is perfectly clear: 'Mr. Horace Button shall act as guardian without the execution of any further instrument.' Period. I watched your sister sign it."

"But surely there's someone on the father's side," Horace said. "Someone more suited to raising a little crumb-cruncher..."

"David was an only child. His parents are dead."

"I'll give her to the Girl Scouts, then," Horace said. "Offer those bull dykes a sizable bequest to take her off my hands."

"They don't take boarders," Rosalind said.

"Check her into a convent. Let the soul-savers have her."

"She's a little young for that."

"Then Semester at Sea. I'll pay for a lifetime passage."

"Shame on you, Mr. Button!" Rosalind said. "This poor child has lost everything. You need to buck up. There are more important considerations than your personal inconvenience."

"I must tell you, I'm unfit to parent," Horace said. "In *Hansel and Gretel* I've always rooted for the witch. In *Little Red Riding Hood* I side with the wolf."

"You'll just have to rethink your fairy-tale loyalties. You're a parent now. You need to start acting like one."

Horace turned to me. "I could use a stiffy, Jack. Shake me the world's biggest martini. Throw it down in a fire pail."

I was already at work. I planted a highball glass of gin on the dining table in front of him.

Rosalind's eyes popped. "Is he really going to drink that?"

"My dear woman," Horace said. "I intend to insinuate alcohol into my system until my entire person smacks of a basket of busted bung-holes." He brought the glass to his lips and took a brawny pull.

"This is no time for getting soused," Rosalind said. "We need you respectable."

Suddenly Horace's face lit up. He turned to Rosalind.

"I'll pay you to raise her," he said. "A monthly stipend. I'm sure the little subversive could benefit from a female touch."

"Show some backbone, Mr. Button."

"Name your price. Anything—"

"Your self-centeredness at a time like this is contemptible." Rosalind went to a window, lifted a drape, and surveyed the reporters on the platform. She made a sour face and gave the heavy crimson fabric a theatrical sniff. She turned to Horace. "This place stinks like a casino. Don't tell me you smoke cigarettes in here?"

"Cigars," Horace said.

"Even worse. You must dispose of those poisonous things at once. The harm of secondhand smoke is common knowledge—"

"Now see here, you odious meddler. I won't be told what to do in my own private railcar!"

"Malarkey, Mr. Button. These are healthy young lungs you've been entrusted with. You must jettison your vices—all of them. I expect you to turn over a new leaf, starting right now. Dump the tobacco and alcohol."

"Heresy! You risk being burned as a witch!"

"Oh, get over yourself, you old fool. Don't you understand? You're about to become the focal point of a nation. America has opened its heart to this little girl. Your every step is going to be scrutinized, every foible judged—"

"Honestly, do you really think I care what any of those dreary people think? The unwashed masses—they aren't worth a damn!"

"And what about your sister? What was she worth?"

Horace leveled an angry finger at Rosalind. "How dare you! I'll throw you out!"

He froze, his face blood-red, his mouth half open.

Rosalind returned his murderous stare. "This child needs you," she said in a firm, measured tone. "Raising her is your moral obligation."

Horace looked as though he'd just been delivered a death sentence. He slumped in his chair and his eyes went glassy.

Wanda and I traded astonished looks.

Rosalind said, "Now, let's talk about how we're going to choreograph this homecoming with Jane."

"I don't see what there is to talk about," Horace said, defeated. "You say it's a fait accompli."

"Consider this, Mr. Button. All those photographers out there—whatever scene we play out is going to make every newscast in the country, and the front page of every newspaper, to boot. We can't let little Jane Pepper walk up and knock on the door like some poor waif out of a Dickens novel. Those camera shutters can move a lot faster than you or I can open that door. It'll make you look like the Scrooge of the century, not to mention the negative image it'll convey about the Republican Party—a young female victim petitioning her rich uncle for a roof over her head. The symbolism would set us back a hundred years."

Horace bristled. "Is that what this is about? Furthering the image of the Republican Party?"

"It's the photo op of the decade, Mr. Button," Rosalind said. "We'd be remiss not to manage it to our political benefit."

THIRTY-ONE

WANDA AND I HURRIEDLY PREPARED the *Pioneer Mother's* guest stateroom for its new occupant, relocating the remaining cases of Pérignon Cuvée to the storage locker at the head-end of the railcar. We made up the bed and stocked the lav with fresh soaps and towels. Wanda dressed the writing desk with a vase of flowers she'd purchased in Denver for the trip home.

"Do these look okay?" she said.

"They look fine," I said.

She kept fiddling with the flowers. "I'm afraid they're past their prime."

"What are you so worried about?" I said. "She's just a kid."

Wanda looked at me with indignation. "I'm worried I'll get stuck taking care of her—that's what I'm worried about. And everyone else will be long gone, including you."

What could I possibly say to that?

I returned to the observation lounge. Horace sat at the bar, his hands wrapped around the big glass of gin. Rosalind was looking out the window.

"Where is he?" she was saying.

"Where's who?" Horace said.

"Arthur."

Horace scowled. "Don't tell me I have a nephew, too."

Rosalind checked her watch. "Arthur's a staffer. He was supposed to be here by now."

Horace looked at me and lifted his glass, which was nearly empty.

"This wiener could stand a little more schnitzel," he said.

"Someone needs to take away the punch bowl," Rosalind told me.

"Check for a hatchet, Jack," Horace said. "She's delusional. She thinks she's Carrie Nation."

I went behind the bar, took the bottle of gin, and refilled Horace's glass.

"What are you doing?" Rosalind said to me. "You need to go out there and get those bags—"

"Don't do it, Jack," Horace said. "Don't bring those infernal things in here. There'll be no turning back."

"Believe me, you're way past the point of no return—*Uncle* Horace." Rosalind returned to the window. She pressed her forehead against the glass, studying the baggage handler, who had his arms crossed and appeared to be dozing. "Look at that disgrace, napping on the job. I swear these union people could sleep through a waterboarding." Her forehead left a powdery mark on the glass. She marched intrepidly to the bar and said to Horace, "All right, here's the plan. When the time is right, the staff will go out and form a receiving line. I'll walk Jane up from the Grand Concourse. As we approach I'll give you a sign, which means you'll emerge from the railroad car. You'll come down the steps and greet Jane at the head of the receiving line. You'll get down on one knee, look her in the eye, and present her with a teddy bear. Play the part broadly. Look happy yet melancholy. Make certain the cameras see the bear. Treat it as a symbol of your undying affection for Jane."

Horace frowned. "I don't have a teddy bear."

"Arthur's bringing you one."

"It's disingenuous," Horace said. "If I cared a whit for the little monkey I'd give her a bottle of gin."

"Be careful what you say in this town," Rosalind warned. "Reckless talk can come back and bite you." She looked at me. "What are you waiting for? Go get the suitcases! And I don't want the black guy lifting a finger, hear me? He stays in the cart. That's one photo I'm not going to give the Party of Absolute Corruption—an African American carrying Jane Pepper's suitcases into her uncle's private railroad car."

I came out from behind the bar. "Should I tip him?"

Horace and Rosalind looked at each other.

"Of course." Horace reached into a pocket, drawing out a thick wad of cash. He counted out five twenty dollar bills.

Rosalind blocked me from taking the money.

"Are you crazy?" she said to Horace. "A hundred dollars? You'll come across as filthy rich and totally out of touch—just the kind of people they want to tax."

Horace shot her a fierce look. "Must everything with you be a political calculation?" He pushed the cash into my hand. "Just give him the damn money, Jack."

Rosalind took me by the arm and ushered me to the door. "At least use your body as a shield. Don't let the media see how much you're giving him."

"Gentle lady, among decent people, generosity is nothing to apologize for," Horace said.

Rosalind wheeled around. "Spare me the lecture on decency. I'm not the one getting three sheets to the wind in the middle of the afternoon!"

I went out onto the open platform. The reporters immediately began shouting questions: "Where's Mr. Button?"; "What's his state of mind?"; "Any word from the president?"; "Who does Mr. Button blame for the assassination?" From inside the railcar a finger tapped urgently on the window glass. Rosalind had a stern expression. She pointed to the golf cart. Without looking again at the hectoring reporters, I descended the steps.

I touched the baggage handler on the shoulder, waking him up. Heedful of keeping my back to the media, I showed him the money.

"Here's the deal," I said. "My boss is paying you to stay in the cart. I'll take the bags."

As I counted out the money, the baggage handler's eyes grew big.

"Hold on," he said. "You're giving me all that not to work? That's crazy."

"Not crazy," I said. "Politics."

With the baggage handler looking on, I unloaded the hot pink suitcases from the back of the golf cart and hoisted them up to the open platform. Wanda helped me take the bags inside. We carried the suit-cases through the observation lounge and stacked them in the hallway outside the second stateroom.

About this time Arthur showed up. His jet-black hair stood up in jagged tufts, and his gray pinstriped suit hung limply on his tall frame. His eyes were vaguely Asian. He carried a yellow plastic shopping bag that had the seal of the National Park Service.

"For crying out loud," Rosalind said, "what took so long?"

"Do you know how hard it is to find a bear in this town? It's all video games and Transformers," Arthur said. He spoke in a high, screechy voice. "Here, check this out."

He reached into the bag and pulled out a chocolate brown teddy bear. The bear wore a trooper hat that said "Smokey." Smokey sported denim jeans and had a ranger's badge affixed to his chest. In one paw he held a plastic shovel. His prominent muzzle was that of a grizzly. His yellow eyes glowed menacingly.

"That's supposed to be cute?" Rosalind said.

"You said get a bear."

"I didn't say a federal officer."

"Listen to this. He talks!" Arthur pressed the bear's belt buckle. Smokey the Bear came to life. His eyes blinked and he spoke in the deep bass voice of a radio announcer.

"Only *you* can prevent wildfires," Smokey said.

Arthur gave the belt another jab.

"If you start a fire, put it out," Smokey said. "If it's too hot to touch, it's too hot to leave."

Rosalind shook her head and covered her eyes with a hand.

"Leave it to you, Arthur," she said. "This child's entire world has been atomized into a single smoldering crater, and you bring her Smokey the Bear. This may go down as the most insensitive gift in the annals of human history."

"Hey, I'm a legislative analyst," Arthur protested, his voice going up another octave. "What do I know about bears?"

"I can't believe you've put us in this position," Rosalind said. "What, the massive central government is the solution to our problems? It takes

Smokey the Storm-trooper Bear to fix all that ails society? It's anathema to everything Ruth ever stood for."

"Maybe you're overthinking it," Arthur said.

Rosalind looked at her watch. "It's too late now. We'll just have to make this ludicrous thing work." She turned to Wanda. "Can you sew?"

"Me?" Wanda said. "I can barely cook."

Rosalind scrutinized the bear. "There must be something we can do to cover up all this ranger jazz." She looked at Wanda. "Get me a pillowcase."

"A pillowcase?" Wanda said.

"You know, to dress the bear in. We'll give him a nightgown. Make him our cute little sleepy bear, all ready for bed."

Horace regarded the scene with mirthful eyes. I must have smiled too, because Rosalind looked daggers at me.

"Unless you have a better idea," she said.

"Not me," I said.

A couple minutes later, under Rosalind's supervision, Wanda was cutting a white pillowcase along lines carefully inked with one of Horace's writing pens. The two women worked the broad-brimmed ranger hat through a small hole in the pillowcase until the bear's head came popping out. The pillowcase settled squarely atop Smokey's powerful shoulders, concealing the badge and shovel. The bear's heavy black boots showed beneath the hem of his new nightgown.

"Perfect," Rosalind said. "But we still need to do something about the hat."

"Just cut it off," Arthur said.

Rosalind faced him wrathfully. "Leaving us with what, Arthur? A brain-damaged bear?"

"Not if you cut it at the seams."

"No," Rosalind said. "That's a terrible idea. It risks leaving Smokey with half his head. Or worse, the batting coming out like brains. Is that what you want, Arthur? Smokey Bear with his brains pouring out like cotton candy? Oh, how the media would have a field day with that!"

Arthur became sullen. He shook his head and stared at the floor.

Rosalind turned to Wanda. "Can you make a sleeping cap?"

"I'm not sure how..."

"Not freakishly, Pope-ishly huge. Just big enough to cover the ranger hat. Sew it out of a napkin."

"Like I said, I don't really sew."

"What's the big deal? You cut a napkin in the shape of a cone and go in and out with the needle. He'll look adorable."

Ten minutes later Wanda and Rosalind stood back and admired their work. The cone-shaped cap came to a sharp point high above the bear's head. The white of the cap matched the white of the gown. When Horace saw the bear, he slammed his glass on the bar and hooted with delight. He and I must have been thinking the same thing.

"It looks like a King Kleagle of the Ku Klux Klan," I said.

Rosalind and Wanda both stared at me with hatred.

THIRTY-TWO

STANDING IN THE STICKY AIR of the covered train shed, Arthur, Wanda, and I formed a receiving line at the steps of the railcar. The last in line, I stood next to the *Pioneer Mother*'s monogrammed welcome mat.

Minutes later I had my first look at Jane Pepper: tall for an eleven-year-old, lanky as a colt, a strawberry blonde with pale skin and freckles covering her pretty face, walking with her shoulders erect and her blue eyes fixed straight ahead. She wore a yellow dress and white Mary Jane shoes. Her bobbed hair made her look like a tomboy.

Rosalind gave a single nod and the next thing I knew, Horace was standing on the *Pioneer Mother*'s open platform. He had his hair slicked back and his suit jacket smartly buttoned. He carried the highball glass in one hand and the nightgown-clad bear in the other. I held my breath as he descended the steps without benefit of the handrail. He took each step gracefully, seemingly effortlessly.

But the moment Horace's black oxfords touched the welcome mat, one of his knees buckled. He pitched into my arms. A wave of cold gin splashed me in the eye. My football instincts—the dexterity to absorb a blow while holding my ground—helped save my employer from a nasty spill.

Reeking of alcohol, Horace pushed the glass into my hand. "Hold this."

I took the glass and what I thought was the cocktail napkin. Horace continued on his way. A split second later I realized my mistake. The white linen napkin I was now holding was actually the pointed tip of Smokey's sleeping cap. As Horace walked away, the cap pulled free from the bear's head.

"Uh-oh," I said.

Wanda glanced at me, then at Horace. She covered her mouth with her hand.

Oblivious to the bear's missing sleeping cap, Horace held the stuffed animal out in front of him and up high as though he were an acolyte carrying a processional cross. From the bank of reporters came a barrage of shutter clicks. Rosalind froze and stared at the scene with horror. Jane approached her uncle.

"Look at you," Horace said. "Just like your mother."

Jane gazed quizzically from the bear to Horace.

With a contorted face and the throaty, involuntary groan of a man pushing his physical limits, Horace got down on one knee, balancing the bear atop his kneecap. He held this precarious pose for a second and then collapsed into a heap on the ground. He rolled onto his back and lay there, looking up at the rafters of the train shed.

Jane stood over him.

"What was that, Uncle?" she said.

"What was what, urchin?"

"Was that a bear?"

Horace looked perplexed. He dug the stuffed animal out from under his body and studied it. Smokey's muzzle was pushed in and its ranger hat was smashed.

"Yep, it's a bear all right," he said.

"Why is he wearing a dress?"

Horace looked at the bear and then at Jane. "Beats the hell out of me, kiddo." He rolled onto his side. "But get this. He talks." Horace fumbled up and down Smokey's gown for the on switch.

"What does he say?" Jane asked.

"I'm trying to show you."

"But he isn't talking."

"Hold on, he will." With one eye closed, Horace stuck an arm up the bear's dress. He groped around blindly. Suddenly the bear came to life.

"Always hike with a friend," Smokey said. "If you get lost, stay in one place. Blow your whistle."

Jane smiled. "What else does he say?"

"Let's see." Horace gave the button another push.

"Get lost... blow," Smokey said.

Horace beamed with delight. Something in the bear's voice mechanism had jammed. He pushed the button again.

"Get lost... blow."

Still on his back, Horace roared with laughter. He kept pressing the button.

"Get lost... blow....Get lost... blow."

He waved the bear in the air. He kicked his feet and howled. Then, he passed a loud, long rip of gas—it sounded like cardboard tearing—which only made him guffaw even harder.

"Uncle," Jane said, "did you just fart?"

Rosalind came up behind me and cuffed me on the shoulder.

"Don't just stand there, you big oaf," she said. "Help him up!"

I handed the cocktail glass to Arthur and went to assist Horace.

Meanwhile, Rosalind planted herself between Horace and the reporters. She spread her arms out wide.

"There's nothing wrong with Mr. Button!" she shouted. "He has a trick knee, that's all!"

I got behind Horace and tried lifting him by his shoulders, but he was dead weight.

"Unhand me, you ignorant hamburger muncher!" he said. "Leave me be!"

"You need to get up, Mr. Button," I said in a low voice. "You're making a scene." I had hold of him under his arms.

"Fish heads!" he railed. "I am Professor John Henry Cluttermush, dean of the Harvard Divinity School!"

"Come on, be a good scout and get up." I lifted with all my might and finally got Horace standing. He turned to the reporters.

"Get lost, you bastards!" he roared. "Blow!"

"Let's get you inside." I turned him the other way and walked him toward the *Pioneer Mother.*

Jane scooped up the bear and followed us.

"What's the matter with him?" she asked me.

"He must have hit his funny bone," I said.

Ahead of us, Wanda ascended the steps of the open platform. She grasped Horace's wrists and pulled from above while I pushed from below. The back of Horace's jacket was covered with gravel. An old scuffed food wrapper clung to his coattail.

Rosalind looked on with a gaping mouth and bugging eyes.

"Come on, Mr. Button," I said. "Up the stairs you go."

Jane came up behind me. "People don't really have a funny bone. It's just an expression, right?"

"That's right," I said. "It's just an expression."

"Who are you?"

"I'm Jack."

Even with my pushing and Wanda's tugging, Horace couldn't muster the strength to climb the steps.

"Lift my legs," he said to me.

I bent down and manipulated Horace's feet, placing them one at a time on the steps like concrete blocks.

"This is very exciting," Jane said, looking at the old Pullman. "To think we get to go all the way across the country in a train."

We finally got Horace onto the open platform. Jane followed me up the steps.

"Does Uncle have many books inside?" she asked.

"Lots," I said, turning Horace toward the doorway. "Do you like to read?"

"Yes," Jane said. "I especially like to read about Eleanor Roosevelt."

"Eleanor Roosevelt!" Horace thundered. "Fuck Eleanor Roooo-sevelt!"

THIRTY-THREE

I PULLED THE CASHMERE BLANKET up to Horace's chin and gathered his suit jacket and pants from the floor for the dry cleaner. By the time I turned out the light my employer was snoring. As I left, I shut the door behind me with a click.

I found Wanda down the narrow hallway, working in the guest stateroom. She sat on the floor amid a host of open suitcases and yawning dresser drawers, organizing shirts, pants, and sweaters. The bed was covered with sealed bags of underwear and socks, summer dresses with their price tags still affixed, and shoes in boxes.

"Is he asleep?" Wanda asked.

"Dead to the world," I said. The window blind was down, so I lifted it for a moment to survey the station platform outside. A few reporters remained, facing bright lights, doing their stand-up stories with the *Pioneer Mother* as a backdrop. I lowered the blind and turned to Wanda. "What about Rosalind? Is she gone?"

"She had a dinner reservation at Morton's," Wanda said. "I'm supposed to tell you she's picking Mr. Button up at ten o'clock tomorrow morning to meet with the funeral director."

"Where's Jane?" I said.

"In the powder room, changing."

Suddenly, Jane pushed past me into the stateroom, carrying an armful of stuffed animals.

"I've never heard such a loud toilet," she said. "It makes an awful swoosh!"

She wore floral pedal pushers, a pink V-necked T-shirt, and rubber sandals. She went back and forth across the room, in and out of the lavatory, dividing the animals into families and giving them names, this gangling girl who weighed little more than a paper doll herself. She plucked the animals from a large cardboard box parked temporarily in the hallway. The box had been delivered to our railcar on the heels of Horace's fiasco on the train platform. The white and pink rabbits, the cats, dogs, bears, the musical swan and the giant green anaconda—the plush toys were gifts from Senator Pepper's grief-stricken staffers. Jane gave Smokey Bear a place of honor at the head of the bed, next to her Dunlop tennis racket. Smokey still wore his dress.

"Why do you eat so late?" she said. Her animals arranged, she lay across the bed, her hair touching the floor, looking at the world upside down.

"Are you hungry?" Wanda said.

"I'm dying of thirst." Jane clutched her throat and pretended to be stricken.

Wanda's eyes pleaded at me. "Maybe Jack can take you to the lounge—"

"Sure," I said. "Let's go." I held out a hand, urging Jane from the stateroom.

She followed me down the hallway.

"Is Uncle going to be all right?"

"He should be fine by morning."

"What's the matter with him?"

"It's his artistic temperament. Sometimes it gets the better of him and he needs a good rest."

"He seems a little crazy. Has he written a lot of books?"

"Probably a dozen or more." I pointed out the row of books lined up on a glass shelf in the built-in breakfront behind the dining table. "Those are all his."

"Can I read one?" Jane said.

"Help yourself."

She carefully pulled a book out and brought it to the bar. It was a collection of Horace's essays titled *Turkeys I Have Fathered*. She sat on her knees on the middle barstool, opened the book, and began skimming the pages.

I presented her with a cold drink. "Try this."

Jane set the book aside. "Pink. My favorite color." She sat eagerly forward and sucked the straw. Her hair swept ahead at a rakish angle, accentuating the severity of her bob haircut.

The poor thing. *Did they go after her with garden shears?*

"It's very good," Jane said. "What is it?"

"A Shirley Temple."

"Mmm." She took a long sip. "Miss Snodgrass-Smith has a nice bar, but yours is nicer."

"Think so?"

"Your bottles are much prettier. Hers are mostly clear."

"Your uncle likes colorful things."

"Miss Snodgrass-Smith wouldn't allow me behind her bar. I stayed with her the last two nights. I think she was afraid I'd drink her wine."

"Would you have?"

"Oh, no, never." Jane looked at me earnestly, and then somewhat defensively. "It isn't so far-fetched, you know. At summer camp we drank Irish car bombs."

I was skeptical. "Irish car bombs? Who gave you those?"

"Wilbur Sheridan Padgett. He's a very wicked boy. He sold cigarettes, too, and taught the young ones to play blackjack for money. He paid me ten dollars to kiss him."

"I don't think that's a good idea—kissing boys for money."

"Miss Snodgrass-Smith said the same thing. I think she's a bit of a prude."

"What kind of a camp was this?"

"Golf and tennis. In Bethlehem, New Hampshire."

"Tell me about the camp," I said.

Jane worked the straw. She looked cross-eyed into her glass, watching the level of the Shirley Temple drop. "It's a bastion of moral turpitude, seething with rebellious kids."

"Pretty sophisticated observation—"

"Madison Murphy's mom wrote that in a Yelp review. It means a hotbed of depravity. At least we think it was Madison's mom. They made her go home early."

"Your camp sounds like quite a place."

"I've been going there my whole life. I'm working on my tennis stroke. Brushing up on the egg." Jane took the cherry from her glass and dangled it by the stem. Tilting her head, she chomped it in one bite. She chewed with an exaggerated manner, eyeing me keenly. "Do you play tennis?"

"Too clumsy," I said. "I'd never make it jumping over the net."

"It must be fun being a bartender."

"I meet a lot of interesting people. Especially working for your uncle."

Jane slurped through her straw at the bottom of the glass and pushed the ice cubes around.

"Another Shirley Temple?" I asked.

"Please." She rested her elbows on the granite bar counter, leaning forward, watching me make the drink.

I showed her how to fill a glass with ice, pour ginger ale, and add a splash of grenadine. Stir with a swizzle stick. Drop in a maraschino cherry as garnish.

"Help yourself," I said. "Anytime."

Jane looked at me, astonished.

"You mean I'm allowed to go back there and fix my own drink whenever I want?"

"I'm sure your uncle wouldn't mind," I said.

"It's like having my own restaurant!"

"Just promise me you won't go making any Irish car bombs," I said.

Our young live-aboard passenger forced us to alter our routine, starting with dinner that night. By this time we had been uncoupled from the Capitol Limited and moved to Track 1, which was at a remote end of the Union Station platform, far removed from the busy commuter tracks. The Pioneer Mother camped in a perpetual dusk.

"I don't think cow's tongue and sautéed lambs' hearts will cut it for an eleven-year-old," Wanda said as she inspected the contents of the refrigerator. "Ditto calves' brains."

We were running short on everything, but Wanda got creative. There were leftovers from the previous night's forcemeat-stuffed crayfish shells, and packages of ground chuck and pork in a freezer. She found flour tortillas in a cupboard in the pantry and decided we'd have forcemeat tacos.

"The disgrace of every gringo who ever ran a hack Mexican restaurant," she said. "We'll have our own Taco Tuesday."

She filled bowls with fresh guacamole, pico de gallo, shredded cheddar cheese, iceberg lettuce, sour cream, and black olives. It was the sort of casual, serve-yourself dinner that Horace would never allow—and we were doing it right under his nose.

I set the dining table for three.

"We can't do that," Wanda said, pulling me into the galley, speaking in a stage whisper. "We can't eat with her."

"Why not?"

"Because she's a guest."

"Wanda, she's a kid."

"That doesn't make it right."

"We can't make her eat by herself."

"It's a line we don't cross."

"I can't accept that."

"It's not our problem."

"Problem? She's a kid!"

"We're not entertainers and we're not babysitters," Wanda said. "You want her to have company for dinner, hire a clown."

"You're being completely insensitive."

"Shh. Not so loud. And I am not."

"This is ridiculous. What's your big objection?"

"My big objection is that I don't want to get too close to that kid. I told you. I'm not the parenting type. And rules are rules."

"Come on, Wanda. Have a heart."

"She hasn't cried. Have you noticed that?"

"People grieve in different ways."

"I'm putting my foot down," Wanda said. "You and I are not eating with that kid."

"You won't eat with me?" Jane stood in the doorway. She looked from Wanda to me, her eyes brimming with tears.

Wanda said, "Oh, no, hon—"

"Nobody ever wants me!" Jane said. She turned to run away.

Wanda nabbed her by her narrow shoulders. "Wait. That isn't true."

"Everybody hates me!"

"No, honey. You're wrong."

Jane writhed in Wanda's arms. "Nobody likes me. No one cares!"

"Hey," Wanda said. "Stop."

Jane broke free of Wanda's grasp, backed blindly into the hallway, and crumpled against the wall. She sank to the floor, all arms and legs. "The whole world hates me. Everyone's always trying to get rid of me!" She covered her face with her hands and sobbed.

Wanda followed Jane into the hallway and dropped to her knees. She wrapped an arm around Jane's shoulders.

"Listen to me. Jane. We're not trying to get rid of you."

Jane wailed. The tighter Wanda tried to hold her, the harder Jane tossed and turned and kicked her colt's legs. A rubber sandal flew off her foot.

"I wish I was never born!" she cried. "I wish I was dead like Mommy and Daddy!"

Wanda held Jane tightly. "No, baby. Don't say that. Please. Don't ever say that." She held her and rocked her. "We want you. Your uncle wants you. We all want you."

Wanda kept rocking her.

Sniveling and mewling, Jane finally lay still.

"It's okay, baby," Wanda was saying. "I've got you. We've all got you." She blinked up at the ceiling. She was crying, too.

That night, the three of us ate dinner together. I sat at the head of the dining table. Jane lit the candles in the sterling silver candelabra, and she brought Wanda and me Shirley Temples on a tray. She served us with a white linen napkin folded over one arm.

Had Horace awakened and come down the hallway in his robe, he would have been horrified by the breach of etiquette playing out on the old Pullman.

Horace Button, gourmet, gastronome, and member of the Confrérie des Chevaliers du Tastevin, likely wouldn't have recognized his own dining table.

THIRTY-FOUR

THE SOUND CAME FROM A GAP in the upper corner of the upholstered bulkhead that separated Jane's stateroom from our double bedroom, where you could see a crack of light whenever the lamp in Jane's room was on. It arrived in soft, anguished waves, the wailing of a wounded animal. After more than a week of sleeping aboard the *Pioneer Mother*, I had grown accustomed to the peculiar sounds of nighttime on this old Pullman—Horace's guttural snoring, the insistent rush of a flushing toilet, the low rumble of a locomotive departing on an adjacent track—but this muffled sobbing was new to me, and despite longing for sleep, I found myself listening.

Wanda was obviously listening, too. We both lay motionless in our bunks, staring up at nothingness, praying this quiet squall would pass.

Finally, Wanda sighed, threw off her covers, and left our double bedroom, floating out the doorway, ghostlike in her white cotton nightgown. Twice she did this, and twice she returned after a few minutes.

"I feel so powerless," she complained. "What can I possibly do or say to comfort that kid?"

"It's a terrible situation, Wanda," I said. "There's nothing you can do or say."

When she got up for the third time, I checked the display on my cell phone: 1:37 a.m. For a few minutes I listened to Jane's muted crying and to Wanda's voice murmuring on the other side of the bulkhead. The nighttime burden struck me as unfair. By virtue of being female, Wanda was the one stepping up to comfort this grieving child. And where was

Horace? Sleeping soundly through the night, plastered and oblivious. I climbed down from my bunk and stepped into the hallway. I paused at the open door to Jane's room.

The light from the corridor partially illuminated the scene. Wanda sat on the edge of the bed and gently rubbed Jane's back. Jane lay face down, clutching her pillow.

"It's okay, baby," Wanda was saying. "Let it out." Her helpless eyes found mine.

"I'll get some water," I said, backing out of the doorway.

At the bar, I filled a glass. When I returned, Jane was lying in the fetal position with her eyes closed. She gulped air in deep, convulsive breaths.

"Shh." Wanda stroked Jane's hair. "You're a smart, able, beautiful girl. You're going to be all right."

I set the glass of water on the desk.

"Jack just brought you some water," Wanda said. "It's next to the bed, okay?"

"Okay," Jane said in a small voice.

"Anything else I can do?" I said to Wanda.

"No," she said. "Just close the door on your way out."

I hesitated in the doorway. There was something extraordinary about this abused, wounded, persevering chef, something I saw revealed in this darkened bedroom: her wholehearted kindness, her selflessness, the way she sat with this orphaned girl and consoled her in her grief.

I went back to the observation lounge to turn out the lights. Behind the bar, I reached for a rare XO cognac. I filled a heavy crystal snifter and carried it down the hallway, passing Horace's door, passing Jane's. All was quiet.

In our double bedroom the lights were on. Wanda sat somberly on the bed.

"She's sleeping again?" I said.

"Hopefully for good this time." Wanda eyed the snifter in my hand reproachfully.

"This is for you," I said. "To help you sleep."

Wanda studied my face, at first puzzled, and then she got up quickly.

"Wait, give me a second." She tripped the toggle switch on the wall, and the light in the bathroom flickered on. She checked her face in the mirror and finger-combed her hair. I sat on the lower berth. The silhouette of Wanda's body was plainly visible through her backlit nightgown. I forced myself to look away.

"Jane thinks she's to blame," Wanda said, speaking softly into the mirror. "She thinks it's all her fault."

"What makes her think that?"

"Something to do with a boy at camp. Wilbur somebody."

"Wilbur Sheridan Padgett."

"You know about him?" Wanda shut off the bathroom light.

"He made Irish car bombs and taught kids to gamble."

Wanda sat beside me on the bed. "Well, apparently he was her first crush."

"So what does that have to do with—"

"She begged to stay one more week at camp. Her parents said okay. Otherwise they would've been in New Hampshire last Saturday, picking her up."

"Oh, God."

"I just want to scoop her up and cry," Wanda said.

I handed her the cognac.

"Am I drinking alone?" she said.

"I don't need it," I said.

Wanda brought the snifter to her mouth and took a sip, then cradled the glass in her lap and for a long minute said nothing. Cognac glistened on her upper lip.

"All right," I said. "Just a taste."

Wanda passed me the snifter. The cognac burned pleasantly in my mouth. In the quiet night its strong tones of ripe oranges and vanilla were almost startling. I gave the glass back to her.

She curled her legs beneath her. "He won't lift a finger to help her. You know that, right?"

On a nearby track, a train was arriving. The pulse of the locomotive reverberated in my bones.

"It's hard to imagine being so callous," I said.

"It's denial," Wanda said. "He can't stand the thought of sharing his life with anyone." She pushed a tangle of hair away from her face. "What will happen to her, do you think?"

"He's talking about boarding school. Or a convent."

"From a legal standpoint, does he have to take her?"

"I'm assuming he could always resign as her guardian."

"What then?"

"She'd be out in the cold. A foster family, maybe."

We both meditated on this.

"So, how do you convince someone to raise a child when it's the last thing he wants to do?" I said.

"You don't. Not with Mr. Button."

"Maybe Billy Whitehead can talk to him."

"He won't listen to Billy."

"Or Mrs. Whitehead."

"I doubt it."

"Maybe I can talk to him."

"No offense," Wanda said. "But why should he care what you think?"

"I like to think we've developed a little mutual respect."

"Have you told him yet? That you're leaving?"

"No."

Wanda sneered at me. "You're afraid."

"It isn't that."

"Then why haven't you told him?"

"I don't know, with all this commotion and upheaval, it feels like I'd be piling on."

"Maybe you're having second thoughts about leaving."

I shook my head. "Don't think so."

Wanda stared down at the snifter. "She'll pay a terrible price for her uncle's selfishness. It's so incredibly sad."

I put an arm around her shoulders and drew her close. "Hey, you were great tonight, by the way."

"Then why do I feel so inept?"

"You're doing what you can. You care. It means you're human."

"Really?" Wanda said. "You think I'm human?"

Our heads came together. Our foreheads touched.

It began tentatively, a brushing of our lips, and then we kissed.

Wanda drew back and looked at me curiously.

"I've been wondering what that would be like," she said.

"And?"

"Not bad. For a jock."

I kissed her again. I savored the taste of cognac on her lips and tongue. Wanda set the snifter aside. We scrunched down, lying side by side. It took some shifting before our bodies meshed comfortably on the narrow berth.

"Do you fit?" Wanda said.

"Except for this ladder trying to crawl up my ass."

She laughed and we kissed some more. From a midpoint between her shoulder blades I ran a finger down her spine, following it to the delicate swooping saddle that was the small of her back. With the same hand I fished for the hem of her nightgown and found a landing pad of warm skin. When I dipped two fingers beneath the waistband of her panties, Wanda tensed.

"No?" I said.

"Not now, okay?"

"Whatever you say, Wanda. It's your show."

"Let's just stay here, like this. Can we?"

We lay together the rest of the night, clinging to each other, our bodies barely fitting on the bed. I finally reached over and turned out the light. I dozed. Wanda woke me. She scrambled over me and a minute later returned with a bottle of water from the galley refrigerator. When she'd had enough I set the bottle on the floor and took her in my arms again. Facing her, clutching her, I nodded off, and then I slept hard.

The next thing I knew Wanda's alarm was sounding.

I tightened my hold on her. She pulled free, clambered over me, and flicked on the bathroom light. Moments later, she grabbed her chef's whites from the small closet. She turned out the light and opened the door to the hallway.

"That's it?" I said. "You're leaving?"

"The kitchen department never rests."

I got up on an elbow. "I've decided. I'll talk to Mr. Button. I'm going to call him on his attitude toward Jane."

"Pretty tough talk for a guy on his way to a luau." Wanda stepped into the hallway and pulled the door closed behind her.

The door opened again.

"For the record, we didn't sleep together," Wanda said. "Exhaustion and cognac—that's all it was."

She shut the door, leaving me in total darkness.

THIRTY-FIVE

"MR. BUTTON, I NEED TO SPEAK TO YOU about your niece,"
I said.

Horace slumped in his desk chair, taking a breather from the page
that was clenched in the platen of his old IBM Selectric typewriter. He'd
hardly touched the eggs Benedict and skillet potatoes that I'd delivered
to his stateroom earlier and that now congealed on a tray next to his
bed.

Horace turned to me woefully. "I'm really in Dutch on this one," he
said. "What in blazes am I going to do?"

"You can talk to her, for one. Acknowledge that she exists."

"I'm not interested in raising a child. Not at this point in my life."

"Just take a minute. Sit with her."

"And say what?"

"Ask how she's doing."

Horace looked away. He stared obstinately at a point on the wall.

"At least *pretend* to care," I said.

Horace's gaze returned to the piece of paper in the typewriter. He
pinched a corner between his thumb and index finger and plucked it
from the roller's grip.

"I was just writing about Chez Patrice," he said. "Do you know it?
A West End landmark. Monsieur Patrice serves a whacking good meal."

"Mr. Button—"

"His oxtail ragout and lobster Thermidor are indispensable. We'd
knock off a couple of Armagnacs, Patrice and I, after a dinner of

two dozen Wellfleet Harbor oysters, a bucket of soft-shell crabs, and *chateaubriand*."

"Mr. Button, your niece—"

"I intend to visit Chez Patrice this evening. It's imperative that I return to work."

"Are you serious?"

"I must," Horace said. "You see, there was a big scare not long ago, word that Patrice's brook trout had slipped. A fish is alive in water but dead in oil. I fear for the worst. And as long as I'm in Washington, I must see for myself. Why are you looking at me as if I have three heads?"

"You can't just go about your life pretending she doesn't exist."

"I don't know whom you're talking about—"

"Your niece, Mr. Button. You can't just ignore her. You have responsibilities now. You need to provide for her."

"Wanda's a perfectly capable chef. She'll provide."

"Wanda? I should tell you that Wanda hardly slept at all last night."

"Tell her I recommend a gin sling and a good nap."

"Palming your niece off on your chef isn't the answer—not in the long run."

"In the long run I'll be dead and that little girl will be a baroness who outlives a score of husbands."

"That doesn't excuse your behavior now."

"I fought terrible nightmares last night, did I tell you? The Dark Camel was stalking in the driveway. It gave me heart palpitations. I woke up this morning with a bad case of *delirium tremens*."

I glanced at my watch. "Which reminds me. You have an appointment at the funeral home this morning."

"That's another thing, Jack. I don't get on well with hearse jockeys. My criticism of their deceitful business practices has made me a sworn enemy of the industry. I need you to come along as protection."

"I'm afraid I can't do that."

"Oh? Why not?"

"Technically I no longer work for you."

Horace appeared dumbfounded. "What are you saying? Have you gotten into the liquor cabinet?"

"If you'll remember, I was brought on by you and Mr. Whitehead strictly as a temporary. My contract expired two days ago."

"Then we'll simply extend it."

"I'm sorry, Mr. Button. You've been wonderful to work for and very good to me, but I have to move on."

"This comes as a particularly lethal shock. I don't know what to say. Is it about money?"

"Money's got nothing to do with it. It's just that I'm already committed to this other thing, and I need to leave as soon as Wanda finds my replacement."

"I don't want a replacement, Jack. I want you. And not as a bartender, either. I'll make you my executive assistant."

"That's a great compliment—"

"I'll mentor you on everything I know—business, writing, the pleasures of good food and good wine. No other position could possibly rival that."

"You might be surprised."

"You're what I most need right now—someone with a clear head to look after my interests."

"That's very flattering, Mr. Button, but—"

"They're also asking me to meet this afternoon with the estate attorneys. God knows what kind of snake pit they'll try and hurl me into. Please, Jack. I implore you. There must be some compromise. At least give me a few more days."

I hesitated. "What about Jane?" I asked.

"What about her?"

"I really think you need to sit down and talk with her."

"I can't do it, I can't take the time."

"You've still got fifteen minutes before Rosalind arrives."

"Forget it," Horace said. "You might as well ask an orangutan to dance the Charleston—"

"That's it." I turned for the door. "I'm finished."

"Wait, Jack!" Horace said. "It's just… I don't know how to speak to a child."

"You can start by apologizing to her for yesterday afternoon."

"Yesterday afternoon?"

"You very publicly denounced her hero, Eleanor Roosevelt. And in quite colorful terms."

Horace's face grew red. He licked his lips.

I went to him and put a hand on his shoulder. "Just take a few minutes," I said. "You'll do great."

Ten minutes later Horace sat stiffly at the dining table, drumming his fingers, looking blankly at Jane. She stared back at him. On the table before her lay *Turkeys I Have Fathered*, which she'd been reading in her room. From between two pages of the book, the painted eyes of a pink flamingo looked on—a plastic swizzle stick from the bar that served as Jane's bookmark.

Horace cleared his throat. "I see you're globe-trotting with a chronicle of my failings."

Jane knitted her brows and looked at her uncle.

"You're reading my book," Horace said.

"Oh, yes," Jane said. "It's very funny. I had no idea you were so clever with words."

"Ah. Well." Horace turned to me with a horrified expression.

From my post behind the bar, where I pretended to be working, I nodded my encouragement.

He transferred his gaze back to his niece.

The seconds ticked by.

"You're eleven," Horace said.

"Almost twelve," Jane corrected.

He smiled curtly. "Teenage years, right around the corner."

"I wish they'd make the driving age thirteen. If you're old enough to babysit, you're old enough to drive, don't you think?"

"Makes sense to me," Horace said. "I'm surprised they haven't changed it already."

He stared at Jane a moment too long and then grimaced.

Jane got up on her knees in the chair. She planted her elbows on the table and gawked at her uncle without embarrassment, as if she were studying a large zoo animal behind glass.

Horace took umbrage. "Is something wrong?" he said.

"Are you Italian?"

"My girl, I'm English and Scottish, just like you. What makes you think I could be Italian?"

"My best friend's grandfather was a swarthy Italian," Jane said. "He was so fat he had to be buried in a piano crate. They lifted him into the grave with a crane."

Horace stared at Jane, his eyes growing dark. Suddenly he let out a hearty laugh.

"Ha! That's jolly good!" he said. "Reminds me of the story of the famous Italian tenor Enrico Caruso. He was a notoriously demanding guest, a thorn in the side to hotel management on every continent. He was performing in San Francisco the night of the great earthquake, staying at the Palace Hotel, which of course burned to the ground. Caruso made his getaway using the Montgomery Street exit, wearing nothing but a top hat and a Turkish towel. Wags later remarked it was easier to burn the place down than to adapt it to the tenor's demands."

Jane narrowed her eyes coolly at Horace.

"Ha! You see!" Horace smiled merrily and slapped the table. "Easier to burn the place down than to adapt it to the tenor's demands!"

"He must have looked very silly, walking around in a top hat and towel," Jane said.

Silence.

Jane regarded her uncle impassively.

"Have you ever been to Europe?" she asked.

"Of course, many times. Always by Atlantic crossing, and always on the Cunard Line. Once you've been indoctrinated to the Queens Grill, you'll never feel at home on any other ship. But I'll tell you something. Never order the Maine lobster on the east-west passage, or the Dover sole crossing west to east."

"I'd like to speak French," Jane said. "Eleanor Roosevelt spoke fluent French."

"I'll give you some advice about France," Horace said. "Never get in a fistfight with a Frenchman. It's degrading. You must always strike him with your walking stick."

"Fighting isn't allowed at school. We'd get sent home for that." Jane pushed back in her chair and put her ear to the table.

Horace raised his eyebrows. "What, pray tell, are you doing?"

"I'm listening for termites."

"You won't find any termites here, I can assure you."

"I went to a restaurant once. You could hear termites chomping the table."

"Mortifying thought."

"I like going to restaurants."

Horace's face lit up. "Then we have something in common, you and I."

"Mother never took me to restaurants. She was too much in the public eye, she said. Have you ever been to Captain Jim's Treasure Trove and Seafood Palace?"

"I've never even heard of it."

"It's the best place for dinner in the whole world. I went for a birth-day party once. They take your picture and set the food on fire. All the waiters dress like pirates. They even have a gift shop."

"Suddenly I feel faint."

"We had a sword fight on the bridge over the lagoon."

Horace forced a smile. "A gift shop and a lagoon. When I see Patrice tonight I'll suggest a makeover of the premises."

"Who's Patrice?"

"Patrice is a man who weeps easily and charges like Van Cleef and Arpels. But he knows his seafood. They say he can tell if a mackerel had a happy childhood."

Jane regarded her uncle suspiciously. "How can you tell if a fish had a happy childhood?"

"Perhaps one of these days I'll introduce you to Patrice," Horace said. "He's a true culinary genius. His proficiency with escargots, for exam-ple, is legendary."

"Es-car-go?"

"Snails."

Jane wrinkled her nose. "People eat snails?"

"Snails are a wonderful delicacy. You remove them from their shells and bake them in sizzling garlic-herb butter, then put them back in the shell for serving."

"The poor snails. What if they get put back in the wrong shell?"

"It's immaterial, since the shell is strictly for viewing pleasure. I happen to know the cooked snail is perfectly happy to be infused with butter and heading for the gastronome's gullet. It's his raison d'être. Any shell will do."

THIRTY-SIX

AT TEN O'CLOCK HORACE AND I were making our way through the cavernous Main Hall of Union Station, past the glittering shop windows and street-level restaurants. Horace wore his derby and carried a walking stick. I gripped a heavy black briefcase that contained a portable bar.

"I thought that thing with my niece went rather well," Horace said.

"It did," I said.

"Then why do I feel as though I am about to descend into a swamp?"

The moment we stepped into the muggy sunshine, my senses were assaulted by a crush of people and the cacophonous babel of gridlock traffic around Columbus Circle—buses, cars, a sea of yellow taxis. We dodged stacks of suitcases and flocks of pigeons.

"Always so many birds," Horace said, looking around. "For a memorable meal you'd be hard-pressed to top squab and a good claret."

Across the plaza three enormous American flags flew at half-staff. A contingent of National Guard armored Humvees occupied the concrete apron in front of Columbus Fountain.

At the curb, a black Lincoln Town Car honked its horn, a window rolled down, and a woman's sleek arm beckoned from the passenger seat. As Horace and I slid into the backseat, a policewoman's whistle chided Arthur for blocking traffic.

"All right, all right, I'm going," Arthur said. He maneuvered the car forward, working us into a line of traffic moving toward Massachusetts Avenue Northwest.

"How is everyone this morning?" I said cheerily.

"Don't ask," Arthur said.

In the front seat, Rosalind focused on a cell phone in one hand and an iPad on her lap. Her hair was pulled back in a tight bun, the way she'd worn it the day before. Without looking up she said, "Have you seen the newspapers?"

Horace gazed out the window. Not two feet away, on the other side of the glass, a construction worker pulverized the concrete with a jackhammer.

"Why bother?" Horace said. "The damn things elude my comprehension anymore."

Rosalind turned in the seat. "Then I'll summarize," she said. "A complete and utter debacle. They're calling for an investigation."

"An investigation?" Horace said.

"Child and Family Services," Rosalind said.

"They're wondering if the girl's safe," Arthur said.

Horace chortled. "That's what a little stumble gets me in this town? An investigation?"

"Stumble?" Rosalind said. "You were falling-down drunk. And cursing everyone in sight, including the press. Have I mentioned the people in this town play hardball?"

"So what's all the pother?" Horace said. "I've nothing to hide."

"And when they declare you unfit to be guardian and you lose custody of your niece, then what?" Rosalind said.

Horace pondered a moment. "You're telling me if I drink enough, they'll take that child off my hands? Open up the bar, Jack."

Rosalind glanced at the briefcase on the seat between us.

"Don't you dare," she said, glowering at me. "And why are you here, anyway?"

"Me?" I looked at Horace.

"Jack's my executive assistant," Horace said. "In case decisions need to be made."

"That's the whole point of our meetings today," Rosalind said. "To make decisions."

"Good, we can rely on Jack."

"Not for our meeting with the attorneys, we can't," Rosalind said. "We're discussing the senator's will."

"It's the stiff-stacker I have the antipathy for," Horace said. "I'm bowing out of the meeting at the mortuary and giving Jack my proxy."

Rosalind was incredulous. "You're delegating your sister's funeral arrangements to a bartender?"

Horace said, "Madam, I assure you, I have no desire to enmesh myself in the gory details of a double funeral. I intend to spend the morning getting drunk as a lord."

"Surely you're pulling my leg, Mr. Button," Rosalind said. "Because if you're serious, that is the most irresponsible thing I have ever heard."

"My responsibility is to my readers," Horace said. "No one else. Come on, Jack. Hit me with a bourbon toddy."

Rosalind turned to me. "Don't you dare!"

"Put some hair on it, Jack," Horace said. "And give it an inch of your thumb."

My thumb?

Under Rosalind's scornful glare I opened the briefcase, pulled out a rocks glass and a bottle of bourbon, and poured Horace a stiff one.

"Shame on you both," Rosalind said, facing forward.

Horace winked at me. "It's uncanny, Miss Snipperhooch," he said to Rosalind. "Jack's sweet-smelling thumb lends a certain piquancy to a morning shot. You should try it. You might like it."

Rosalind spun around. "The name is Snodgrass-Smith, Mr. Button. Snod. Grass. Smith. You can drop the *Smith* if it's too much for your addled brain to handle—God knows I'd like to drop it myself—but I'd appreciate your showing respect for a surname signed on the Declaration of Independence. My direct lineal ancestor, Mr. Samuel Abraham Snodgrass, also happened to sign the Articles of Confederation, and would have signed the Constitution, too, had he not contracted swamp fever in his fight against Lord Cornwallis's army and departed suddenly for the south of France. So you will address me by my proper name, Snodgrass. Or Snodgrass-Smith if you want to convince me you're still sober enough to read your mail. Do I make myself clear?"

For a moment Horace stared at Rosalind without blinking, and then he turned and looked out the window. He took a sip of bourbon.

"This old fellow Snodgrass," Horace said a minute later. "You say he left for the south of France?"

Rosalind's iPad dinged. She looked down at the screen. "They thought the warmer climate might cure his fever."

"*Cuisine française* and an abundance of reliable table wines," Horace observed. "A fine remedy for swamp fever, no doubt."

"As it turns out he never made it to France. Whether he perished at sea or was taken by pirates we'll never know." Rosalind navigated to the newly arrived e-mail and became engrossed in the message.

Horace said to me, "Pirates. Nefarious mercenaries in slouch hats and morning coats. Everything always in costume."

"Shit," Rosalind said.

"More bad news?" Arthur said.

"It's the L.G.B.T. branch of the National Park Rangers Association. They're demanding an apology." Rosalind turned to Horace. "From you," she said.

"An apology from me?" Horace said. "For what?"

"For mocking them in public. The ranger bear in a dress. Apparently the Forest Service's drag queens were offended."

"But it was a nightgown!" Arthur said.

"You and I know that, Arthur," Rosalind said. "But try convincing a bunch of gay, lesbian, and transgender park rangers that it was a harmless gesture. They're on a hair trigger when it comes to microaggressions. They see a conservative waving Smokey Bear in a dress, and it's Armageddon." She sighed heavily. "I knew that bear was a mistake."

"What are we going to do?" Arthur said.

"I don't know," Rosalind said. "They say if they don't get an immediate apology, they'll petition Child and Family Services to award custody to the state—whatever it takes to keep Jane Pepper from being brought up in a homophobic household."

"That's rubbish!" Horace snapped.

"I know how these people think," Rosalind said. "To them, your sister was the enemy—Republican or Democrat, it didn't matter. She was hands down the best politician to hit this town in thirty years, and she had the political establishment shaking in their boots. She had to be stopped, one way or another. And now that she's passed, God rest her soul, they'll do or say anything to discredit her legacy, and that includes demonizing you. They'd love nothing better than to see Ruth Pepper's daughter made a ward of the state. You'd better change your ways, Mr. Button, or this town will hand you your head on a platter."

"I covered Capitol Hill as a reporter for many years, Miss Snodgrass. I'm familiar with its politics."

"Times have changed. Washington is a blood sport now, a zero-sum game with no rules. It's all about money and power."

"It's always *been* about money and power," Horace said. "Why, the stories I could tell you about any given day: grand larceny with breakfast and embezzlement by noon. I once watched an administration with overalls and a hillbilly accent trying to load the Lincoln Memorial into a truck."

At this Rosalind smiled. She braced her right elbow against the window and pressed a hand to her forehead.

"You're probably right," she said. "Nothing's changed. And I'm still the militia, trying to beat back Lord Cornwallis's army. Oh, God. Could things get any more dire?" She shook her head, sighed, and said to Horace and me, "Let me be blunt, gentlemen. If we don't get on the same page, things will turn out very badly for all of us. Don't talk to the press. Don't talk to the forest rangers. We simply must project the visage of one big happy family. Got it?" She looked at Horace and said, "If you have too much to drink, steer clear of your niece until you've sobered up. No more scenes like yesterday. Period."

Rosalind's iPad dinged again. She read the new message.

"Oh, this is interesting," she said.

Arthur glanced away from the road. "What is it?"

"The White House. I'm invited to a six o'clock briefing on the murder investigation."

"Do they know who did it?"

"Doesn't say. But I know who I'd put my money on."

THIRTY-SEVEN

THE CARVED WOODEN SIGN at the entrance to the long driveway said "Burton Bannister & Son's Funeral Home and Mortuary." The funeral home was a stately red brick mansion with a white-columned portico, a domed entry, and an expansive green lawn. Soaring shade trees abounded. We were in Bethesda, Maryland.

As Arthur parked the car, the front door of the funeral home opened, and a white-haired man came out onto the wide porch.

"There he is, Jack," Horace said. "Our high-pressure undertaker. Right out of central casting."

Rosalind said, "Let's leave the liquor in the car, please."

"Good idea," Horace said. "I'll stay and keep an eye on it."

Rosalind looked as though she wanted to throttle Horace. "Do me a favor, Mr. Button, and keep the flippant remarks to yourself. At this point your alcohol-fueled babble is irritating and highly inappropriate." She opened her door.

"Be vigilant, Jack," Horace said to me in a low voice. "The place is probably rife with trapdoors and body snatchers."

Rosalind spun around.

"Mr. Button, your sister meant the world to me," she said, her eyes brimming. "I worshiped her, in fact, and I'm absolutely numb with grief right now. But I have a very public service to put on, and a lot of extra logistical details to attend to, which means I can afford neither to fall apart nor to scream out loud, which is what I feel like doing at the moment—at you. I'll be grateful for your cooperation and as much decency as you can muster, given that you've consumed half a liter of bourbon and abdicated your decision-making responsibilities to a bartender. Please. For the next hour or so, grow the hell up."

Burt Bannister, the funeral director, materialized at Rosalind's open car door.

"Rosalind, you made it!" he said. He had a big Irish head. The impeccable part in his hair was a pink line glistening with sweat.

We made introductions standing by the car. The scent of sun-baked asphalt intermingled with the fragrance of freshly mowed grass, and birds sang in the pine trees. Burt shook our hands. He wore a large diamond ring and dove-shaped gold cufflinks.

"Please," he said, "everyone, come inside."

Burt led Horace and Rosalind up the steps to the mansion. Arthur and I followed.

"Tell me," Horace said to Burt. "Is this place already rented out for Halloween?"

Burt did a double take, then clapped Horace on the back. "A sense of humor," he said with a laugh. "We could use more of that around here."

The funeral home smelled like an old church: candle wax and floor polish and the musty scent of old books. A worn Oriental rug adorned the foyer's hardwood floor. Hanging on the walls were large portraits done in oil—four generations of Bannisters.

"Quick history," Burt said. "Great-granddad was a cabinetmaker. There was a big outbreak of flu, so he moonlighted making coffins. Grandfather joined the family business out of the army. Mastered the technique of embalming. At that point we stopped making coffins and focused exclusively on operating the funeral home. Do you have time to meet the team?"

Rosalind glanced at her watch. "We're a little pressed."

Burt seemed disappointed. "They were hoping to meet Mr. Button."

Horace said, "Why of course we'll meet them, Burt. Just lead the way."

Burt looked to Rosalind for approval.

"Good," Rosalind said quickly. "Let's do it."

The four of us trailed Burt down a hallway and around a corner. Standing in a perfect line, like soldiers awaiting a military review, was Burt Bannister's staff. In their conservative, semi-formal attire they could have been the hospitality committee of the neighborhood Presbyterian church.

The first employee, a woman in her forties with limp black hair, had her hands clasped demurely in front of her. The furrows in her high, blunted forehead made her appear fretful. She wore a tasteful blue dress and a silver cross pendant.

"Dagny Di Fransesco is my administrative assistant," Burt said. "She'll be sitting in on our meeting this morning."

Dagny shook Horace's hand. "My condolences on the loss of the senator and your brother-in-law," she said.

"Thank you, Dagny." Horace smiled back warmly.

"In her spare time Dagny enjoys listening to jazz," Burt said. "She also devours mystery novels like a fiend—"

"Mr. Bannister, please don't—"

Burt had a glint in his eye. He placed a hand on Dagny's shoulder. "The only mystery to me is why the single men haven't devoured Dagny."

Dagny blushed. "I'm so sorry, Mr. Button. He always does this." She looked at Burt and mouthed the words: "You're such an ass."

Horace put on a brave smile.

We continued down the line, meeting the rest of the staff: the senior mortician, a smallish man with a black Luciferian beard; the funeral director assistant, a recent Ohio State graduate and a rabid Redskins fan; the greeter, an elderly widow who rescued cats and played the accordion. The groundskeeper was a skeletal old black man who washed the cars and ran the crematorium.

Rosalind kept looking at her watch.

"There," Burt said. "You've met the team. Now we'll go to the conference room and talk specifics."

We continued down the hallway. Arthur sidled up to me.

"God, this place is so freaky," he said under his breath.

The conference room was one you'd find in a stockbroker's office—federal-style furniture, including a long mahogany table. The room was stocked with glossy Bannister & Son's brochures: *Living with Loss; Coping with Grief; A Checklist for Death.* I took one of each, thinking Wanda might glean tips for dealing with Jane. The morning's *Washington Post* lay prominently on the conference table. The picture on the front page, above the fold, showed Horace on his back on the train station platform, arms in the air, holding Smokey Bear in the dress while Jane looked on, mystified. "Officials Concerned Over Pepper Child's Welfare," said the headline.

Burt opened a bookcase that turned out to be a fully stocked wet bar. "Who'd like a drink?" he said.

Across the room, Rosalind looked at me wide-eyed.

"Mr. Button," Burt was saying. "Can I pour you anything?"

Horace scanned the line of bottles. "Four fingers of bourbon, if it wouldn't be too much trouble."

"No trouble at all," Burt said. "Anyone else? We've got coffee, too."

"Coffee's fine for the rest of us," Rosalind said.

Burt poured a liberal whiskey for Horace and something for himself, too—vodka, by the looks of the bottle. Dagny came in with a stainless steel thermos of coffee, which we passed around the table. Burt took the seat next to Dagny's. He deftly slid the newspaper onto the floor.

"We've got a lot of ground to cover," he said, "so let's get started. Rosalind, you said on the phone that the funeral plan is in place?"

"It is." Rosalind brought her coffee cup to her lips and took a sip. Her eyebrows fluttered. She set down the cup—it bore a red imprint of her lower lip. "We finalized the last details this morning with the majority leader's office. Starting tomorrow the caskets will lie in state in the Capitol Rotunda for twenty-four hours. The sergeant at arms is coordinating with the Defense Department about the honor guard. The service is Friday morning at the National Cathedral. Then, starting Saturday we'll travel by special train back to Nevada for burial at a cemetery in Winnemucca."

This was the first I'd heard of a special train. Horace's face was impassive.

"Good," Burt said. "Then you aren't expecting a viewing of any kind?"

"I think we all understand the condition of the remains," Rosalind said.

I shifted my gaze to Arthur. He sat stock-still, his eyes focused on Burt.

"Is it important to you that the hearses be of matching color?" Burt said.

Rosalind looked past me to Horace. "What do you think? Matching hearses?"

"I can give you black or white," Burt offered. "Or one of each."

"Your call, Mr. Button," Rosalind said. "What's your preference?"

Horace jabbed a thumb in my direction. "Check with Jack. His department."

All eyes turned to me.

"We haven't talked about it," I stammered. "Seriously? Hearses come in colors?"

Rosalind said to Burt, "Let's go with matching black. White strikes me as a bit... effeminate."

Burt turned to me, seeking my agreement.

"Fine," I said. "Matching black."

Dagny made a note of it.

"Will you require any additional automotive resources?" Burt said, looking from Rosalind to Horace to me. "Limousines for family or close friends?"

Rosalind jumped in. "Family only. The rest of us have our own limousines."

"Of course, you're government," Burt said. "How many in the family party?"

"Just two," Rosalind said. "Mr. Button and Jane."

"What about extended family? Or will anyone else be sharing the limousine?" Burt put the question to Rosalind and then looked at me.

Rosalind looked down the table at Horace.

Horace shrugged. I shrugged, too.

Burt said to Dagny, "Make it a stretch, black. Maximum flexibility." He turned to Rosalind. "What about the flowers? Will we be transporting those as well?"

"Only from the Rotunda to the National Cathedral," Rosalind said. "After that we're donating everything to Walter Reed."

Burt focused his attention on Dagny's notepad. He waited until she stopped writing and then turned back to Rosalind.

"What about newspaper notices?" Burt said. "Will you be relying on us for any obituary information?"

Rosalind gave him a contemptuous look. "Please. This is a United States senator we're talking about."

"Of course," Burt said. "My apologies. Death certificates the same?"

"Same. Our office will handle it."

"So transportation of both caskets to the Capitol, the National Cathedral, and then the train station?

"Correct."

"Which train station?"

"Union Station. Massachusetts Avenue Northeast."

"Do you need us to secure a railroad car for the trip west?"

"Amtrak's already given us a baggage car for the caskets. We'll get the rest once we know the size of the delegation."

"Delegation?"

"The majority leader's calling for a member delegation to accompany the remains to Winnemucca. A number of us will be on that train."

"A funeral train." Burt smiled. "Wonderful tradition."

"Senator Pepper was a servant of the people," Rosalind said. "This gives them a chance to pay their respects. By the way, I want some mortuary people on that train. In case of an emergency."

"An emergency?"

"You know," Rosalind said. "In case a coffin pops open, something like that."

Dagny stopped writing.

Burt bridled. "I guarantee you, Rosalind, our coffins do not pop open."

"Humor me, Burt," Rosalind said. "I want some of your people on that train."

"I'm not sure you understand what you're asking. It'll add a great deal of expense—"

"Just schedule it. Please." Rosalind rubbed her temples.

"And this extra expense," Burt said. "It'll be paid by whom?"

"Like everything else, the costs will be paid by the government. Submit the invoice for your time to the Senate sergeant at arms."

Horace banged his whiskey glass on the table. He turned angrily to Rosalind.

"Something wrong?" she asked.

"This country's flat broke, Miss Snodgrass," Horace said. "And you're saying my sister's final act as a public servant will be to embark for the Styx with a dead hand planted firmly in the public till?"

"I assure you, Mr. Button, it's customary practice," Rosalind said.

Horace looked at me. "New marching orders, Jack. No Rolls-Royce coffins, no big-ticket grave monuments, no beluga caviar. We're going strictly el cheapo here."

Rosalind blanched. The room fell silent.

Burt smiled sympathetically. "I hear you, Mr. Button. Yours is not an uncommon reaction. My purpose today isn't to sell you monuments and caviar. It's to make a difficult time a little more bearable."

"They're asking me to raise an eleven-year-old child," Horace said. "Next to that, death is hilarious."

Burt chortled. "May I suggest cryonics? There's a machine in back. We can deep-freeze her now and resuscitate her when she turns twenty-one."

"I like it," Horace said. "Let's you and I talk."

"Can we please get back to the subject at hand?" Rosalind said. "I need some mortuary people on that train."

Burt ruminated. "How many days are we talking about?"

"Four days. And three nights."

"That won't be cheap."

Rosalind fixed her eyes on Burt. "As I said, it all comes out of the Senate's contingency fund. You'll be paid top dollar for your people's time, including hotel and airfare for the return to D.C."

"Interesting proposition." Burt shifted in his chair and turned his gaze to the ceiling for a moment. He looked back at Rosalind and smiled. "All right. You'll have two of us on the train. Most likely Dagny and me."

Dagny fingered her silver cross. "Mr. Bannister, it's your anniversary weekend. You're taking Mrs. Bannister to Cape Cod, remember?"

"Screw Cape Cod," Burt said. "She can go by herself. All she does is sit in front of an easel and paint kelp, anyway." He pushed back his chair and stood. "Shall we convene to the showroom?"

Rosalind looked at him. "Showroom?"

"To pick out the coffins," Burt said.

With a final gulp of coffee I stood with the rest. Horace made no effort to move.

Incredulous, Rosalind scowled at him. "You're not coming?"

"Jack's in charge," Horace said. "Whatever he says, goes."

"He wears a waiter's jacket and serves you poison all day!" Rosalind said. "What does he know about picking out coffins?"

But Horace hung fast. We left him sitting alone in the conference room, nursing a fresh drink.

"You said both caskets will lie in state in the Rotunda?" Burt said to Rosalind as we walked as a group down the hallway. "A civilian? Isn't that a bit unusual?"

"Unusual but not unprecedented," she said. "Senate practice is that prominent citizens may lie in state. David Pepper falls under that category."

"I'm quite familiar with the Rotunda setting, actually," Burt said. "I can show you some product that'll look absolutely spectacular there."

We stopped at a set of wide double doors, and Burt used a key to unlock the deadbolt. He opened the door and switched on the lights. The windowless room was the size of a two-car garage. On the walls, coffins hung two-up like bunk beds; others were arranged on the floor in a chevron pattern that reminded me of the Midland bicycle shops I had visited as a boy. Most of the coffins were displayed with their lids open, revealing tufted velvet interiors.

"You can disregard that entire bunch," Burt said, indicating the coffins at the far end of the room. "Those are all cremation caskets." He stepped forward and drew our attention to some copper and bronze caskets. "I'm thinking that either the Brougham, here, or the Monte Sereno, over here, would make stellar choices. As you can see, both are superbly attractive metals. A one-piece top, continuous-seam bottom. Over time they'll withstand entry of outside elements to a remarkable degree. And over here is our Imperial Cutlass, if money's no object and you really want to honor your loved ones."

"Excuse me," Rosalind said, "can you give Jack and me a minute?" She had her head down and her back turned.

"Of course," Burt said. "Take all the time you need."

The moment the others left the room, Rosalind's shoulders slumped, and she began to shake. She covered her eyes with one hand and braced herself on an open coffin lid with the other.

"God help me," she said. "This is so horrible."

I went to her and touched her lightly on the back. "Hey."

She turned. Her lips trembled and mascara streamed down her cheeks. I took her in my arms.

"They're so ... so cold."

"What's cold, Rosalind?"

"The metal caskets." She could barely choke out the words.

"You don't like the metal caskets because they're cold?"

"They're abhorrent. I hate them." Her back felt lean and muscular in my hands. Her perfume smelled strongly floral.

I reached into a pocket and pulled out an embroidered handkerchief—an extra one of Horace's. "Take this."

She lifted her head, saw the handkerchief, and gripped it.

"Thank you," she said. She brushed the handkerchief across her eyes.

"Listen, Rosalind. If you don't want metal caskets we won't get metal caskets."

She smiled at me through her tears. "You think Mr. Button will go along with that?"

"Don't worry about Mr. Button. I'll handle Mr. Button."

Rosalind dabbed her eyes, patted her cheeks, and wiped her mouth.

"I'm sorry I said that—about you dishing out poison," she said. "I know you're just being a loyal employee."

"I've been called a lot worse."

Rosalind was relaxed in my arms. She made no effort to budge.

"Tell me something," she said. "Why does that man—your boss—have to be so difficult? Doesn't he realize that that bomb shattered a lot of other people's lives, too?"

"I know."

"I could just shake him. I don't think he comprehends how much Jane needs a home right now." She folded the handkerchief and offered it to me.

"Keep it," I said.

"I promised the senator, if anything ever happened..." Rosalind's gaze went glassy, but then she snapped out of it. "From now on, you and I should be on the same team, all right?"

"I agree."

"Will you work on him? Get him to see the light?"

"I'll do what I can."

Rosalind surveyed the room.

"All these caskets," she said. "Can I make one request?"

I looked at her.

"Let's not be impetuous," she said. "Let's take our time and get it right, okay?"

THIRTY-EIGHT

ARTHUR AND I SAT COOLING OUR HEELS in brown leather armchairs in the reception area of the law offices of Weiss, Rosenthal, and French. From twenty-one stories up, the view was spectacular: lush green vegetation, blue water, all those white monuments.

"Look at them in there, eating finger sandwiches and sipping tea," Arthur said. He stared past the receptionist and into the glass conference room where Horace and Rosalind were meeting with a team of estate attorneys. "I could tell them exactly what the senator's will says. I practically wrote it."

I kept my nose buried in the *Wall Street Journal.* A front-page article speculated about who killed Ruth Pepper. A foreign terror organization, a domestic political enemy, a lone-wolf nut—there were any number of theories, but government sources were being tight-lipped, and so far no one had taken credit for the killings.

"So who do you think killed Senator Pepper?" I said.

Arthur frowned. "Who knows? She probably got ten death threats a day."

I returned to the newspaper article. The FBI was on the case. The construction of the I.E.D. amounted to a signature, the director said.

"Pity the common man," Arthur said. "I wrote that, too."

I looked up from my newspaper.

"Excuse me?"

"Senator Pepper's famous line," Arthur said. "'Pity the common man who believes in Socialism, because he believes in something that doesn't believe in him.' I wrote that."

"I think I've heard that before," I said.

"I know. Because Senator Pepper always said it."

I went back to my newspaper.

"That bear wasn't my fault," Arthur said suddenly. "I could've brought a hundred bears and it wouldn't have made any difference."

"No, probably not." I kept reading.

Arthur's hostile eyes bored into me. "Don't you people have a code of ethics?"

I turned to him. "I'm sorry?"

"Aren't there certain rules for bartenders? Like if someone drinks too much and gets in an accident, can't you be held personally liable?"

"Are you saying yesterday was my fault?"

"The guy was bombed out of his gourd, and you were the one serving him."

"Mr. Button does what he wants. He's his own man."

"But you could have cut him off."

"Not really."

"Yes."

I turned my back to Arthur. The law-office receptionist was a doe-eyed brunette with horn-rimmed glasses, wearing a low-cut silk blouse. She looked like a stripper trying to look like a receptionist.

Arthur had a sinus problem, or perhaps a cold. He kept blowing his nose into a tissue, and I could sense him breathing through his mouth. He stuffed the tissue into a side pocket of his suit jacket.

"I really should be in there," he said, indicating the conference room.

"Then go," I said.

"I can't. Rosalind told me to stay out here. In deference to you."

"To me?"

"You're the only one who doesn't know the contents of the will. She thought you'd feel like the odd man out. Net-net, I'm sitting here, and it's costing me lunch."

"Maybe the receptionist has jelly beans."

"I'll tell you this much," Arthur said. "The will pours everything into a trust. You wouldn't believe what that Pepper girl is worth."

"It's really none of my business."

"I'm a lawyer, did I tell you that? Yale Law School. Public interest. I helped strategize the instruments, both the will and the trust. I can tell you pretty much to the penny what she's worth—"

I cut him short. "I'd rather not know—"

"Somewhere north of twelve million dollars. She's the beneficiary of the trust."

"Dammit, Arthur," I said. "I asked you not to tell me."

"It's public record. Stocks, bonds, a working cattle ranch in Nevada. The senator's autobiography generates pretty serious royalty income, too, and I mean *serious*. Ridiculous, huh? About to start seventh grade and you're already a multimillionaire."

"I'd rather think of her as a kid."

"I'm not a gossip. I have an underlying moral justification for telling you this."

I glared at him.

"Your boss is the sole trustee," Arthur said. "That's what they're in there telling him right now. Little Jane doesn't get her hands on a dime until she turns thirty."

I continued to scowl, but the extent of Jane's wealth staggered me.

"Her uncle holds all the power for the next twenty years," Arthur continued. "Can you imagine? Being that close to big money—and it's in the hands of some drunk."

"I can imagine," I said. "My drunk rode a motorcycle."

"What?"

"Never mind."

"The point is, your boss is under a lot of scrutiny right now."

"I know. Child services—"

"More than that. They're assessing his fitness to serve as guardian. Someone could always petition the court to have him removed."

"On what grounds?"

"Being mentally unfit to serve. Chronic abuse of alcohol, for example."

I eyed Arthur suspiciously. "Like who could argue that, for example?"

"Like Rosalind, for example."

We sat for the next few minutes without talking. Arthur attended to his dripping nose. I tried turning my attention back to the newspaper, but conflicting versions of my future began circulating through my head, and I couldn't concentrate on the words.

"So tell me this," I finally said. "What are the chances Rosalind would petition the court to have Mr. Button removed as guardian?"

"Right now, I'd say fifty-fifty."

"And what are the chances Child Services would try to take Jane?"

"That one's a little different. It depends on the polls."

"The polls?"

"They're actively polling it right now. So far it's strictly down party lines. Democrats want to see the government intervene. Republicans say leave her with her uncle, even if he's a raging alcoholic. At the moment Independents are leaning with Republicans, but if that changes, you'll see Child Services pay a visit to your railroad car sooner rather than later."

"You're saying a government agency can be influenced by a national poll?"

"This is Washington, D.C.," Arthur said. "Everything is polled. Everything is politics."

In the conference room, Horace and Rosalind sat with their backs to us, eating and talking and nodding their heads.

I tried another newspaper. This one had a sports section. Football season was underway.

"What's it cost to operate that railroad car?" Arthur said.

"I have no idea," I said without looking up.

"Winter fuel prices are going through the roof. I know. I'm tight with the guy who handles policy for the Energy Committee."

"My boss doesn't care about gas prices. The price of *foie gras*, on the other hand..."

"What do you know about private railcars?" he asked.

"How to set a handbrake and where to top off the fresh water. That's about it."

"What about chartering one?"

"Not a clue. Call Amtrak."

"You know the term *bicameral*?"

I glowered at Arthur.

"It means involving both legislative chambers," he said. "That funeral train we're putting together—it'll have bicameral representation. God, it's causing me such a headache. Getting all the right equipment lined up, I mean. Vista domes. Sleeper cars. Coaches. It's so complicated, I could scream."

"What's so complicated about it?" I said.

"Because Democrats won't ride with Republicans—hell, half the Republicans won't ride with one another. And senators won't ride with congressmen. Members of the press need their own accommodations. And everyone has staff. See what I mean? And it's up to me to make it all happen."

"Sounds like a long train."

"A *very* long train," Arthur agreed. "A lot of high-ranking people are going to be on it, serious names, but you didn't hear that from me."

Arthur pulled his hair and laughed so maniacally that the receptionist looked over. "Three days!" he said. "A comprehensive solution that makes everyone happy in three days! Are you kidding? " He rocked his head back and banged it several times against the wall. The framed print above his head—an Indian camp by Bierstadt—quivered on its wire. Arthur was close to getting beaned by an encampment of Ojibwa Indians.

Arthur said, "And to think five days ago I was working on Medicare reform."

Where was *I* five days ago? I turned back to the sports section and immediately fixed on the date: Wednesday, August 30. Giselle's first day of filming in Hawaii. I hadn't spoken to her since Sunday.

Arthur scrutinized me again.

"You'll be on that train, you know," he said.

"I doubt it."

"No question in my mind. Because your boss's railroad car will be hooked on the back, the rear of the rear. That's the plan."

"That doesn't mean I'll be on it," I said. "I'm leaving town."

"You're leaving town?"

"I'm on my way to Hawaii," I said.

Arthur stared at me gravely. "When?"

"Soon. Maybe very soon."

"I wouldn't do that if I were you."

"What do you mean, you wouldn't do it?"

"Just clear it with Rosalind first."

"I'm not clearing anything with Rosalind first. What's she got to do with it?"

"Look, I'm just telling you. Talk to her before you do anything."

I stood up and flung the newspaper onto the coffee table.

"What am I, her servant?" I said. "I don't even work for her. That's the problem. I don't work for anyone."

"Where are you going?"

"Stretching my legs. I need to make a call."

I went out to the hallway. Giselle picked up on the fourth ring.

"This is Herr Fritz," I said in my best German accent. "From the Grand Harvey Hotel. I need *boeuf en croûte* for five hundred people, *sehr schnell.*"

"Sorry, Herr Fritz," Giselle said. "You'll have to hang up. I'm expecting a call from a handsome young man in Washington, D.C."

"It's good to hear your voice. How are you, Giselle?"

"I'm fine, but Hawaii's been problematic, to say the least."

"Why? What's going on?"

"My God, our dress rehearsal was positively cataclysmic! The wind was howling and sand kept blowing in my eyes. My hair was a complete mess. Then we lost gas to the outdoor stove, and one of the stage backdrops blew completely over. That was all in the span of maybe an hour, can you believe it?"

"Where are you now?"

"I'm holed up in the coffee shop of the Coconut Edgewater Hotel, doing a postmortem with Hakeem and Yuri."

"Hakeem and Yuri?"

"My producer and my director. Yuri's eating what may be the worst macadamia-nut pancakes anyone's ever put on a plate, I might add. He's nodding yes. And the mystique of Hawaiian coffee is a positive joke, I can tell you that. We're thinking we'll have to postpone the luau. The wind's already coming back." Giselle shrieked suddenly. "Look! Oh my gosh! A seat cushion just flew into the pool!"

For a moment the cell signal weakened, and static filled the line.

"Giselle, can you hear me?"

"I'm here."

"I'm sorry I couldn't call sooner."

"But you're on your way?"

"Well, that's what I'm calling about."

"We could do grilled flattened quails and sautéed wild mushrooms."

"Grilled flattened quails?" I said.

"I'm talking to Hakeem and Yuri. In the hotel kitchen, Yuri. Sure, why not? A kitchen's a kitchen. So, Jack, I'm here. When do you arrive? I'll send a car to meet your plane."

"Giselle, there's something I have to tell you. It turns out Ruth Pepper has an eleven-year-old daughter, and she's been sent to live with Mr. Button."

Giselle went silent a moment. "I'm sorry, but what does that have to do with anything?"

"Everyone's in a panic," I said. "Mr. Button wants nothing to do with her. Wanda's terrified. I'm still trying to figure out Ruth Pepper's chief of staff—she's up to something. But, mainly, I'm worried for this poor girl."

"Jack, she isn't your responsibility."

"I know, but she's going through hell."

"You can't save the world."

"I need to be sensitive to the circumstances."

"I don't understand why you're bringing this up. What're you saying?"

"I'm saying these people need me right now. I can't just walk out."

"You're a bartender, Jack. I doubt you've properly construed the situation. You're expendable. And I'm offering you everything. Good God! Don't you get that?"

"Giselle, I spent the morning picking out caskets. For Ruth Pepper and her husband."

A pause.

"Why you?" Giselle said.

"Long story."

"Listen, you've done your job. You delivered him to Washington. Now here's what I want you to do. Fly out of D.C. tomorrow. My office can arrange the ticket. You're going east to west, so if you leave early enough in the morning you can be here before sundown."

"Tomorrow is too soon."

Silence.

"You know what, Jack? Maybe you shouldn't come at all. It's getting to the point where I really don't care."

"But I want to see you."

"Whatever. Decide."

"I can probably make this weekend work. Saturday. Sunday at the latest."

"I need a commitment."

"Saturday for sure, then. I'll see you Saturday night."

"Just get here, okay? Wait, Hakeem and Yuri are signaling... They're here? Now? Sorry, Jack. I need to go..."

When I returned to the law office I found Arthur at the reception desk, getting the parking ticket validated. In the conference room everyone was standing. Horace donned his derby, took up his walking stick, and came out glum-faced. Passing me, he made saucer eyes that only I could see.

THIRTY-NINE

THE BRIGHTLY LIT STOREFRONTS; the cool, musty air; the coffered plaster ceiling of the Main Hall that echoed the din of the streaming crowd—Washington's Union Station was like a great underground city. Slogging against early afternoon commuters, Horace and I made our way through the concourse, dodging clusters of loitering travelers sitting with their suitcases.

Seeing our gate, Horace came to an abrupt stop.

"Holy God," he said.

A knot of reporters blocked our way. They saw Horace and converged on us, switching on the lights of their video cameras. The Amtrak agent who monitored the boarding gate stood at a podium just beyond a metal detector. Short and broad with a Hitler mustache, he hailed us to forge ahead. I pushed through the reporters, pulling Horace with me.

"Have you heard anything from the president?" a reporter asked.

"Not a word," Horace said.

"Any idea who killed Senator Pepper?" another reporter asked.

"I'm a writer, not a sleuth."

"What'll you do if Family Services tries to take Jane?" called a reporter.

Horace stopped and swung his head around. "I'll fight them tooth and nail."

"Were you intoxicated yesterday?"

"No comment."

Two uniformed policemen manned the metal detector. They directed us to empty our pockets into waiting plastic tubs. Horace balked.

"This is Mr. Button," the Amtrak agent said to the policemen. "He's traveling private." He signaled to Horace and me. "You two come on through—"

A woman reporter shouted, "Is Jane safe?"

"Perfectly safe," Horace said.

"Do you have any guns aboard the *Pioneer Mother*?" a reporter said.

"No comment."

Horace gave me a nudge in the back. I stepped aside and let him go ahead of me. He braved the detection device, squeezing his broad shoulders together and clutching his silver-headed stick to his body. The alarm sounded.

"Come on, keep coming!" the Amtrak agent called to me.

I ducked my head and went through. The alarm sounded again—the portable bar.

"Don't stop," the Amtrak agent said. "You're good to go."

The automatic doors closed behind us, drowning out the reporters' shouted questions.

We found the *Pioneer Mother* locked and its alarm set. I let us inside and circulated through the observation lounge, turning on lights as I went. Horace shed his derby hat on a side table and planted his walking stick in the umbrella stand. He settled onto a barstool.

"You've hardly said a word since we left the attorney's office," I said. "Are you all right?"

"All this Sturm und Drang has left me exhausted," he said. "Where do you think our little cattle baroness has gone? I don't suppose she's joined the circus—that would be asking too much."

"Grocery shopping with Wanda would be my guess." I went behind the bar and started to unpack the briefcase. "Can I get you anything?"

"No, I think I'll go for a nap."

"You haven't had a proper drink since the funeral home. Are you turning over a new leaf?"

"I have to tell you, Jack, the review of my sister's estate was heart-rending. I give her credit. When it came to her financial affairs she was smart enough to follow our father's advice. That's one of my greater regrets. I was so headstrong when it came to listening to him—always so insensitive, even when he was trying to help. He backed *Sunshine Trails* financially in the early years and saved us with some loans when we needed them."

"Maybe this is your opportunity to pay him back," I said. "By looking after his granddaughter."

"I know my place, Jack, and it's among the pots." Horace stared out the window. Clusters of commuters passed on the distant platforms. "Just thinking of Patrice's braised sweetbreads smothered in truffle makes my mouth water. And the idea of raising that little girl leaves me feeling unsettled, almost sick to my stomach."

"Do you want me to accompany you tonight to the restaurant?" I asked.

"It's not necessary. I know the way."

"What would you like us to do with Jane?"

"Find a good boarding school in France. God knows the little ragamuffin can afford one."

"I meant this evening."

"Oh." Horace turned back from the window and looked at me. "Of course you did. Forgive me. Take her to dinner somewhere—whatever you'd like."

"You know, the world would forgive you for taking a night off," I said. "Why don't you join us?"

"No, I owe it to Patrice. His reputation is on the line." Horace smiled tersely. "I believe I'll pack off, Jack. The sand in my eyes tells me it's time for a snooze."

Horace retired to his stateroom.

I was about to go out for a sandwich when the chime in the galley sounded.

I knocked on Horace's door. "Mr. Button, you called?"

Horace pulled open the door. He stood in his white boxer shorts, high black socks, and a white T-shirt. He had a bath towel wrapped around his neck. "I'm feeling a bit rocky, vertiginous you could almost say. The heart palpitations are back."

"Shall I call the paramedics?"

"No, it isn't that serious. But something's a little off, I can feel it. My personal physician is Dr. Henry Rose, in San Francisco—"

"I know Dr. Rose very well."

Horace smiled quickly. "Of course you do. I think we should summon him."

"To Washington, D.C.?"

"If it can be arranged. He might already be flying in for the funeral, I can't remember. In fact, never mind. Give me your cell phone. I'll call him myself. Just show me how the damn thing works."

I gave him my phone and showed him how to make a call.

"Are you experiencing any pain in your chest or arms?" I said. "A squeezing sensation, anything like that?"

"No, nothing like that." Horace scrutinized the phone's keypad.

"Jaw pain, shortness of breath, nausea?"

"You say I just input the number and press this little green button?"

"That's it." I studied his forehead for signs of perspiration. His scalp and forehead were dry. "Sure you don't want me to call the paramedics?"

"I couldn't be more positive." Horace took the phone into his state-room and shut the door behind him.

It occurred to me that I might never see him again alive.

I felt a ripple of panic. *Where would that leave Jane?*

I left the railcar, envisioning a big fat submarine sandwich spilling lettuce and tomatoes, but the tumescent mutations I saw being made behind glass in the delicatessens around Union Station looked tasteless and unhealthy, so I kept walking. I finally settled for a bowl of miso soup and a tuna roll at a Japanese take-out restaurant.

On my way back to the *Pioneer Mother*, among the street-level shops of the train station, I discovered a bookstore and went inside. I easily found a number of Giselle's cookbooks—her titles dominated a display shelf in the cooking section. I leafed through the pages of a heavy volume entitled *Giselle Every Day at Home*, dazzled by the cavalcade of strik-ing airbrushed photographs: Giselle pouring wine; Giselle sitting with friends at a rustic outdoor table; Giselle cutting, peeling, and chopping in a kitchen. The thought of spending time with this stunning woman rekindled my resolve to leave the *Pioneer Mother* as soon as possible.

I found a thin paperback biography of Eleanor Roosevelt, for young readers, and bought the book for Jane—a gift by which she might remember me.

Inside train stations I always displayed a lanyard with a *Pioneer Mother* identification badge around my neck. This allowed me to pass through the secured gates and out to the train platform. As I approached our railroad car, the scene at Track 1 gave me pause. At first I feared Horace had had a heart attack.

Police officers, Red Caps, and car attendants all gawked into the dark chasm behind the coupler of the *Pioneer Mother*. I hurried for a look.

On the tracks a silver baggage trolley lay on its side. Around it, cardboard boxes spilled heads of lettuce, packages of meat, milk, and eggs.

"Looks like Mr. Button's gonna have to go on a strict diet," one grinning Red Cap said to me. Safety rules prohibited him from venturing into the pit to retrieve the groceries, he said. Only maintenance could do that.

Wanda sat with Jane on the steps of the old Pullman. Like Wanda, Jane wore a kitchen bandana tied across her head. She had her arms wrapped around her knees and looked as if she'd been crying.

"Don't worry about it, baby," Wanda was saying to Jane. "Next time just try to hold onto the cart, okay?"

I soon got the story: Wanda and Jane had gone grocery shopping. The Red Cap brought the bulk of the provisions up from the curbside loading zone on his luggage cart; Wanda and Jane followed, each pushing a grocery-laden baggage trolley. The little parade made its way discreetly through the crowded train station. No one noticed Jane Pepper in her bandana, doing the work of a train steward. Everything had gone smoothly until they reached the *Pioneer Mother*, when suddenly Jane screamed and her cart plunged into the void.

We all took one last look at the spilled provisions. No one could say how long the trolley would be there. Wanda's dinner plan was ruined. Still bundled in their slick plastic bags, two whole young chickens brooded beneath the coupler.

"It doesn't matter anyway," I said to Wanda in our double bedroom. "I'm taking you and Jane out to dinner." I faced the back of the door, tying my necktie in the mirror.

"Fraternizing with the help, Majordomo. Strictly off limits."

"I have the boss's permission. Carte blanche, as long as we take Jane."

"He's feeling better?"

"Obviously." I looked at Wanda in the mirror. "So can we go out?"

"No, I have way too much to do."

"Like what?"

"Billy and Mrs. Whitehead are flying in for the funeral. They're coming to dinner tomorrow night."

I turned back to Wanda. "How's our liquor supply?"

"We'll restock tomorrow," Wanda said. "After our little accident we need to restock a lot of things. And I hear Dr. Rose is coming, too."

"Is he? Good. What else is going on?" I buttoned my shirt collar.

"I got a lead on a bartender today."

"Tell me."

"A friend of a friend," Wanda said. "Sounds like a good candidate. I'm assuming you're still leaving?"

"I have no choice. Giselle pretty much said get there or else."

"You talked to her?" Wanda said.

"Earlier this afternoon." I reached into the closet and pulled out my waiter's jacket. I needed to prep the bar for Horace's standing six o'clock cocktail hour. "What do you think? Am I making a mistake going to Hawaii?"

"A mistake? Why would it be a mistake?"

I donned the jacket and straightened my cuffs. "I don't know. She seemed a little… dismissive. Maybe she was just distracted. The filming wasn't going well, and—"

"It's your life, Jack. Go screw TV stars and sit on your ass on the beach, if that's what you want to do."

I stopped and looked at her. "Whoa! Where did that come from?"

"Here's the good news," Wanda said. "Pierre says he can start Friday. So nothing's keeping you here. In fact, feel free to use the laptop to make your plane reservations—"

"Wait a minute. His name is Pierre?"

"Why, you got a problem with Pierre?"

"Not a problem. I just can't believe—really? You're going to share a bedroom with a guy named Pierre?"

Wanda had a sparkle in her eye. "Jealous?"

"I'm not jealous," I said. "And for the record, last night was about a lot more than exhaustion and cognac."

"Sleep deprivation and delirium, then—"

"You dismiss these things in your head, Wanda, because you know you're safe on this train." I buttoned my jacket. "But life is about a lot more than being safe. It's also about taking chances, about putting yourself out there."

"I told you, I can't go out to dinner tonight."

"Or any other night, for that matter, because all you ever do is work." I opened the door to the hallway. I quickly closed it again. "See, I think there's a lot more to you than being a chef. I think that your friend Max knew that. I just hate to think I'll leave here without knowing who you really are."

Wanda cocked her head slightly.

"I see you cracking," I said. "Come on, Wanda, what do you say? Take a night off. Do it for Jane. I've got a special place picked out and everything."

"What's this special place?" Her eyes turned playful.

"It's a surprise," I said. "But trust me, you'll love it."

FORTY

OUTSIDE THE SOARING WHITE GRANITE ARCHES of Union Station, the setting sun cast a hazy pink light around Columbus Circle. Pigeons moved in waves across the esplanade, spurred by the passing crowd.

"It's quite intriguing, really," Horace said, a little breathless from our walk through the train station. "You could reach someone from almost anywhere. Without going through an operator or a switchboard."

"That's very true," I said.

"For example, you could have a lawyer on one coast talking to a lawyer on the other, and you could be listening from any point in between."

"We call that a conference call..."

"Not to mention the safety aspects. If you found yourself locked out at night or being stalked by a brigand with a bomb, you could simply call for help."

"Easy as that."

Horace stopped and gave me an earnest look.

"Could you get me one, Jack?"

"You want me to get you a cell phone?"

"Is that a silly request? Does one need a permit, or to pass some sort of test?"

"No, no, there's no test," I said. "I can have one for you tomorrow."

"Tomorrow!" Horace said. "That would be splendid. Just do me a favor and keep it in strict confidence. If word got out that I've gone so... futuristic... it could damage my brand, if you know what I mean."

At the passenger loading zone, we found a long taxi line. Horace bypassed the line. He went directly to the curb and commandeered the first cab that pulled up.

"I'm getting married in an hour," he said, opening the door and climbing into the backseat. A number of people shot me hostile stares, including the businesswoman at the head of the line.

"Sorry," I said. "He's very rude sometimes. It's inexcusable." I turned and looked inside the taxi. "Sure you don't want me to come with you?"

"I'd rather you attend to the ladies." Horace raised his walking stick to the scraggly, dark-skinned driver. "Chez Patrice. Take the direct route."

The driver wheeled around, his eyes black with indignation. He spoke in a heavy Indian accent. "Good sir, I have never heard of this place Chez Patrice. I do not understand where you want me to go."

"Then I shall tell you, you ignorant outlander," Horace said. "Just drive!"

I slammed the door shut as the car leapt forward.

A tomboy decked out for dinner at a posh restaurant—that's what popped into my mind when Jane came strolling down the hallway. She wore a long, dark skirt and a white monkey jacket with ceramic tigers for buttons. She sat on the barstool beside me, her wheat-colored hair as straight and blunt as the bristles on a whisk broom.

"Nice jacket—I especially like the buttons," I said.

"Thanks," Jane said. "Miss Snodgrass-Smith took me shopping and said I could get two nice outfits. I'm saving the other one for Friday. Have you tried a cookie?"

"Not yet."

Jane sprang up from the barstool. "I'll get you one." She dashed into the galley and returned with a cookie. She watched carefully as I took a bite. "It's lemon ricotta with a lemon glaze. I cracked some of the eggs myself."

"Delicious."

"Wanda knew the recipe by heart. She let me work the mixer, too—at least part of the time. You have to keep the beaters in the bowl or it splatters. Where is she, anyway?"

"Still getting ready. Would you like a Shirley Temple while we wait?"

"Can I make it?"

"Of course."

Jane went behind the bar and mixed a Shirley Temple. She set the drink on the middle of the counter and came around and sat on the same barstool. She unsheathed a plastic straw and planted it in the drink.

"Here, I got this for you." I gave her the Eleanor Roosevelt biography. "I found it this afternoon in a bookstore."

Jane's eyes grew wide. She leafed through the pages.

"I've never seen this one before," she said. "I can't wait to read it." She leaned forward, sucked her straw, and studied the book. "She became an orphan at the age of nine, did you know that? She used to cry herself to sleep."

"All set?" Wanda came around the corner, graceful on high heels. Her layered hair fell past her shoulders. She wore lipstick and eye shadow. On her wrist was a silver bracelet. She walked past me with the trace of a smile, trailing a faint scent of perfume. In her black dress, with her athletic frame, she was both chic and guilelessly clean, a wholesome Midwestern beauty.

"My gosh," I said. "You look great."

Wanda said to Jane, "And aren't we lucky to be in the company of such a handsome gentleman?"

Jane turned her eyes up to me. "Very lucky."

Wanda stood near the door. "All right, Majordomo. Show us this great place you're taking us to."

The taxi dropped us in the busy parking lot of a super-regional mall in McLean, Virginia. By this time darkness had fallen. We were greeted by a cluster of young parking lot attendants stationed at a valet's podium.

"Hooray! My favorite restaurant!" Jane gushed, running for the wooden foot bridge that crossed a gleaming blue lagoon and led to a faux weather-beaten clapboard building. High above the roof, a garish neon sign flashed the words "Captain Jim's Treasure Trove and Seafood Palace."

Wanda looked at me and laughed. "This is your idea of a special place?"

"They don't take reservations," I said. "But they told me the wait shouldn't be too bad on a Wednesday night."

Jane stopped in the middle of the bridge and gazed at the water.

"I wonder if this is where they get their fish?" she said.

The lagoon was nothing more than a shallow wading pool with multicolored lights and a painted bottom.

Wanda sauntered up close to me and discreetly gave my hand a squeeze. "I suspect Captain Jim gets his fish at the back loading dock like everybody else."

A throng of people stood just inside the door. Every seat in the reception area was taken. People sat on lava rocks. Children congregated on the floor. A pounding waterfall saturated the air with the sharp smell of chlorine. At the outer edges of the raised plank flooring, a koi pond wound around planters thick with bamboo. An arched bridge led to a busy cocktail lounge. Drinkers stood on the bridge and tossed coins into the stream.

While Wanda and Jane waited off to the side, I got in line at the hostess stand, where two attractive pirate girls entered names into the restaurant's computer system and handed out red pagers.

"May I help you?" one of the hostesses said when my turn finally came.

Before I could speak, a woman in a leopard-print top interrupted—a bottle blond, slightly overweight, pushing forty.

"What the hell is going on?" she said to the hostess. "You claimed twenty minutes and it's been almost an hour."

The hostess put her fingers on the computer keyboard and gazed down at her screen. "Let me check. What's your name again?"

"Dee Dee," the woman said. "Dr. Dee Dee. Party of four." She turned to me and shook her head.

"Your table should be ready in a few minutes," the hostess said. "A party's about to leave. You're welcome to browse the gift shop."

"No way," Dr. Dee Dee said. "I'm not paying eighteen dollars for a plastic fish."

The hostess turned away from Dr. Dee Dee and looked at me expectantly.

"Jack," I said. "Three for dinner."

With downcast eyes the hostess started typing.

Dr. Dee Dee studied my face. "Football player?"

"Not anymore," I said.

"Let me guess. Sidelined by injury."

"You're pretty good."

"Perceptive. I saw you coming across the bridge."

The hostess handed me a pager. "Should be about twenty minutes," she said.

"Gee, where have I heard that one before?" Dr. Dee Dee said. She cornered me at the arched bridge. "So, Jack, where'd you play football?"

"Stanford."

"Small world. Do you know a Dr. Milton Pappajohn? Guest lecturer in art history?"

"Doesn't ring a bell."

"No loss. He's my ex."

"Sorry."

"He's in Palo Alto computer-dating coeds, and I'm stuck here, taking ten-year-olds to this cockamamie place for a birthday party."

"I feel your pain."

"And what brings an educated man like you to such a ridiculous mise-en-scène?"

"A going away party. Mine."

"Going away where?"

"To find peace and happiness in paradise. Maybe love."

Dr. Dee Dee handed me her card. "Love's my specialty. Call me before you leave town. I might be able to help."

"You probably wouldn't like where I sleep," I said. I studied the card. She was a professor of film studies. I'd never heard of the university.

Thirty minutes later Wanda, Jane, and I were seated in a deep leather booth halfway down the sizable dining room. Jane's face gleamed.

"Don't you think Uncle Horace would love this?" she said.

"Absolutely." I took in the details of the room—ruffled fan palms, hurricane wall sconces, gurgling lobster tanks atop pony walls. The servers were decked out in elaborate pirate garb: men in billowy shirts with vests and head scarves; women in long dresses with hip sashes and corsets. They carried great trays of food, much of it afire.

A woman in a wench costume came by to take our picture. A black-haired wig sat askew on her head. Under her ragged peasant's dress she wore white New Balance athletic shoes. She spoke with an accent I mistook for Russian.

"Where are you from?" I asked her.

"I am from Poland," she said. "Okay, everybody, look this way." She raised her camera.

We leaned in, Wanda and I on either side of Jane. My hand found Wanda's bare shoulder.

"Ah, such a beautiful family," the photographer said. "Squeeze closer now, please?"

We pressed together even more.

"That's good," said the photographer. "Smile for the camera."

We smiled and there was a bright flash.

"You can find the photograph in the gift shop later, yes?"

"Can we get three copies?" I said to the woman.

"Three copies? Yes, of course." She noted our table number and moved on.

Wanda leaned across the table. "Three?"

"Guess I'm already feeling sentimental," I said.

Jane knitted her brow. She turned to Wanda.

"Don't ask me," Wanda said. "Ask Jack."

Jane looked at me. "What does that mean? Why are you sentimental?"

"It means nothing lasts forever," I said. "Enjoy it while you can." I glanced at Wanda.

Jane wrinkled her nose.

"Hi, I'm Dennis. I'm your server. I'll be taking care of you tonight." Dennis wore a ruffled shirt over red-and-black striped trousers and had a do-rag tied across his head. He sweated profusely. "Special occasion? Birthday or anniversary?"

"Just a night out," Wanda said.

"Nothing wrong with that," Dennis said. He put his palms together. "Who's dined with us before?"

Jane's hand shot up. "I have!"

Dennis glanced at her. "Then you know we fire you from a cannon if you don't finish your vegetables. Start anyone with a cocktail?"

We ordered a round of drinks: a gin martini, a glass of champagne, a Shirley Temple. The serving staff traversed the dining room in what amounted to raucous dinner theater. They joked, they laughed, they formed lines and sang sea chanteys. Delivering our appetizers in long-handled skillets, they stayed in character as they surrounded our table and auctioned off food ("Shiver me timbers, what landlubber gets the coconut shrimp?"; "Which scurvy bilge rat craves the fried calamari?").

Jane loved it.

When a hollow-cheeked surfer-type went by holding a flaming dessert, Jane's mouth fell open.

"That's a cherries Jubilee," Wanda said. "Would you like to try one?"

"If I'm allowed," Jane said.

"Of course you're allowed. Maybe we'll even make it on the railroad car one of these nights."

I was on my second martini. I kept staring in wonder at Wanda. This was not the same woman I'd been living with for ten days.

Dennis came by and planted his hairy knuckles on our table. "I just saw Captain Jim at the helm. He says you can report to the salad bar anytime. Just don't make a wrong turn and walk the plank." He winked at Jane.

I set my napkin on the table. "Shall we go?"

We located the salad bar in a bustling anteroom off the main dining room. "Something for Every*Booty!*" exclaimed a rustic sign beside a leaning tiki torch. In two long lines, diners inched their way up a double-sided buffet. They pressed their noses to the sneeze guard; they grappled for serving tongs. A group of wild boys stuck pitted black olives on their fingers and then threw the olives back in the bowls.

Wanda touched me on the shoulder and whispered in my ear: "Look for drains. They must hose this place out at night."

I followed Wanda and Jane into line. The plate I took was still warm from the dishwasher. Someone jostled me in the back, and a small, pale hand reached past me and seized the next plate on the stack. I turned to face a stout woman with skin the hue of a radish. She wore her hair short. "Thank a Teacher," said her glittery white T-shirt. A silver crucifix rested against her breastbone.

I smiled at the schoolteacher and she smiled back.

When my turn came at the lettuce station, I wielded a pair of plastic tongs and planted a clump of mixed greens onto my plate.

"Hey, Stanford." Dr. Dee Dee beamed at me across the way. One of the boys putting olives on his fingers was hers.

I nodded and smiled politely. From that point on, I scrupulously avoided eye contact. At the crab cakes, the schoolteacher tapped me on the shoulder.

"Do you know your daughter looks an awful lot like that Pepper girl?" she said.

"Excuse me?"

"Ruth Pepper's daughter—your girl looks just like her."

In front of me, Jane scooped pear slices with a slotted spoon.

I patted her on the head. "We hear that a lot," I said. "Must be the haircut."

Jane turned and peered at me curiously.

"We're from California," I added. "Just visiting."

"I should apologize for our city," the schoolteacher said. "They've got things really turned upside down around here—all the street closures and barricades. It's even worse than usual."

I put a dry-looking crab cake on my plate. "It hasn't really affected us. We've been doing a lot of walking." I pressed Jane to keep up with Wanda in line.

"The little girl's uncle," the schoolteacher said. "That man she's been sent to live with, I know he's supposed to be a celebrity and all, but I'm afraid he's a no-good drunk."

"Is he?" I said. "I haven't seen him."

The schoolteacher clucked. "Someone needs to give that poor child a home."

Across the way, Dr. Dee Dee held up the line, eavesdropping. She put an artichoke heart on her plate and feigned interest in the chow mein noodles.

The schoolteacher persisted. "How old did you say your daughter was?"

"Eleven, almost twelve," I said.

"Same age. Such a pointless tragedy. Not only for that family but for our nation as a whole."

Dr. Dee Dee glowered at the schoolteacher. "As far as I'm concerned she got what she deserved."

The schoolteacher blinked at Dr. Dee Dee across the salad bar. "Surely you can't mean that."

"Ruth Pepper was a bloodthirsty piece of shit," Dr. Dee Dee said. "I'm glad she's gone."

Oh God, I thought. *Here we go.*

"That's a vile thing to say," the schoolteacher replied.

"Ladies—" I said.

"She was a war-mongering psychopath," Dr. Dee Dee said. "She can rot in hell."

Jane gaped wide-eyed at Dr. Dee Dee.

"Hey, girlfriend," Wanda said to Dr. Dee Dee. "Cork it."

"No one's talking to you, momma," Dr. Dee Dee said.

The schoolteacher turned to me and said, "Isn't that just like a Washington liberal—resort to name-calling when truth isn't on your side."

"Truth?" Dr. Dee Dee said. "She wanted to bust the unions, to deny people their voting rights."

"You're misinformed—"

"She was Islamophobic and anti-feminist—"

"Bunk."

"—a gun-toting idiot, a global warming denialist—"

"You don't know your facts."

"She tried to ban books from the library."

"A myth—it never happened."

"Of course it happened. God. What rock did you crawl out from under?"

"Ladies, stop," I said.

Infuriated, Dr. Dee Dee took the artichoke heart from her plate and threw it at the schoolteacher. It bounced off her forehead.

"That's assault!" the schoolteacher said.

"Blow me, bitch," Dr. Dee Dee said. "Any day I wake up and Ruth *Idiot* Pepper is dead is a great day, as far as I'm concerned!"

A salad plate shattered at my feet.

"What's the matter with her?" Jane screamed. "Why is she saying these horrible things?" She pressed her hands over her ears.

Wanda glared at Dr. Dee Dee. "Lady, shut the fuck up, before I shove these kitchen tongs down your throat! Can't you see there's a kid here?"

The room fell silent. Everyone looked at Wanda.

Still covering her ears, Jane sank to a squatting position and began to wail.

Wanda turned to me. "Get her out of here!"

I gathered Jane in my arms. A stabbing pain shot up my side as I made my way to a fire exit.

"Oh, my Lord in Heaven," the schoolteacher said. "Was that really who I think it was?"

I burst through the fire door. The alarm rang as I carried Jane into the night.

In the end we got hamburgers at a stand on the lower level of Union Station. We sat at a café table on the perimeter of the food court. No one recognized Jane. A burly black janitor with gray hair made his way around the mostly vacant pavilion, stripping soggy plastic bags from trash cans and running a damp mop over sections of tile floor.

Jane quietly ate her cheeseburger. Wanda picked at fries. It struck me that I was in the company of two extraordinary women. Contemplating my shiftless future, I was revisited by that same sense of forlornness I'd felt when I woke up in the hospital after my accident—the realization that a once-in-a-lifetime opportunity was being squandered, and it was all of my own doing. I wished I had the photograph of the three of us in the booth at Captain Jim's, when for a moment a tumultuous world was at bay, and we were all happy.

FORTY-ONE

Special to *Sunshine Trails*
"Window on the West," by Horace Button
"RIP Chez Patrice"

WASHINGTON, D.C.—I have a recurring nightmare to which I often awake screaming: the lobster population is declining at an alarming rate. This doomsday reverie is fueled, no doubt, by the disappearance of terrapin dishes from the menus of the better restaurants of the Eastern Seaboard some years back—mass hysteria whipped up by the dark auguries of pseudoscientists of the environmental-whacko variety, deliriously designating the common marsh turtle an endangered species.

But if the lobster population were ever truly in decline, I would point the finger of blame at Chez Patrice, the landmark French bistro located in Washington, D.C.'s fashionable West End. Monsieur Patrice's lobster Thermidor is the stuff of legends—right up there with his oxtail ragout and *escargots à la Bourguignonne*.

With its lusty cuisine, stone fireplace, formal tablecloths and entirely tolerable sound level, Chez Patrice served as my home away from home in the days I covered Capitol Hill as a cub reporter for the *New York Herald Tribune*. Monsieur Patrice himself introduced me—a youth in the City of Magnificent Intentions for the first time—to the wonders of a blazing fire, a snifter of Armagnac and a dozen Wellfleet Harbor oysters, all enjoyed in the hours before dawn, while the townspeople slept.

I scrupulously avoid Washington, D.C., anytime a Democrat administration is in power, on general principles, but when an obligatory trip to the Federal City materialized without warning, muscle memory drew me back to the familiar block where Monsieur Patrice performs his daily miracles of gastronomy.

I knew the block and I knew the door, but something was horribly wrong. A temporary banner above the restaurant's classic sign witlessly boasted new ownership.

At the maître d's lectern I was greeted by a stylish manager with a shaved head and a slippery temperament. This, the spot where Patrice always stood.

"What happened to Monsieur Patrice?" I said.

"Monsieur Patrice passed quite unexpectedly," the man said. "His great-nephew has taken over. When it comes to food, he has a wonderful vision."

"I'm really more interested in the dinner menu than his vision," I said. "I hope he kept the Thermidor."

"He dropped most of that French stuff, which nobody liked," the manager said. "He's repositioning the restaurant as more of an Asian steak house—a cultural hybrid featuring combinations of tempura, yakitori, sukiyaki and modern renditions of Sri Lankan comfort food."

I turned on my heels, flagged down a passing taxi and hotfooted it to the bar at the Hay-Adams Hotel, where I said ten Hail Marys and then raised a weighty snifter of Armagnac to Monsieur Patrice.

In this day and age, the only truly endangered species is the first-class dining establishment.

Signed,
Your ace reporter,
HB

FORTY-TWO

ON THE OTHER SIDE OF THE DOOR, the toilet flushed and I heard water running in the sink. A minute later, Wanda came out of the lav, still wearing her black dress.

"Here." She took me by the hands and coaxed me into a sitting position on the lower berth.

"What are you doing?" I said.

She stood over me, her fingers intertwined with mine.

"This is against my better judgment." She leaned in and kissed me.

I shook my head. "Wanda, it's too late."

"You asked what I thought about Hawaii. Here's your answer." She kissed me again.

"I can't change my mind," I said.

She wrapped my head in her arms and drew my face against her chest.

"This isn't about changing your mind," she said. "I can take care of myself, okay?" She gazed down at me. "You look confused."

"I feel like I'm on the verge of a terrible mistake. I just don't know what it is."

With a finger she traced the scar on my face, from my cheekbone to my jaw. "Does it hurt?"

I just looked at her.

"No strings, Majordomo," she said. "I promise."

"What if we wake Jane?"

"We'll be quiet."

"The bedsprings squeak."

"There are other things we can do." Wanda lowered herself slowly onto my lap. She put her arms around my neck. The mass of her weight surprised me and stifled my first impulse, which was to push her away for her own good.

"We shouldn't do this," I said.

"Let's just see what happens." She reached for the light switch. The bedroom went dark. Her hair brushed my face as she found my mouth with hers.

Suddenly, there was a boom like a thunderclap. Our lips parted. We both sat perfectly still, blinking into darkness.

"What was that?" Wanda said.

"It sounded like a gunshot," I said.

The sound repeated—the unmistakable, resonant explosion of a gun firing. It was exceedingly close—inside the *Pioneer Mother*, even.

My heart pounded as scenarios raced through my head: Ruth Pepper's killers coming to finish off a family vendetta; kidnappers; a Child Services raid gone horribly wrong.

I gave Wanda a prod and sprang to my feet. I reached in the darkness for the door handle. The empty hallway was quiet.

I went to Jane's door, listened, and then opened it. Jane was asleep in her bed.

Wanda stood behind me. "She's there?"

I nodded. "Stay with her and keep the door locked."

"Be careful." Wanda went inside Jane's stateroom. I heard the click of the lock.

I peeked into Horace's bedroom. The lights were on. The bed hadn't been slept in. Horace had yet to return from his night at Chez Patrice.

I crept to the galley, pulled open a drawer, and grabbed the biggest kitchen knife I could find. I'd grown up proficient with firearms and understood too well the peril of being on the wrong end of a gun. If someone was coming after Jane or Horace, I was in for a lopsided fight. I held the knife upright and close to my body as I went around the corner and investigated the bar, the dining room, and the observation lounge. Nothing. The shades were all drawn.

I was coming up the narrow hallway, about to check on the head-end of the railcar, when a third shot rang out. In the window of the door to the vestibule, I saw the muzzle flash. The shooter was aboard the *Pioneer Mother.*

In the next moment, I saw that big head, the red face, and those wide shoulders. Horace stood in the tight space of the vestibule, aiming his two-shot derringer at the train shed rafters like a lunatic. I opened the door and hauled him inside before he could get off another shot.

"Goddammit, Horace, what the hell are you doing!"

"I think I got one, Jack."

"One what?"

"A pigeon squab."

"Are you kidding me?" I snatched the pearl-handled derringer away from him and released the barrel latch. "This is a train station on high alert. These people don't screw around!" One chamber contained a bullet, the other a brass shell that smelled of spent gunpowder. I pocketed the live round.

"He shall not wonder where he sleeps tonight," Horace said. "He sleeps wrapped in his Father's arms."

"What are you talking about?"

"Patrice. He's dead."

I looked at Horace. "Don't tell me you shot him."

"He passed a short time ago. His idiot nephew ruined the place. In fact, give me the gun and I'll go finish him off."

"You're not going anywhere. Jesus Christ. I can't believe this."

"The bird dropped behind the little signal shack. Do you think Wanda could whip up a roast pigeon? I'm famished."

"I think we better get you some coffee." I took Horace by the arm and dragged him the length of the hallway. I planted him on a barstool and put the unloaded derringer in my pocket. "Stay there and don't move."

I tapped on the door of Jane's room. "It's safe," I said in a low voice. "You can come out."

Wanda opened the door cautiously.

"Our hotel child," I said. "Shooting at pigeons."

"Seriously?" Wanda pulled the door closed behind her. Miraculously,

Jane had slept through it all.

"Says he's hungry," I said. "Keep an eye on him. I'll go out and do damage control."

I went to the open platform. The police were already there in force. They were heavily armed, sweeping the tracks with their flashlights.

"Everything okay?" I said to the policewoman nearest me, who shined her light on the baggage trolley in the ditch.

"We had reports of shots fired," she said.

"Yeah, we heard it, too," I said. "Sounded like they came from farther up the tracks."

The officer got on her radio. The other officers converged near our railroad car and began shining their lights past the *Pioneer Mother*, to the tracks and railroad yard ahead.

As the hour approached midnight I had Horace seated at the dining table, nursing a bourbon soda and eating cocktail peanuts from a can.

"Sukiyaki, yakitori, and Sri Lankan comfort food," he kept saying, shaking his head, bringing the glass of whiskey to his mouth.

In the galley, Wanda prepared a tomato and cheese omelet, the product of my negotiations with Horace. I was in no mood to retrieve a dead pigeon from behind a signal shack.

Wanda gave the omelet a flip.

I came up behind her and took her by the shoulders. "I like seeing you cook in a black dress and bare feet. You should do it more often."

"Don't distract me, Majordomo. I'll burn the eggs." She used a spatula to coax the omelet onto a plate, which she handed to me. "Hopefully he's still drunk enough to choke this down." As an afterthought she gave me a bottle of ketchup. "He can always smother it with this."

I turned to leave the galley but then hesitated. In the past four hours I'd nearly slept with Wanda, disarmed my employer, and lied to the police.

"Listen, Wanda, I've been thinking," I said. "It's time I got out of here."

She glanced down. "I know."

"I should make travel plans."

"Use the laptop."

"Okay. Thanks."

"Jack, about tonight—I'm sorry. I feel like such an idiot."

I forced a smile. "You'd have hated me in the morning. That much I know."

"Yeah," Wanda said. "Now I just hate myself."

FORTY-THREE

THE NEXT MORNING Horace and Jane ate an early breakfast. They said little at the table. Bach's Mass in B Minor played softly in the background. Somewhat bleary-eyed, Horace asked for an extra cup of coffee.

At the appointed hour I walked Horace and Jane through the Main Hall of the train station and out to the street. Rosalind would be their minder for the day; it was agreed I'd stay back and help Wanda restock the railcar. Unbeknownst to Horace, my future hinged on a stranger named Pierre Bruneau.

In front of Union Station, a small crowd of protesters marched in a loose oval. They carried handmade signs: "Shame on Horace Button!"; "Slay the Patriarchy!"; "Foster Love Not Hate!"

They chanted, "Hey, hey! Ho, ho! Jane Pepper has got to go!"

Onlookers ringed the protesters. Across the square, a line of police in riot gear watched with deadpan expressions.

"Hey, hey! Ho, ho! Jane Pepper has got to go!"

A phalanx of reporters followed as we pushed through the crowd. Jane cowered in the presence of so many people. Looking over her shoulder at the demonstrators, she clutched my arm and stayed close. Arthur and Rosalind had the Town Car waiting in a red zone, flanked by an escort of D.C. motorcycle officers. I packed Horace and Jane into the backseat, and the motorcade sped off, sirens wailing.

On my way back inside the train station, I glared at the protesters. One of them, a gaunt, shirtless man with a beard, jeered at me and gave me the finger.

By noon, Wanda and I were five miles away, provisioning at a Costco. The shoppers gave Wanda a wide berth as she assertively stalked the aisles in her chef's whites, her list written in longhand on a legal pad. I followed, pushing an overloaded cart.

"Why are you scowling at the meatballs?" I said.

"I'm not scowling, I'm thinking."

"Think about this. What if you hate this guy—Pierre?"

"He comes highly recommended by a friend," Wanda said. "That tells me I won't hate him." She crossed something off her list with a black Sharpie and pressed on.

"Who's your friend?" I said.

"Her name's Chastity Newhouse," Wanda said. "She's from Harlem. She worked with Pierre in New Orleans before he moved to Washington." We stopped in an aisle stacked high with condiments. Wanda placed a plastic jug of red wine vinegar in our cart and pointed me in another direction. "Cell phones are over there. You've got the credit card?"

"Right here."

"I'll see you at the food court," Wanda said. "Whenever."

"We're done?" I said.

"We're done," she said, barely giving me a glance.

I stood there for a few seconds, watching her walk away.

Done.

In the electronics department, I wended my way to the cell phone counter, zigging and zagging my shopping cart around scores of enormous flat-panel televisions perched atop shipping crates. Seeing so many big screens in sync, being bombarded by identical images, was like being trapped in a hall of mirrors. The muted TVs showed two flag-draped coffins in the center of the Capitol Rotunda, with occasional cutaway shots to Horace and Jane, who sat side by side in a special VIP section. A steady stream of mourners passed through the Rotunda, following a velvet rope line, pausing at the caskets. Many people left flowers.

The sales associate behind the counter looked at me with concern. She was a pretty African American about my age.

"Are you all right?" she said.

My gaze reluctantly left the giant screens and I turned to her.

"Fine," I said.

I put the cell phone, a two-year service agreement, and the groceries all on a *Sunshine Trails* credit card.

At the food court I parked the shopping cart near a bank of soda dispensers where I could keep an eye on it.

I found Wanda and Pierre sitting at a plastic cafeteria table, chatting amiably. Small in stature, clean-shaven, and impeccably groomed, Pierre looked to be thirty. His features were dark. With his plaid bow tie and double-breasted blue blazer, he stood out in the casual food-court crowd. I squeezed next to Wanda on the narrow bench.

"Hope I'm not interrupting," I said.

Wanda smiled. "I think we found our new majordomo."

"Congratulations," I said to Pierre.

"Wanda tells me you're on your way to Hawaii," Pierre said. "Lucky me."

"Lucky you?" I said.

Pierre gave Wanda a knowing smile. He had a slight snaggletooth. "That means I get to oversee table service on the *Pioneer Mother*. A dream come true."

"You're familiar with Mr. Button's work?" I said.

"Are you kidding? He's iconic."

Wanda turned to me. "We were just going over some of Pierre's ideas about upgrading the service."

"Upgrading?" I looked at Pierre.

"I'd like to go white-glove, for one," Pierre said.

"We were talking about a full butler's uniform, too," Wanda said. "Black tie and tails. What do you think?"

"Lose the white waiter's jacket?" I said.

"That's what Pierre's thinking," Wanda said.

"Formal tails are so much more elegant," Pierre said. "This is a big week for me. I'd like to put my best foot forward."

"I don't know," I said. "The white jacket has such a great history when it comes to railroads—Pullman stewards and all that."

"We wouldn't do it without running it by Mr. Button," Wanda said. "But I kind of like the idea, especially for dinner service." She turned to

Pierre. "I say pack the tails."

Pierre looked at me. "I'd also like to start putting out compotes with chocolates and candied fruits as a matter of policy. Wanda says you aren't doing that now."

I shot Wanda a dark look.

"I don't even know what a compote is," I said to Pierre.

Pierre showed his snaggletoothed smile. "Well, not the time to panic. Maybe in Hawaii they use coconuts instead." He took out his smartphone and made a note. "I'll add it to my packing list."

"Pierre confirmed that he can start tomorrow," Wanda said. "And he's available the full week, so I guess we're set."

The three of us ruminated on this in silence. I think we all breathed a collective sigh of relief. For the first time I noticed the people in line for food. They came away with plates of hot dogs, pizza, and jumbo sodas.

"What do you do normally?" I asked Pierre.

"I work at a bookstore."

"Got out of the restaurant business?"

"Burned out. I needed a change."

"Tell him about your website," Wanda said.

Pierre turned to me. "The website's more of a hobby, really. I blog about the etiquette of formal table service."

"He's an etiquette expert," Wanda said.

"Self-taught," Pierre said. "For the most part."

"You should check it out," Wanda said. "It's amazing."

"What about you?" Pierre said to me. "How long does it take to get to Hawaii?"

"I could do it in a day, but I'm taking two," I said. "I stop and repack in San Jose tomorrow night, then fly to Kauai on Saturday."

"Wanda tells me you're going to work for Giselle Lebeau."

"Know much about her?"

Pierre snorted. "I know enough to wonder why you're trading a Rolls-Royce for a Ford." He stopped. "I'm sorry, that came off sounding rather bitchy. It's just that I'm not so enamored with television chefs in general. Horace Button is the Rolls-Royce of the food and wine scene, as far as I'm concerned."

"And Giselle's a Ford?" I said.

Pierre smirked. "More like a Peugeot scooter, as much as she's been ridden."

My face flushed. "Excuse me?"

"She has a reputation in the industry," Pierre said. "For collecting young men. Then after a week or two she gets bored and spits them out like cherry pits." He gave me a sardonic smile. "If I were you, I'd pack a return ticket and a lot of pepper spray."

Wanda must have kicked him under the table because suddenly he jumped. He turned and looked at her.

"What, darling?" he said. "Am I talking out of school?"

By the time we said goodbye to Pierre and left the food court, I felt blindsided. Pushing our shopping cart toward the exit, I grew increasingly angry.

"Have you ever heard that before about Giselle?" I said to Wanda.

"Maybe something along those lines," Wanda said. "Once or twice through the grapevine."

"Jesus, Wanda. Were you ever going to tell me?"

"None of my business. It's your life. Do what you want."

We stopped at the door while a Costco employee checked our receipt.

Wanda turned to me and flashed a sly grin. "It'll look good on your résumé: majordomo-slash-gigolo—"

"All right—"

"—seeks multiple positions with horny older woman."

"Enough."

"Formal dining room preferred."

"Wanda, stop!"

FORTY-FOUR

"DON'T ASK ME HOW," Dr. Rose said, listening to his stethoscope. "But the old jalopy's still chuggin' along." His black medical bag sat open on a side table in the middle of the observation lounge. The stethoscope dangled from his hairy ears.

Horace sat regally in a parlor chair, his leather oxfords planted firmly on the floor. He had consented to taking off his suit jacket for the old doctor, but that's where he drew the line. Even the cuff links stayed on. He watched suspiciously as Dr. Rose moved the stethoscope to another landing spot.

"When's the last time you had this spurious thing calibrated?" Horace said.

"There's nothing wrong with my stethoscope," Dr. Rose said. "Are you still taking your pills?"

Horace gave a dismissive grunt.

"Eh? You don't forget?" Dr. Rose said.

"No, I don't forget."

Dr. Rose worked the stethoscope's gleaming silver diaphragm beneath Horace's long silk necktie and listened intently. Horace looked at me and rolled his eyes. Finally, Dr. Rose pulled the stethoscope from his ears and stuffed it into his bag.

"Not bad for a condemned building," he said.

"Speak for yourself, you old goat," Horace said.

Dr. Rose picked up a lit cigarette from a glass ashtray, took a deep drag, put it down, reached into his bag, and pulled out a blood pressure gauge. He wrapped the cuff around Horace's arm. It took him forever to do this. He moved like he was underwater.

"Cutting back on salt?" Dr. Rose said.

"Ask Wanda. I don't count salt granules."

Dr. Rose squeezed the rubber bulb that was attached to the blood pressure gauge. The cuff tightened around Horace's arm.

"What about alcohol?" Dr. Rose said.

"What about it?" Horace said.

"Are you cutting back?"

"Ask Jack. He's the stingiest bartender I've ever known. Makes me beg for every single drink."

"Will he make me beg for a vodka martini in about three minutes?"

"He's leaving us, Henry. Did you know that? First thing in the morning."

Dr. Rose turned and looked at me. "Oh? Something better come along for your star protégé?"

From behind the bar I nodded and gave a thumbs-up.

"As if a murdered sister, raising a niece, and weathering the ire of gay and lesbian forest rangers weren't enough," Horace said. "I have to cope with a treasonous bartender. No wonder I'm having heart palpitations."

I'd told him of my imminent departure for Hawaii. The shock of finding out my new benefactor was Giselle rendered him lightheaded and blind with rage, but Dr. Rose's arrival forestalled an irreversible rift developing between us. Horace quickly focused on enumerating the symptoms of his dizzy spells for the old doctor.

Dr. Rose peered at the gauge of his blood pressure meter, then removed the cuff from Horace's arm. "Blood pressure's a little elevated, but I can live with it."

He tried rolling the blood pressure gauge into a neat little package, but in his trembling hands the pliant rubber hose wriggled uncontrollably. He dumped the contraption into his medical bag like a snake into a gunnysack. Next he fished out an ophthalmoscope.

"So what else can you tell me about these spells?" Dr. Rose said to Horace.

"What is there to tell? I had another episode today. While I was sitting with the coffins and Democrats."

Dr. Rose lifted Horace's right eyelid and shone the bright light directly into the pupil. "You're a walking contradiction to the collective wisdom of medical science. According to the Surgeon General, you should be dead."

"That's what they told my Granny Kitty McKinnon. Everyone said she'd come to a bad end from alcohol. And she did, too—at the age of ninety-four."

Dr. Rose moved the light to Horace's other eye. "I'm warning you, Horace. You haven't done a whit to lose weight. If you don't start taking care of yourself, you'll be the one in the coffin."

"Maybe. But I'll enjoy a certain *schadenfreude* when I deliver the eulogy at your funeral first."

Dr. Rose placed the scope back in his bag and zipped the bag shut. He stopped to take another drag off his cigarette, exhaling out his nose, dragonlike.

"My advice remains the same," he said to Horace. "Exercise. Lose weight. Drink in moderation."

"Stop with the superstitious twaddle," Horace said. "What's the diagnosis?"

"You have to give it time. You've suffered a major trauma to your ancestral constellation."

"My ancestral constellation?"

"Your sister still lives in your brain chemicals and body chemistry, along with all the hatreds, wars, and prejudices of your ancestors," Dr. Rose said. "Why do you think you're such a narrow-minded bigot?"

"I'm being stalked by the Grim Reaper and you give me a fairy story about pixies in my brain chemicals."

"There's nothing wrong with you, Horace. What can I say?"

"Write me a doctor's note. Say I'm terminal. Address it to the probate court."

"I don't inject myself into my patients' legal affairs."

"I'm telling you, Henry, it's a death sentence: cotillion, pizza parties, birthday sleepovers. Raising this child's going to kill me."

"Nonsense. It'll probably add fifteen years to your life."

"They think they know who killed Ruth, did I tell you that?" Horace said. "Her chief of staff confided to me today. If not for my failing health I'd hunt down the miscreants myself and bring them to justice—"

Suddenly an urgent alarm sounded.

Gonnng! Gonnng! Gonnng!

Horace looked at me with wide eyes.

"What the hell is that infernal racket?" he said.

"Your phone, Mr. Button," I said. "You've got an incoming call."

"Quick! In the pocket of my jacket. Can you get it?" Horace said.

I retrieved the phone and answered the call before it went to voicemail.

"Mr. Button's phone," I said. "Jack speaking."

"This is Lisa French calling," said a woman's voice. "From the law firm Weiss, Rosenthal, and French. Is Mr. Button available?"

"One moment, please…" I turned to Horace. "Lisa French?"

"That's the call. I'll take it!" Horace grabbed the phone and held it to his ear. "Lisa, so good to hear from you…" He listened for a long minute. He raised his eyebrows and tilted his face upward, scanning the ornate ceiling. "Well, isn't that interesting?… Yes, yes, of course I will, anytime you can bring it by… After work tonight is perfect … No, no, it won't be too late for us. We're entertaining. We're on track number one. I'll have Jack leave your name with the Amtrak agent… Of course, Lisa. Thank you, too."

He passed the phone back to me and I hit the red button.

"Good news?" Dr. Rose said.

"So good I can't jinx it," Horace said. "How about passing me one of those cigarettes, Henry? And Jack, let's get busy shaking a pair of vodka martinis. We're about to bury my sister, but it's no time to throw in the towel."

FORTY-FIVE

FRANK SINATRA SANG "FLY ME TO THE MOON." On the dining table, five settings of flatware, crystal stemware, and china plates gleamed beneath a silver candelabra. The low lighting brought out the railroad car's rich mahogany paneling.

Wanda set a platter of iced caviar on the bar. It had all the condiments: lemon wedges, crème fraîche, egg whites, minced red onion, sour cream.

I popped the cork on a chilled bottle of Dom Pérignon and showed the bottle to Wanda. "A swig? In honor of my last night here?"

"No. Thank you."

"I may be moving on, Wanda, but I'll never forget this time. I want you to know that."

She concentrated on arranging the caviar. "Let's not make a big deal out of this," she said. "You were never supposed to be more than a temp, anyway."

Horace came around the corner, freshly showered and dressed for dinner. He planted himself on his favorite barstool and took a handful of cashews from a pewter dish. His citrusy, woodsy cologne suddenly permeated the air around the bar.

"No sign of our guests yet?" he asked.

"Not yet," Wanda said.

"Where's Jane?"

"Behind you," I said. "Reading."

Horace looked over his shoulder. Jane sat buried in a parlor chair, lost in her Eleanor Roosevelt book. Horace turned back to Wanda and me. He popped a cashew into his mouth and gazed at us with spirited eyes. "I see my essays have been superseded by the biography of a horse-faced woman. I'll start with a glass of that, Jack." He nodded at the bottle in my hands.

I pulled a champagne flute from the rack and filled it three-quarters full.

Horace lifted the glass by its stem. "Whimpering, the eunuchs cluster behind the door. I am the lion at the threshold." He took a healthy slug.

Wanda and I looked at each other, baffled. Jane came up behind her uncle and laid her book on the bar counter. She climbed onto the second barstool.

"Where are you going?" she said to me.

I glanced at Wanda. She turned away.

"Hawaii," I said.

"When?"

"Tomorrow," I said. "At about the time you'll be going to the service."

"A vacation?" Jane said.

"More of a job," I said.

Wanda sighed, shook her head, and left the bar.

"The benefits are enticing," Horace said to Jane. "But the hours are lousy." He took another sip of champagne.

Jane looked disappointed. "I think you should stay here."

"I think so, too," Horace said.

At the other end of the railcar, Dr. Rose pushed open the heavy door and held it for Poppy and Billy. "Look who I found in the lobby of my hotel!"

Wearing a silver lamé dinner dress and a stunning diamond necklace, Poppy trooped theatrically through the observation lounge. She spotted Jane at the bar. "Dear, poor child. What a ghastly ordeal you've been through. But they say you're tough as nails!"

Wide-eyed, Jane stared back at Poppy.

"Your uncle tells me you're doing exceptionally well," Poppy said. "I must ask. What's your secret?"

"My secret?" Jane said.

"For coping with this hideous turn of events. My Lord in Heaven, you've lost everything!"

Jane hesitated. "Well, it helps to think of other things."

"Yes, distractions can be good."

"Sometimes I think about people I admire."

"Like who, for instance?"

"Like Eleanor Roosevelt. I thought about her a lot today."

"I know exactly what you mean. When I'm blue I think of Cartier and Coco Chanel, and that always perks me up." Poppy settled on the end barstool.

Billy approached Horace breathlessly. "Mother's been the talk of the town. Have you heard the story?"

Poppy turned. "Oh, shut it, Billy! These people don't want to hear about me. Can't you see they're in mourning?" She looked back at Jane. "You're staring at my necklace. It's worth seventy-five thousand dollars. I'm supposed to notify those boobs over at Lloyd's of London every time I take it out of the vault. Can you imagine? Who's got that kind of time?"

"Jack, you and I need to talk," Billy said. "In private. Before the night's over."

"Anytime, Mr. Whitehead. Champagne to start?"

"Yes, fine."

I lined up two champagne flutes on the bar and poured out the glasses. I put the first flute in front of Poppy and handed the second one to Billy.

Horace used a mother-of-pearl spoon to top a cracker with minced onion and caviar. "Jack, pour a glass of that bubbly for our country doctor, won't you? He has the palate of a bumpkin—chicken pot pie and Mexican casserole. We need to acquaint him with a higher end of the hog. Come join us, Henry. I'd like to make a toast."

Dr. Rose had stopped at the parlor chairs to light a cigarette. He came to the bar.

I poured him a glass of champagne.

"Thank you, Jack," Dr. Rose said.

Poppy eyed the cigarette in his hand. "My God, Henry. Since when have you taken up smoking?"

"Since my eighty-second birthday," Dr. Rose said. "I decided I needed some excitement in my life. I tried a circus class, but I couldn't hang on to the trapeze."

"Well, I wish you'd quit. Cigarettes are the territory of pimps and the Irish."

"I'd happily quit if you'd go out with me," Dr. Rose said.

Poppy cupped Dr. Rose's chin. "Never, Henry. You have an ass like a string bean."

Jane covered her mouth and laughed. I put a Shirley Temple in front of her.

"All right, everyone, I have an announcement," Horace said, raising his glass. "Ruth's chief of staff confided to me today they've identified the murderous savages who planted the bomb. With luck, our boys will have them in custody before we leave for Winnemucca."

Wanda came out of the galley and stood at the edge of the bar.

"Who are they?" Billy asked. "Did she say?"

"Foreign-born terrorists, some medieval form of rug merchants intent on jihad," Horace said. "That's all I know. The point is, we can sleep tonight knowing those monsters will soon get their just desserts. A toast."

Everyone raised a glass.

"Righteousness is no shield against fate or the reckless acts of cowards," Horace said. "Here's to Ruth and David."

"Here, here," said the others.

They tilted their heads back and drank champagne. Jane looked down at the floor. She was crying.

Wanda wrapped an arm around Jane's shoulders. "Hey, you okay?"

"Have your uncle take you shopping," Poppy said. "It has wonderful therapeutic effects."

Billy leaned in sympathetically. "*Holiday on Ice* is coming to the Cow Palace. When you're in San Francisco I'll get you front-row passes. I know the chap who mounts the show."

Poppy said, "In a few years we can make you an intern at the magazine."

"We'll put you to work in the mailroom," Billy said. "Would you like that?"

Wiping her eyes, Jane nodded.

Wanda said, "Hey, can you help me in the galley a minute?"

Taking Wanda's hand, Jane sprang from her perch at the bar and followed Wanda around the corner.

The tenor of the party shifted into high gear. Conversation flourished. I poured a lot of champagne and shook a number of martinis. Horace's punch lines were followed by great belly laughs. The caviar vanished.

"Now, everyone, listen," Billy said. "You must hear Mother's story. She really put her foot in it this time—the society columnists are having a field day."

Horace turned to Poppy. He planted a black shoe on the footrest of the middle barstool.

"All right, steno gal," he said. "Let's hear it."

"If you absolutely insist," Poppy said. "But steward, prime my pump first." She gave me her martini glass. I placed a fresh Gibson in front of her. She took a sip. "Ah! Good. Now where was I?"

"The museum dinner," Billy said.

"Yes, right! This was one of those horrible planning dinners," Poppy said. "All they want is your money. It was a long, drawn-out affair—simply interminable. I dodged the business but apparently not the gin. I don't even remember getting home, but being August in the City, it was freezing. I had on my beaver frock coat from Spungen's in Berlin. I blacked out in the bathroom. When I came to, I was flat on my back in my claw-foot tub, beaver coat and all. For the life of me I couldn't get out. So, I thought I'd draw some warm water and sleep it off there. Next thing I know it's God-knows-what hour and I'm up to my neck in this chilly drink. I called Cecily the maid and gave her a good bawling out for leaving me in a cold tub. She'd been sound asleep. She got knee-deep in the water and had her hands around my neck before she realized what she was doing. We both fell into hysterics over the whole ridiculous situation. She helped me out of the tub, but by then I'd ruined a perfectly good beaver coat. I swear to God, I don't know how these things keep happening to me."

"Because you thrive on sensation and scandal," Horace said. "You always have."

Poppy plucked a lit cigarette from Dr. Rose's lips. "Well, at least I'm not a G.D. stick-in-the-mud." She took a drag, turned to her left, blew a cloud of smoke in Horace's face, and stamped out the butt in an ashtray.

Outside on the open platform, Lisa French knocked on the door.

Horace quickly got up from his barstool and went to let her in. He brought her to the bar. She was businesslike and struck me as somewhat mannish: her tailored pinstriped suit, her stocky build, her thick brown hair combed back in a stylized mullet. She carried a heavy lawyer's briefcase.

Horace introduced his dinner guests.

"You're a medical doctor?" Lisa said to Dr. Rose, glancing at his cigarette.

"Not a very good one, I'm afraid," Dr. Rose said, looking glum.

"May I offer you a drink?" Horace said to Lisa.

"Not a thing, thank you." Lisa took in the interior of the railcar. "So this is it. The *Pioneer Mother*. It's splendid."

"And possibly my salvation, if what you're telling me is true," Horace said.

"Is there somewhere we can talk in private?"

"My stateroom," Horace said. "If you don't mind tight quarters."

"I don't mind at all." Lisa looked toward the galley. "Whatever's cooking, it smells wonderful."

"Wanda's stuffing a breast of lamb," Horace said. "Can we talk you into staying for dinner?"

"Not tonight, I'm afraid…"

Horace and Lisa started up the hallway.

Several minutes later I was opening an Alsace Riesling when Billy came behind the bar.

"I need a word with you," he said.

He led me up the hallway, past Horace's closed stateroom door. He turned angrily.

"What the hell, Jack? What are you doing?"

"Dinner, Mr. Whitehead. I'm opening wine—"

"I mean, why aren't you in Hawaii?"

I gave him my best blank stare.

"Come on, Jack. Cut the B.S. I talk to her practically every day."

I remained expressionless.

"She says you're on your way," Billy said. "Finally."

"Saturday."

"Make it tomorrow." Billy produced a white envelope from an inside pocket of his suit jacket. He tried handing it to me, but I had the bottle of Riesling in one hand and the corkscrew in the other.

"This is for you," he said. "Take it."

I transferred the corkscrew to my other hand and took the envelope.

"That's a first-class ticket," Billy said. "You leave at eight o'clock in the morning, arrive Hawaii tomorrow night."

"But I need to stop in San Jose first."

"Forget San Jose. I promised Giselle I'd get you there posthaste."

"But I have to pull my stuff together and pack—"

"Buy whatever you need when you get there. Send me the bill."

"—and pay my rent."

"I'll pay your goddamn rent—"

Horace's stateroom door opened.

"I should be able to contact him yet this evening," Lisa was saying to Horace. "They're on Pacific time." Seeing Billy and me standing in the hallway, she managed a curt smile. "Gentlemen."

Horace regarded Billy with disdain. "Eavesdropping? Or are you simply firing the bartender again?"

"Actually I'm giving him a promotion," Billy said. "I'm accelerating his departure for Hawaii."

Horace shook his head. "You're a disgrace. Just leave him alone, why don't you? Here, Lisa, let me see you out."

Billy waited until they had left.

"Go on," he said to me. "Open the envelope. There's something I want you to see."

I set the bottle on the floor and slipped the corkscrew into my pocket. The envelope contained two printed sheets of paper. The first was a reservation confirmation: Alaska Airlines; Reagan National, connecting through Seattle to Lihue, Kauai Island, Hawaii.

"The next one," Billy said.

The second sheet spelled out coded sentences and their meanings: "The flight was long" meant Giselle was still interested in pursuing a deal with *Sunshine Trails*. "I slept the whole way" meant the deal was off. "I'm hoping to snorkel" indicated the two parties were far apart on the terms of the deal. "I hear helicopter tours are good" meant Giselle was agreeable to contributing future cookbook projects to the company. In the sentence "I'd like to rent a surfboard for x hours," x equaled the number of future books she was willing to contribute.

I looked at Billy coldly. "You want me to be a spy."

"Sex as a weapon in the corporate arsenal. Makes life interesting, don't you think?"

"I can't do it, Mr. Whitehead."

"Of course you can. I'll call you Saturday afternoon. That should give you plenty of time to pump your girlfriend for information." He smiled smugly. "Come on, Jack. Don't look so ungrateful. I'm sending you to goddamned Hawaii."

FORTY-SIX

BY ELEVEN O'CLOCK I had the bar cleaned and stocked for Pierre's first shift in the morning. In just over seven hours, according to Billy Whitehead's itinerary, I'd be on my way to the airport. I pulled the shades in the observation lounge and was about to turn out the lights when Horace came padding down the hallway in a silk robe and slippers. He carried a writing pad and a pen.

"Can't sleep?" I said.

"Some unfinished business," he said. "Pour two cognacs, would you, Jack? And bring me a couple of stogies from the humidor."

Horace went to the end of the car, settled into his favorite parlor chair, and turned the table lamp on. I carried the cognac and cigars on a silver serving tray, which I placed on the side table next to Horace. He nodded at the adjacent chair.

"Sit, won't you?" he said.

I sat.

Horace smiled self-consciously and passed me a snifter of cognac. "This is for you. You've just poured your last drink as bartender on the *Pioneer Mother*. How does it feel?"

I took the snifter. "You must think I'm an ingrate for leaving."

"No," Horace said. "I've thought it over. I was hasty in my anger. An alluring beauty awaits you in Shangri-La. I can't blame you one bit."

"Well, if you've got any wisdom, I'd love to hear it."

Horace's eyes sparkled. "What I can offer is the humble musing of an old tosspot, but it's late. I'd be keeping you from packing your bags."

I smiled. "I can sleep on the plane."

"Then, cheers." Horace touched his snifter to mine.

I took a sip of cognac. Those familiar tones of orange and vanilla—for a moment I was lying with Wanda on the lower berth in our bedroom.

"This journal you were telling me about the other night," Horace said. "I hope you're going easy on me. Your words may be the only enduring account of my days on earth."

"I doubt that. In fact, while I was here, I'd hoped to get some tips from you on being a writer."

"Tips. Ha! I'll tell you a story about writing." Horace took one of the cigars. He indicated the second cigar on the tray. "That one's for you. Help yourself."

I picked up the cigar and copied my employer's punctilious ritual: clipping the head just so; wetting the cigar in my mouth and drawing air through it; holding it over the tip of the torch lighter's flame and then getting it going with a succession of quick, shallow puffs. I leaned back in my chair and pretended to savor the experience, but I hadn't smoked a cigar since the night of the football draft two years earlier, and I fought the urge to hack and plant the thing headfirst in the ashtray.

We smoked and meditated to the low rumble of an arriving locomotive.

"I take it that writing is more than a casual interest of yours?" Horace said.

"When I was in the hospital, Dr. Rose urged me to find a new calling. I did some soul-searching and finally landed on becoming a writer. I decided I had to write a novel, one brilliant enough to prompt an ex-fiancée to take me back. How's that for naïve?"

"I'm certain you aren't the first." Horace cradled his snifter in the palm of his hand. He studied the cognac and then turned to me. "Dr. Rose and I had a long talk about you tonight. You've been a good project for him. He's really quite fond of you."

"He was on the board of the Stanford Athletic Department—that's where I first met him," I said. "He took a personal interest in my recovery, especially my emotional state. My eyes were bandaged after some of the facial surgeries, and he spent a lot of time at my bedside, reading me all the newspapers and magazines he could get his hands on. He probably saved my life by getting me to engage with the outside world again. He even had me auditing classes at the graduate schools—his way, I think, of encouraging me to picture a future without football. Becoming a writer was my own stupid idea. By the way, I owe you for a bottle of champagne."

Horace looked at me.

"The other night, leaving Toledo," I said. "Wanda and I split a bottle of Dom."

Horace shrugged. "We've got too much of the stuff anyway. It's coming out our ears."

"She told me her life story."

"Interesting, isn't it?"

"Very."

"She's proof, I think, that good can come from evil, that dreams and hard work can overcome a deep-seated anger, no matter how righteous." Horace puffed his cigar. "Poppy... now there's an interesting case. I call her my darling of diamond-studded disaster. Do you know the story? How we lost Billy's father?"

"No. Should I?"

"Lincoln had heart issues from time to time. He went in for what was described as a routine procedure—a cardiac catheterization, where they look at the arteries around the heart. The doctor mistakenly gave him nitrous oxide instead of oxygen. Killed him on the spot."

"My God."

"Henry was the doctor. He was devastated, of course."

"Dr. Rose?" I was speechless.

"He stopped practicing medicine after that," Horace said. "He still looks after me, of course, as a favor to an old friend."

I ruminated on this for a second and then turned to Horace. "Thank you. A piece of the puzzle just snapped into place. 'Quit looking in the mirror,' he'd say to me when I was at my lowest. 'Get it out of your head that you're supposed to be somebody special. Find someone even more damaged than you, and be of service. That's how you fix a broken life.'"

Horace smiled.

"Was there a lawsuit?" I said.

"For medical malpractice?" Horace said. "No. Poppy wouldn't hear of it. We were all such close friends. Lincoln and Henry started the Biscuit Shooters camp together at Mount Hollow. The three of us spent some wonderful years there." Horace stopped to tap his cigar over the ashtray. "For a while Billy made noise about a lawsuit, but when his mother installed him as C.E.O. and publisher of *Sunshine Trails*, that seemed to satisfy him. He never brought it up again."

"That's an incredible story."

"That's not the half of it," Horace said. "Henry, you see, is hopelessly in love with Poppy. He can't marry her, of course, because it wouldn't look right. So the poor bastard suffers in every imaginable way."

Horace and I smoked in silence for a while, contemplating the misfortune of our mutual friend. I canted my cigar over the ashtray and set loose a chunk of gray ash.

"Here's another one for you, the writing story I promised," Horace said. "I was about your age, working for the *New York Herald Tribune*, covering the halls of Congress. I think I told you that already."

"You did."

"During my days in D.C., it was at Chez Patrice that I felt most at home. Patrice was a gentleman in every sense of the word. He ran a wonderful restaurant, played host to every big-name politician in town. He was also a great supporter of aspiring young artists. Life as a cub reporter left me empty. The vocation of politics always struck me as lowbrow and somewhat undignified—the fundraising and campaigning and so on. I had literary ambitions. I was determined to write Broadway shows. At the time Patrice had a bartender working for him who was an aspiring composer—his name was Sheldon Shaw. Patrice put the two of us together, and our partnership was quickly formed. I'd write the book and lyrics, Sheldon would compose the melodies. Patrice contributed the facility, moral support, and enough libations to keep our creative juices flowing."

"Sounds like the perfect arrangement," I said.

"It was indeed," Horace said. "Every night when the restaurant closed, we'd wheel an upright piano into the middle of the dining room, turn up all the lights, and go to work. We had good chemistry, Button and Shaw. The first act came together almost effortlessly. We called our play *The Lincoln Bedroom*. It was a sex farce set in the White House—a gay president still in the closet, his secret lover comes to a state dinner disguised as the Emir of Afghanistan. The First Lady invites him to stay the night with his harem in the Lincoln Bedroom. Camels and dancing girls and a long mirrored hallway of slamming doors—you can imagine how things play out. Those sleep-deprived times in D.C. were some of the best days of my life."

"So what became of Button and Shaw?" I said.

"Scuttled by the brainless barnyard urge of the human animal," Horace said. "Patrice turned his amorous attention from me to Sheldon, who was a little younger than I, thinner and much prettier. The boy had beautiful eyes. I found out they were having afternoon trysts behind my back. Suddenly the team of Button and Shaw was no more. I was devastated—at the time losing Patrice felt as though I'd lost my soul mate. *The Lincoln Bedroom* remains unfinished to this day."

"I'm sorry."

"In hindsight I got exactly what I deserved. I was using Patrice as much as he was using me. I thought he'd be my ticket out of journalism and onto Easy Street."

"And you left Washington for good?"

The question was met by a moment of silence, and then he said, "I see we're both dangerously low on cognac."

I took Horace's snifter and went to the bar. He puffed his cigar while I refilled his glass. I topped off my snifter, too.

"You asked me about leaving Washington," Horace said through a cloud of smoke when I sat down again. "I'll tell you what happened. I was so angry at Patrice that I made a career out of exacting my revenge."

"A career?" I took a moment to rekindle my cigar. By this time the taste of the smoke on my tongue—hints of dry grass and chocolate—complemented the spicy flavors of the cognac. I was enjoying the pampered life of a media baron.

"I went to New York and started my society column," Horace said. "From day one, every sentence I wrote, every word, was aimed solely at Patrice. I wanted to rub his nose in it—the grand time I was having night after night, painting the town red. The dinner parties, the theater openings, the nightclubs, living in black tie and tails until the sun came up. I also never missed an opportunity to skewer any one of Patrice's famous customers: the politicians, the cabinet secretaries, the K Street lobbyists."

"Does that by any chance include Russell Rawlins?" I asked.

"Russ was one of Patrice's best customers from the early days," Horace said. "Not that anything excuses his abominable politics."

He puffed his cigar thoughtfully.

"I must tell you, Jack. The whole notion of living one's life to prove something to someone else…it seems to me rather pointless. Last night, when I went back to Chez Patrice, my intent was to mend fences. Now I find he's gone. And what do I have to show for my life's work but a dusty collection of ill-tempered essays that ten years from now no one will even see—"

"I wouldn't say that."

"—no masterpiece, no Broadway play, no adoring fans giving a standing ovation."

"Your fans worship you," I said. "I've seen it firsthand from Denver to Toledo to just this afternoon at Costco."

Horace looked at me, surprised and somewhat miffed. "Costco?"

"That's where Wanda and I met with your new bartender today," I said. "He's a huge fan." I looked down and swirled my cognac. "In fact, he told me something interesting about Giselle. She has a reputation in the industry. Apparently she's a bit of a slut."

"A slut?"

"Famously promiscuous. Sexually adventurous. Just what every young man ought to desire."

Horace looked away and pondered this a moment. He turned back to me with mischievous eyes. "You should go to Hawaii and take notes for a salacious memoir. People buy those kinds of books. Your success as a writer would be guaranteed."

"I really don't know what to do. Any advice?"

"The only advice I can offer is that in life, shortcuts rarely work out," Horace said. "Anything easily given can be just as easily taken away."

"You're saying I shouldn't go?"

Horace set his cigar on the ashtray. "You asked earlier for my wisdom. May I be perfectly honest?"

"Please."

"I think in the long run your pride will suffer, being a kept man. All your life you've set goals and worked hard for the successes you've achieved. You and I are a lot alike in that regard. Ours isn't the kind of personality that finds happiness merely by settling for what's easy or convenient. I have something I'd like to run past you, a proposal I think you might find interesting. It's the opportunity to embark on a second act, to make a choice that might turn your life in a new and surprising direction."

"You've got my attention."

"You know I met tonight behind closed doors with my sister's estate attorney, Lisa French," Horace said. "It seems that one of her junior partners was taking an inventory of Ruth's strongbox. He came across something quite momentous…"

FORTY-SEVEN

AT 6:25 A.M. I STOOD on the *Pioneer Mother*'s open platform, sipping coffee, enjoying a rare moment of tranquility while the world bustled around me. The train shed's roof echoed the low rumbles and ringing bells of active locomotives. On a succession of tracks, commuters alighted from arriving trains and crowded the station doors. The humid air, charged with the sharp odor of locomotive exhaust, warned of a brutally hot day to come.

By this time I had moved my things out of the double bedroom. The upper berth was stripped of its sheets and pillowcase. My duffel, packed full of clothes, sat zipped and upright against stacked cases of champagne in the equipment locker.

I finished my coffee and looked one last time at Billy's sheet of coded sentences. I leaned out over the railing and touched the flame of Horace's torch lighter to a corner of the paper. The page flared. As the paper's edges curled inward and grew increasingly black, I let it go. It drifted downward like a fallen leaf, landing on a shiny steel rib of Jane's overturned baggage trolley.

"Burning the canoes," Pierre called. "That means there's no turning back."

He wheeled a big black roller bag and carried a matching garment bag that was nearly bursting at the seams.

"You found us," I said.

"Oh, I found you at five o'clock this morning. I've been waiting in the Main Concourse ever since, counting the minutes. I hope I'm not too early."

"No, no. Let's get you aboard," I said.

As Pierre came up the steps I took the garment bag for him and held open the door. He entered the observation lounge and gasped. He paused to finger an embroidered arm cover on one of the parlor chairs.

"This must be where he sits and writes," he said.

I pointed out the first chair on the starboard side. "That's his favorite."

"Is he up?" Pierre said.

"Maybe in another hour or so. Come on, let's tell Wanda you're here and get you settled."

In the galley Wanda dried her hands on a chef's towel and glanced at the clock on the wall. She smiled at Pierre. "Early. I like that."

Pierre perched in the doorway, taking in the details of the galley.

"What's on the breakfast menu?" he said.

"Scrambled eggs with quail, slices of summer fruit, potato pancakes, English muffins with strawberry jam."

"Sounds delish," Pierre said. "What's my morning uniform?"

Wanda and I exchanged glances.

"I'd stick to the white waiter's jacket for now," I said.

Pierre looked disappointed.

"I hope you brought your black tie and tails, though," Wanda said.

"The first things I packed." Pierre raised his chin and flashed his crooked smile.

"Your bedroom's this way," I said.

I left Pierre unpacking his bags in the double bedroom and returned to the galley.

"What do you think?" Wanda said to me. "Is he up for the job?"

"Are you kidding?" I said. "I thought he was going to dry-hump a parlor chair."

Wanda glanced at the clock and then looked at me. "Aren't you supposed to be heading for the airport by now?"

"Big news, Wanda. I'm not going."

Wanda crossed her arms. "Just like that? You're not going? What about Giselle?"

"Don't worry about Giselle."

Wanda looked at me skeptically. "What, you just suddenly changed your mind?"

Pierre popped his head in the doorway.

"White gloves all right?" He wore a waiter's jacket over his shirt and tie.

"White gloves are fine," Wanda said quickly. She fixed me with a stony stare. "Pierre, would you give us a minute?"

Pierre looked from Wanda to me.

"No problem," he said, retreating. "I'll just check out the living room."

Wanda situated herself directly in front of me. "Should we call him off?" she said in a low voice.

"No, Wanda, the job's his," I said. "Mr. Button made me an interesting proposition last night. I stay and look after Jane's legal and financial affairs. In return I get room and board at the big house in Hillsborough."

Wanda bristled.

"What?" I said. "You don't like that?"

"Do whatever you want," Wanda said. "But don't automatically assume I'm a part of that deal."

"What's that supposed to mean?"

"It means if you want a girlfriend, you should go to Hawaii."

"Here I thought you'd be happy for me," I said. "For us."

"What do you want me to do, throw a parade?"

"Just don't reject me out of hand. Let's see where this goes."

Wanda turned her back to me. "You're in the way. I've got breakfast to cook."

Pierre proved to be a quick study. We prepped the bar, set the dining table, and I showed him the contents of all the drawers and cabinets and how to operate the satellite radio system.

"Seems simple enough," Pierre said.

Jane arrived for breakfast clutching Smokey Bear. She wore a navy blue midi skirt with a white top.

"Jane, say hello to Pierre," I said.

Pierre came out from behind the bar. "If there's anything I can do to make you more comfortable, let me know."

"Thank you," Jane said, glancing at me.

Pierre touched the teddy bear with a white-gloved finger. "And who do we have here in such a pretty summer dress?"

"This is Smokey," Jane said. "He's hungry enough to eat a whole jar of honey."

"Then he's come to the right place. I happen to know that Wanda has prepared a feast. Are we ready to sit?"

Pierre held a chair for Jane. She deposited the bear in the seat next to hers. As Pierre unfurled Jane's napkin, she kept looking over her shoulder at me.

A minute later Horace arrived. I introduced him to Pierre. Horace's eyes darted to Pierre's white gloves. The two men shook hands. They stood and exchanged pleasantries for a minute, mostly about the *Pioneer Mother.*

"I've got champagne chilling," Pierre said. "May I bring you a glass?"

"Thank you, Pierre, but a single Bloody Mary should do," Horace said. "Alcohol and cathedrals are a dangerous mix for me. Too much bottle waving, and I can't distinguish the rectory staff from the pigeon-drop hustlers." Horace turned to me. "Your marching orders for the day, Jack. Have you thought about it?"

"I've thought about it a lot," I said. "But I think you should eat first."

Horace surveyed the dining table.

"Pierre, you've set the table for two," he said. "Now and hereafter set it for three. Jack will be joining us for meals."

From the pass-through window, Wanda looked on quizzically.

Pierre brought the Bloody Mary for Horace and held a chair for him. Horace and I both sat.

Pierre served breakfast.

Horace took a sip of his Bloody Mary and quickly set the drink aside. Jane pushed her scrambled eggs and the quail around on her plate, but she never really brought anything to her mouth.

"You need to eat," Horace said.

"I feel sorry for the quail," Jane said.

"You feel sorry for the quail?"

"What if she's a mother?" Jane said. "Who will sit on her eggs and hatch the little quail babies?"

"The quail is dead," Horace said. "The only thing she can sit on now is a plate."

Jane planted an elbow on the table and pressed her head against her hand. She stared glumly at the small piece of gray meat.

"It makes me sad," she said.

Horace licked his lips. "Wait until you try aspic of quail sometime. Then you'll have no problem devouring the little buggers."

"But what if her family misses her?" Jane said.

"All right, leave the quail," Horace said. "But sit up straight and eat your eggs. And try the potato pancakes. Unless you feel sorry for the potatoes, too."

Horace looked at me and turned his eyes heavenward. He tried another sip of his Bloody Mary, winced, and set the glass down hard. For a minute he watched Jane pick at her scrambled eggs. She had an odd way of eating—whenever she took a bite, she stared dreamily in the distance and waved her fork in tight circles.

"What in blazes are you doing?" Horace said finally.

"I'm counting bites," Jane said. "They say you need to chew your food at least twenty-three times or you'll get fat."

"God almighty," Horace said. "Now I've heard everything."

"That's swearing. It's taking the Lord's name in vain."

Horace opened his mouth and then closed it. His face reddened. He turned toward the bar and took hold of his Bloody Mary.

"Pierre, I can't take this any longer," he said. "Please!"

Pierre came to the table and hovered solicitously. The Bloody Mary was still three-quarters full.

"Is something wrong with your drink, Mr. Button?" Pierre said.

"It tastes like something you'd get in a bowling alley," Horace said. "Have Jack show you how to make a proper one."

Pierre scooped up the glass. "My apologies. As soon as he has a spare minute." He shot me a hostile look and retreated to the bar.

I set my napkin on the table and stood. "Excuse me."

I went behind the bar and made a Bloody Mary for Horace. Pierre watched closely and tried to make notes on his smartphone, but he fell behind.

"Don't bother," I said. "I'll write it out for you."

In the end, Pierre's table service was impeccable. He took good care of us.

Jane finally finished her breakfast. She even asked for a second helping of potato pancakes, once she realized she was allowed to drown them in ketchup.

"All finished?" Pierre said to Jane, standing over her right shoulder.

"Yes, thank you."

"Here, let me show you something about table etiquette." Pierre took Jane's knife and fork, placed them together, and set them diagonally across the plate. "When you've finished eating, put your utensils together like this, blade of the knife facing inward toward the fork, top of the utensils at ten o'clock and handles at four. This signals to me you've finished eating."

Horace glanced at me. We both looked down. Our knives and forks lay strewn haphazardly across our plates, like fallen tree trunks in a forest. We quickly set our utensils on the proper diagonal. Pierre clucked in my ear as he cleared my plate.

After the last cup of coffee had been poured, Horace checked his watch.

"There's a good girl," he said to Jane. "Run and use the washroom. The limousine will be out front in a few minutes, and we can't be late picking up our friends at the hotel."

Jane plucked the stuffed animal from its chair. "Can I take Smokey with me to the church?"

Horace considered this for a moment.

"Let's compromise," he said. "You can have him in the car, but not inside the church. He might agitate the forest rangers. Which reminds me, Jack. We need to add that to our agenda."

"But Uncle," Jane said, "I want Smokey at the service. What if I start to cry?"

"Tell you what," Horace said. "When you feel the tears coming, just give my hand a squeeze, and I'll pass you a sweet to suck. I want you to sit tall this morning and pay close attention. You're going to hear some nice things about your mother and dad, and you'll want to remember it clearly for the rest of your life."

Horace and I both watched Jane carry the bear up the hallway.

"I never thought I'd be the one to say it, Jack, but that child's beginning to grow on me," Horace said. "We can't lose her to the state."

"No."

"You said you had some thoughts."

"In football, there's an old saying," I said. "The best defense is a good offense. Rosalind may not like it, but I think it's time we went on the offensive. We can deal with the forest rangers at the same time."

"Good," Horace said. "Tell me more."

FORTY-EIGHT

"MY NAME IS JACK MARSHALL. I serve as Mr. Button's executive assistant. He asked me to make a few brief remarks this morning on his behalf." I gripped the edges of a restaurant maître d' lectern, which I'd appropriated for our hastily called press conference. Horace and Jane stood somberly behind me.

A crush of reporters encircled us. It had been years since I'd faced the press, and I drew upon the media coaching I'd received as a Stanford athlete—stay calm, ignore hypothetical questions, stick to the facts, and speak of my direct, personal experience. Knowing the scorn these reporters had for Ruth Pepper's politics, seeing their condescending expressions, I was determined to pull this off. They anticipated red meat. Damned if I'd give it to them.

I paused, taking in the architectural details of Union Station's Main Hall: the ceiling's great rococo arches, the towering windows guarded by Roman statues, the white marble floor. The Center Café, an open second-story restaurant framed by two resplendent staircases, loomed in the background. I could hear the faint chants of protesters outside the station.

"First, Mr. Button would like to thank all of you for being here today," I said. "This nation has suffered a terrible attack, an act of terror that has cut short the lives of two remarkable people, one a loving father and husband, the other a beloved mother, sister, and outspoken champion of liberty. Mr. Button and his niece also want to thank everyone across this great nation for their thoughts and prayers. Your sentiments

280

are both humbling and deeply appreciated."

"Will Mr. Button keep Jane?" a reporter shouted from the sidelines.

I ignored him.

"Also, Mr. Button would like to thank Senator Pepper's staff for their tireless work preparing for today's service, even as they battled overwhelming grief," I said. "To Senator Pepper's chief of staff and cherished friend, Rosalind Snodgrass-Smith, Mr. Button is especially grateful for your loving care of Jane in the early hours of this tragedy. He is forever in your debt." I looked up.

The reporters shouted questions.

"Is Mr. Button going to apologize—"

"What makes Mr. Button think—"

"Does he intend to fight for custody if he loses it?"

I locked eyes with that last reporter.

"As to the issue of custody," I said. "Regarding the disposition of his niece, Mr. Button's resolve is firm. He intends to take Jane back to San Francisco and raise her as his own daughter, exactly as David and Senator Pepper wanted. Mr. Button will vigorously fight any effort by any government agency or individual to challenge his guardianship of his niece."

"On what basis does he think he's fit to parent?" a reporter said. "Where's his evidence for that?"

I turned to the reporter. "Mr. Button categorically dismisses any notion that he's unfit to fulfill his obligations as guardian. He's perfectly capable of raising this child."

"What's Mr. Button's position on gay marriage?" a reported said.

"I'm not going to answer that," I said.

"Does he own any guns?"

"Also irrelevant," I said. "We're talking about his fitness to serve as guardian."

"Mr. Button is a notorious cigar smoker," said another reporter. "How would you characterize his level of concern about the effects of secondhand smoke?"

"No concern at all." I looked down at my notes. "Accordingly, and in the interest of complete transparency—"

"Because he doesn't care or because he doesn't believe secondhand smoke is harmful?" the reporter interrupted.

I scoffed at the question. "Mr. Button and his niece are grieving the loss of two close family members. I don't think the morning of their memorial service is the time or place to debate the effects of second-hand smoke."

I returned to my written notes.

"Accordingly, and in the interest of complete transparency, Mr. Button has instructed me to open the doors of the *Pioneer Mother* to any representative from D.C.'s Child and Family Services who wishes to inspect Jane's living conditions." I looked up. "I will be on hand to walk this representative through Jane's multiple levels of adult supervision aboard the *Pioneer Mother*. I'm also prepared to share Mr. Button's plans for raising Jane and for providing for her education and welfare when living in San Francisco. This offer stands for the next three hours, during the time Mr. Button and his niece will be at the National Cathedral attending the service. Upon their return to the railroad car, we ask that Child Services, as well as members of the press, give them their complete privacy for obvious reasons."

"What if Child Services doesn't like what it sees?" a reporter said.

"Mr. Button is confident as to the outcome of any inspection," I said.

A woman reporter directly in front of me said, "You mentioned multiple levels of adult supervision aboard the *Pioneer Mother*. Does that include you? And if so, is Mr. Button aware of your past?"

"I'm not sure what you're referring to—"

"You're Jack Marshall, the former football player. You pled guilty to a very high-profile D.U.I. case a couple of years ago in Silicon Valley."

"I assume…" I turned and looked at Horace. "He's well aware of that fact."

"I am aware," Horace said.

"What about Child and Family Services?" the woman reporter said. "Are they aware?"

I gave her a smile. "If they weren't before, I imagine they are now."

The reporters chuckled.

"So how do you reconcile that?" the woman reporter persisted.

"I mean, is this a good idea? To surround Jane Pepper with two adults who have histories of abusing alcohol? Doesn't that put this child's life in significant jeopardy?"

"Bollocks," Horace said behind me.

"I think we'd dispute your term *abusing*," I said, turning away from her and pointing to another woman reporter.

"Can you quantify the amount of alcohol that's aboard the *Pioneer Mother*?" she said. "And tell us approximately how many drinks Mr. Button consumes on a given night?"

"I'm not going to respond to that," I said. I turned to another reporter. "You've been patient. Let's go to you."

"Back to the issue of firearms," he said. "It's reported Mr. Button may possess a handgun. Can you confirm that fact, and can you give us your unequivocal assurance that the gun is adequately locked away at all times—in a gun safe or some such repository—where Jane can't potentially access the weapon?"

"Look, I'm not going to stand here and give you a complete inventory of everything aboard Mr. Button's private railcar," I said. "I'm also not going to comment on what firearms may or may not be aboard. My purpose here this morning is simply to issue an open invitation for Child Services to evaluate the environment, which we maintain is completely safe and perfectly acceptable for an eleven-year-old."

"Almost twelve," Jane said to me.

"I stand corrected," I said to the reporters. "She's almost twelve."

This garnered more laughs.

"What about you, Jane?" the first woman reporter said. "Do you feel safe with your uncle?"

All eyes turned expectantly to Jane. I stepped back from the lectern and gave her a nod.

Jane blinked back at the reporter. "Do I feel safe?"

"Yes, do you think your uncle can do a good job of raising you?" the woman reporter said.

Jane looked up at Horace. "I think he's a very nice man. He can teach me a lot. I feel lucky I get to live with him."

Horace gave Jane a wooden hug.

"Mr. Button," another reporter shouted, "what about charges that you're homophobic? Are you going to address that? Are you going apologize to the forest rangers?"

Horace frowned. He pointed at me with his thumb.

I glanced at my notes and then leveled my gaze at the reporter.

"With respect to the lesbian, bisexual, gay, and transgender forest rangers who continue to picket outside this train station, Mr. Button has asked me to express his sincere regrets at any offense his actions may have caused," I said. "The intent was to bestow a personal gift on his niece. That in the process he might slight a respected segment of the population was never in his wildest imagination."

"Does that mean he apologizes?" another reporter said.

"If any offense was taken, yes," I said. "You have Mr. Button's sincerest apologies."

"Why won't you disclose Mr. Button's position on gay marriage?" said a reporter in front of me. "What does he have to hide?"

I glared at the man. "Look, Mr. Button has written extensively in his essays, and he's worked tirelessly behind the scenes—*tirelessly*—to ensure that everyone in this country enjoys equal protection under our laws, and that means equal access to life, liberty, and the pursuit of happiness. Go back and read his books, read his material. His position is clear. No one has been a stronger, more consistent advocate of keeping the government out of our bedrooms. And for any single group to take a partisan stance, to attack Horace Button as some backward-thinking, social Neanderthal, based on his belief in lower taxes, smaller government, and increased individual liberty is disingenuous at best. Mr. Button's life's work has been devoted to the belief that all persons, no matter their race, gender, or orientation, deserve to be treated with dignity and respect, especially by their duly elected government. I've spent a considerable amount of time with this man, and I can tell you, he wants nothing more than to see every individual prosper and thrive. This notion that he's a bigoted, homophobic monster couldn't be further from the truth."

I turned and looked at Horace.

He gave me a serious-minded nod and touched his watch—my sign we'd fulfilled our objective and he wanted to move on.

"That's all I've got," I said to the reporters. "Thank you again for coming."

We ignored their shouted questions as I walked Horace and Jane out to the waiting limousine.

I reboarded the *Pioneer Mother* and found Pierre still clearing plates from the table.

"How'd it go?" he said.

"We've set the bait," I said. "Now we just have to wait and see if the fish bite."

Wanda came out of the galley.

"All right," she said, glaring at me. "Will somebody please tell me what the hell is going on?"

I looked at Wanda and Pierre. "Let's huddle up. We have a lot of ground to cover."

FORTY-NINE

PIERRE DRIED A WINE GOBLET with a dishcloth. "I got my true education in the food business by working at different restaurants around Bourbon Street in New Orleans," he said. "That sorry place where so many wonderful restaurants are jammed with people who have such atrocious manners." He held the glass up to the light, scrutinizing the bowl for smudges and giving the rim one last pass with the cloth. "All these insufferable buffoons from all over the country, thinking every day is Mardi Gras. They were so drunk they'd be walking zombies, numb to the once-in-a-lifetime culinary experiences. I'm talking the best of the French Quarter: Antoine's, Galatoire's, Brennan's. I made good money, but the clientele got so impossible that I finally left. I imagine working in Las Vegas would be the same, though I've never been." He hung the glass by its foot in the overhead rack and took down several more wine goblets. He looked at me. "I don't think they're coming, do you?"

"No," I said. "Not at this point."

"Are you disappointed?" Pierre dipped his next wine goblet into the soapy water and took it down the line of chemical solutions behind the bar. His shirtsleeves were rolled up. He had small, pale wrists. His silver watch, pushed up on his forearm, had a simple white face; its hands pointed to straight-up noon.

"More relieved," I said. "When you get right down to it, it's almost impossible to prove a negative."

Pierre snorted. "Right. Like 'When did you stop beating your wife?'"

Wanda came round the corner and looked at me.

"You finally stopped beating your wife?" she said.

"We were just saying what a relief it is that Child Protective Services didn't show," Pierre said.

Wanda fixed her gaze on the glassware at the sink.

"You need to stow that stuff, Pierre," she said. "You've got about one minute before we start moving."

"Yikes," Pierre said. "Those guys work fast."

Not five minutes earlier, three burly trainmen had walked through the *Pioneer Mother*, ostensibly to double-check the emergency brake, but in all likelihood eager for a look inside Horace Button's private railroad car, based on the way their heads swung around as they took their time wandering through. Their switching locomotive would take us out to the staging yard, where the funeral train was being assembled.

Pierre quickly ran the remaining wine goblets through the line. I pitched in and helped, drying glasses and placing them in the overhead rack. I was so busy stowing glasses that I didn't notice the woman on the open platform until she pounded on the door. She had shiny black skin and short-cropped, yellow hair. I assumed she was with the railroad, delivering last-minute orders for the switching crew.

I hustled through the observation lounge and reached for the door. The woman pressed an identification badge against the glass, her mug shot facing me: two black orbs for eyes, a wide, flat nose. I opened the door. The plastic badge, which was attached to a lanyard around the woman's neck, settled in the ample bulges of her lightweight pullover top. The curves of her hips and bottom appeared to test the staying power of her blue jeans.

"What's a matter, you didn't hear me bangin' on that door?" She pushed past me, brushing me aside with her clipboard.

"I'm sorry," I said. "I didn't catch your—"

"Loretta Faye Elder, D.C. Child and Family Services. You can call me Miss Elder. That was quite a stunt you pulled this morning, Mr. Marshall."

"To be honest—Miss Elder, was it?—now isn't a good time."

"Don't tell me what's a good time," she snapped. "I'm the one who dictates the times around here."

"You might want to jump off now while you can—"

Miss Elder eyed me balefully. "Jump off! Who do you think you're talking to? You don't have the standing to tell me to jump off—"

The railcar lurched. Miss Elder shrieked and tumbled backward into a parlor chair. Her stumpy white Keds pitched skyward. We began to roll.

"Hey," Miss Elder said. "This thing's moving!"

"I warned you—"

"Make it stop. Make it stop right now!"

"It's out of my hands."

"Then call someone. There's got to be someone you can call!"

"I wouldn't know who."

Miss Elder looked around frantically as our railroad car emerged from the shed. Sunshine filled the observation lounge.

"Where're we going?" she said. "How long are we gonna be? I have to be in court at one o'clock!"

I settled into the parlor chair across the way. I leaned forward, elbows on knees, hands clasped, and spoke in a calm voice. "Miss Elder, they're making up tomorrow's funeral train. That means you're going to be stuck here a while… an hour, maybe two. Sorry. You may as well sit back and enjoy the ride."

Miss Elder shot me a dirty look.

"Don't patronize me, Mr. Marshall," she said. "Moving or not, I expect you to cooperate fully with my investigation."

"Investigation?"

"I have the legal authority to remove that child from this home. I think you know who I'm talking about. We have a report that she's being neglected."

"Neglected? Says who?"

"By law I can't tell you that. It's strictly confidential."

"In other words, you're here on a bag job."

Miss Elder glowered at me. "You're gonna get your wish, Mr. Marshall… That cocky little speech this morning… You're going to get a thorough investigation from this agency, starting right now with me."

"I'm sorry you mistook the invitation," I said. "Our intent was to be welcoming and accommodating."

"That's baloney and you know it." She pulled out a smartphone from a belt clip. "You said one to two hours? I need to make a call."

Pierre gingerly approached Miss Elder's parlor chair. "May I get you anything from the bar?"

Miss Elder looked at him.

"Very kind of you to ask," she said. "But I don't need a thing." She speed-dialed a number and brought the phone to her ear.

Wanda came out of the galley.

Miss Elder spoke into her phone. "Darnell? Loretta Faye. Guess what? I'm stuck on a damn train... yeah, that's what I'm telling you. It just all of a sudden started going, and now I can't get off... Hey, I have a major problem. Can you cover the Vasquez hearing for me at one o'clock? They're saying it could be as much as two hours before we get back to Union Station... The file's on my desk. The other party wants a continuance... That's fine with me, as long as those kids don't go back to that house in the meantime... The conditions are deplorable... Well, if that happens, call me... No, just call me. Thanks, Darnell. You're a lifesaver... I will... Bye, now." She ended the call and stared distrustfully at the three of us.

During her call, we'd entered the vast railroad yard. The tracks teemed with vintage passenger railroad cars: sleepers from Union Pacific and Canadian National; fluted silver vista domes from Burlington Northern and the California Zephyr; lounge cars from Denver & Rio Grande and Santa Fe; dining cars from Southern Pacific and Atlantic Coast Line; coach cars from New York Central and Pennsylvania. The spectacle of these rolling antiques reduced us to silence. These pageant-like carriages, we realized, would soon constitute Ruth and David Pepper's funeral train.

Wanda ventured as far as the threshold of the observation lounge. Standing in the middle of the railcar, in her white chef's jacket and with a red bandana tied across her forehead, she quietly commanded Miss Elder's attention.

"I'm throwing together a quick crew lunch," Wanda said. "There's plenty of food if you'd like to join us."

Miss Elder gaped at Wanda, looking flabbergasted, then indignant.

"No, absolutely not," Miss Elder said. "I didn't come here to eat."

Our railcar slowed and, with a series of hard lurches, came to a dead stop. On a parallel track, a maroon Norfolk Southern business car blocked our view.

"All right, let's skin this cat." Miss Elder turned to her clipboard. "Be truthful with me, Mr. Marshall, and it'll keep our problems to a minimum."

Our problems?

"Would you like to start with a tour?" I said.

"A tour? No." Miss Elder glanced around uncertainly and sighed. "Though I suppose I should see this thing. Is it safe to stand?"

"If we start moving again," I said, "just grab something and hang on."

I showed her through the railcar. The tour took about ten minutes.

"I've never seen anything like this," she said, shaking her head, running a hand across the textured wallpaper in the hallway. "It's like a sultan's palace."

There was a tremendous crash of metal on metal, and the railcar jolted abruptly.

Miss Elder grabbed my arm. "Sorry, but I don't want to fall. This thing's dangerous!"

Our railroad car was on the move again, crossing turnouts, swaying from side to side. Miss Elder held onto my arm as I led her back to the observation lounge. I sat her down at the dining table.

Wanda and Pierre already had lunch on the table: thick BLT sandwiches and German potato salad. Miss Elder stared hungrily at the food.

"Are you sure you won't join us?" Wanda said.

"Looks good, but I'm sure," Miss Elder said. She turned to me. "So, tell me. What are your plans for Jane when she gets back to San Francisco?"

"Mr. Button's thought long and hard about that," I said. "Do you mind?" I indicated my plate of food.

"No, eat," Miss Elder said. She looked at Wanda and Pierre. "Everyone, please, go ahead and start."

Wanda and Pierre began eating.

"Mr. Button recognizes his limitations, especially when it comes to being guardian to an eleven-year-old girl," I said. "The first thing he wants to do is hire a governess." I took a bite of potato salad.

"A governess?" Miss Elder said.

"You know, someone to serve the traditional role of mother—drive Jane to and from school, help with her homework, arrange after-school activities. Someone to be there for all those personal conversations a growing girl would normally have with her own mother."

"That's a pretty sexist stereotype of motherhood, Mr. Marshall."

I wiped my mouth with a napkin. "Won't argue with you there. The thing is, Mr. Button's determined to give Jane a strong female role model in her life. We have Wanda, but he wants an equally strong mentor for activities outside the house. I can't argue with that, either."

"What about her education?"

"The Jesuits."

"The Jesuits?"

"Mr. Button is a big fan of the Jesuit philosophy," I said. "Conscience and compassion, contributing to society, helping others who might be less fortunate. The plan is to enroll Jane in an appropriate middle school and then send her to a good Jesuit college prep school in San Francisco. After that, a four-year college education, minimum, at a leading university."

"Uh-huh." Miss Elder narrowed her eyes. "And what about you, Mr. Marshall? Will you be involved with the child, or are you just the one who gives the speeches?"

"No, I'll definitely be involved. I'll be paying her bills and administering the trust."

"The trust?"

"The David and Ruth Pepper Family Trust," I said. "On the advice of legal counsel, Mr. Button has resigned as trustee. He's asked me to serve in his place."

"And serving as trustee... what, exactly, does that entail?"

"Mainly a fiduciary responsibility to protect the assets of the trust, to interface with the team of investment advisors, attorneys, and accountants that'll be working on the account. There's a lifestyle component to enforce, too. Jane's parents wanted her to travel, to see the world, to volunteer, to immerse herself in other cultures. I'll make sure she has those opportunities."

"Sounds like a lucky young woman," Miss Elder said. "Not lucky being orphaned, I mean… just lucky, you know… to have people in her life who care."

"We consider ourselves a team," I said. "Wanda serves as Mr. Button's full-time chef, both here and at his home in Hillsborough." I turned to Wanda. "Maybe you'd like to walk Miss Elder through your nutritional philosophy."

Wanda set down her sandwich and turned to Miss Elder.

"Sure," Wanda said. "First you have to understand that as a professional gourmand and food writer, Mr. Button has a huge appetite and a pretty sophisticated palate. In plain language he consumes an ungodly number of calories on any given day, much of it in the form of high-fat meats loaded with melted butter, garlic, and rich sauces. For Jane it will be a much different daily regimen. I'll follow Health and Human Services' dietary guidelines emphasizing nutrient-dense foods: fruits, vegetables, whole grains, seafood, and poultry. I'll limit her intake of sodium and red meats, saturated fats and processed sugars."

"My department includes physical fitness," I said, jumping in. "I'll work with Jane on strength training and developing team-sport skills. I'll also make sure she's exposed to leisure sports she can pursue for a lifetime: golf, tennis, running, cycling, horseback riding."

"The whole idea," Wanda said, "is to teach Jane how to maintain a healthy balance between what she eats and the daily physical stuff she does."

"And you're telling me you're going to cook this girl her own special meals?" Miss Elder said.

"Absolutely," Wanda said. "The things I'd eat myself."

"Wanda's possessed," I said. "Everything has to be fresh and made from scratch."

Wanda nodded. "Mr. Button is a stickler for it. Everything."

"You made that potato salad from scratch?" Miss Elder said.

"I did."

Miss Elder smiled. "I might have to try some after all. It looks delicious."

"I'll get you a bowl. Pierre—"

"On it." Pierre leapt up and brought a fourth place mat and utensils to the table. He laid them out in front of Miss Elder. Wanda soon emerged from the galley carrying a plate with a sandwich and a generous helping of potato salad.

"You may as well join us for lunch," Wanda said, sliding the meal in front of Miss Elder.

Two hours later, our colorful train backed its way down Union Station's Track 16. Miss Elder and I stood on the open platform with the conductor, who guided the train in.

"I have to say, this has turned out to be one of the most interesting days of my career," Miss Elder said, taking pictures with her smartphone.

"And you're comfortable that no one's being neglected?" I said.

"I still need to speak to Jane privately," Miss Elder said. "And with Mr. Button, too. But these are just formalities to close out my report."

I panicked.

The governess, the Jesuits, our exhaustive plans for maintaining Jane's health and well-being—these were all devices dreamed up by Wanda, Pierre, and me in our hastily convened meeting around the dining table earlier that day. We had to Google *Jesuits* and *Health and Human Services' dietary guidelines* in order to come up with our talking points. It wasn't that we were insincere about wanting to implement these strategies, it's just that Horace knew nothing about any of it.

I felt sick, certain I was about to be exposed a contemptible liar.

Our train entered the shed and we were engulfed by a familiar twilight. At the track's termination, a small group awaited our arrival: Horace, Billy, Poppy, Dr. Rose, and Jane.

Horace came to the edge of the track. He brandished his walking stick as if it were a baton.

"Ladies and gentlemen," he said. "Boys and girls, children of all ages... Behold the arrival of this magnificent train, on the eve of its passage to glory, ready to take its rightful place in the *dramatis personae* of American history..." He sang the words in a booming voice and made jazz hands as he spoke. His face was crimson.

God help us, I thought. He's drunk.

FIFTY

OUR INEBRIATED MOURNERS boarded the *Pioneer Mother* with the subtlety of a street riot. Horace asked me to find a favorite Elton John CD and play it over the railcar's sound system. "Make it earsplitting," he said.

"How was the service?" I asked.

"A clown act of exhibitionism. Ward politicians, clergy of every religion, including an imam in white pajamas and a Moses beard, and a sitting president who's taken leave of his senses—the Russians missed a golden opportunity to drop a bomb." Horace went to the bar. "I'll have a double Jack Daniel's," he said to Pierre.

He lit a cigar.

Billy joined Horace at the bar. He perched an Italian leather loafer on the brass footrest and ran a hand through his hair. He looked morose.

"Sad day?" Pierre said, pouring Horace's drink.

Billy's eyes darted to meet Pierre's. "Goddamned politicians. They're like Gypsies. Russ Rawlins put the touch on Mother for a big-ticket contribution to his Super PAC. At a funeral, for God's sake!" He turned and glared at me. "Jesus Christ, Jack. Why aren't you on your way to Hawaii?"

Horace jumped in. "Because your Franco-American beauty got outgunned. I made a better offer."

"Stop. I don't want to hear it." Billy lit a cigarette. He looked at Pierre. "Get me a champagne cocktail."

"Of course." Pierre pulled a champagne bottle from an ice bath.

He popped the cork to "Philadelphia Freedom."

In the observation lounge, with Jane looking on, Dr. Rose and Poppy did the fox-trot.

"Doctor or not, Henry," Poppy said, "get your hand off my derriere!"

Jane covered her mouth and laughed.

Billy eyed a Waterford dish on the bar counter. The dish was filled with candied fruits and chocolates.

"What happened to the nuts?" he said.

Pierre pressed the palms of his white gloves together and spoke cheerily. "I thought we'd offer something a little more elegant—"

"All day, all I've wanted was some goddamned nuts," Billy said. "Get this damned Halloween candy out of my face!"

"Yes, sir. I'm sorry." Pierre quickly shoved the bowl under the counter.

In a shadowy corner of the dining room, standing poker-faced, Miss Elder saw everything.

Jane came up to me. "I met the president! He told me the whole country was watching and I had to be strong."

I introduced Jane to Miss Elder.

"I'd like to talk to you after I have a few words with your uncle," Miss Elder said. "Would that be all right?"

Jane glanced at me uncertainly. I nodded. She turned back to Miss Elder.

"Sure, I guess."

"Good," Miss Elder said. "Then we have a date."

Jane squirmed in place for a moment, enduring Miss Elder's maternal scrutiny.

"Can I go?" Jane said to me. "I want to tell Wanda I met the president."

"Yes," I said. "Go."

Jane darted into the galley.

Miss Elder turned to me. "I'm no fan of Ruth Pepper's politics, but being in the presence of that child makes me extremely sad."

Horace left his cigar in an ashtray and came over to us. "A new face," he said to Miss Elder. The glass in his hand brimmed with sour mash whiskey.

"Mr. Button," I said, "meet Miss Elder."

Horace took Miss Elder's hand and gave her a warm smile. "Welcome to the *Pioneer Mother*. Please. Help yourself to a drink from the bar and join our party."

Miss Elder flashed her identification badge. "Mr. Button, I represent D.C. Child and Family Services. I'm following up on a report we received about Jane. I'd like to ask you a few questions."

"Talk to Jack. He's the authority."

"No, Mr. Button, *I'm* the authority. And I need to speak to you. I can't close out my investigation until we talk."

Horace looked at me, his eyes wide. Behind him, Jane emerged from the galley carrying an ornate silver platter lined with deviled eggs.

"Uncle, try an egg?" she said.

"Absolutely." Horace snatched an egg from the tray and shoved it into his mouth, which suddenly took the form of a balloon about to burst. It rendered him dumb.

"Want one?" Jane held the platter up to Miss Elder.

"Goodness, no," Miss Elder said, touching her collarbone. "I'm still full from lunch."

Jane carried the eggs into the observation lounge and passed them around. Miss Elder watched her for a moment, and then turned back to Horace.

"By law you can have someone accompany you when we meet," she said. "Would that help?"

Horace nodded, swallowed hard, and clasped my shoulder. "I nominate Jack."

We convened in Horace's stateroom, shutting the door. I dialed back the speaker volume until "Rocket Man" was barely audible. The three of us stood facing one another, Horace somewhat unsteady on his feet and swirling his glass of Jack Daniel's.

"To start, Mr. Button, I want to say how very sorry I am for the loss of your sister," Miss Elder said. "I understand that it's been a stressful day, and I want to make this as easy as I can on everyone. The charge is that Jane is being neglected due to a lack of adult supervision."

"Oh?" Horace licked yellow egg remnants from his fingertips.

"It's the report we received," Miss Elder said. "And we have an obligation to follow up. I'm going to ask you a few questions. This shouldn't be a big deal. I have every expectation that your answers will allay the agency's concerns. Does that seem fair?"

"Go ahead," Horace said. "Grill me like a prime New York steak." He looked at me and winked.

"For starters, how much have you had to drink today?" Miss Elder said.

"In conventional bottles or magnums?" Horace took a sip of whiskey.

"You're dodging my question. What about these people who came in with you—have they all been drinking, too?"

"Are you kidding? That bunch would drink Aqua Velva if it meant staying tight."

"Then who was sober enough to supervise Jane?"

"Good question." Horace thought for a moment. "I'd have to say the president."

"The president? The president of the United States was the only one sober enough to supervise your niece? You expect me to believe that?"

"Well, he'd lead you to believe he was sober, anyway. I have it on good authority the sanctimonious S.O.B. does his drinking in the dark of night in the White House pantry."

"Tell me, Mr. Button. What has Jane had to eat today?"

Horace scratched his head. "There was a luncheon at the vice president's house at the Naval Observatory, I remember that. A big spread with an open bar..."

"But you have no idea what she's had to eat?"

"She felt sorry for the quail at breakfast, that's all I can tell you."

"His short-term memory gets a little... you know, foggy... when he's been drinking," I said to Miss Elder. I turned to Horace. "We really need to see Dr. Rose about your memory."

"That doddering old croaker?" Horace said. "I'd be better off with a witch doctor."

"Mr. Button, focus a minute," Miss Elder said. "When Jane comes to live with you in San Francisco, what accommodations do you intend to make?"

"Accommodations?" Horace said.

"You know, changes at home or in your work and travel habits?"

Horace made a face. "Haven't given it a moment's thought."

Miss Elder glanced at me.

"You remember, Mr. Button, how we're going to hire a governess?" I said.

"A governess?" Horace said.

I cleared my throat. Horace looked at me and his face brightened.

"Ah, yes! A governess," he said. Then: "Jack, have Pierre bring me a double Hennessy and soda. This bourbon isn't cutting it. I need a sleep enhancer. I feel a nap coming on."

"Mr. Button, please," Miss Elder said. "I have more questions."

Horace sat heavily on the bed.

"I'm old and I'm tired and it's been a long week," he said. "Whatever's about the girl, it's all in Jack's hands."

Miss Elder looked at me and then back at Horace. "And how long have you known Jack?"

"Oh, I'd say a week or two," Horace said. "Best Bloody Marys in the world. It's what got him the bartending job."

"He's a bartender?"

"More than a bartender—a trusted confidant and a Stanford man. Henry vouches for him. He's known Jack, what, five or six years?" Horace looked up at me. "And the chemistry seems good."

"I'm sorry," Miss Elder said. "Who is Henry?"

"Dr. Rose," Horace said.

"The witch doctor?"

"Ha! Witch doctor would be a step up for him."

Miss Elder glanced at her clipboard.

"Jack tells me you've mandated a Jesuit education for Jane," she said.

"Have I?" Horace said.

"You have, Mr. Button," I said. "Don't you remember?"

"You see," Horace said to Miss Elder. "I get the slightest bit plastered and my capacity to remember rides a steady downhill toboggan."

"But the minute he sobers up, he has a great capacity for recollection," I said. "And his vocabulary is nothing short of amazing—he's a prolific writer."

"I'm well aware of his work as a writer," Miss Elder said. "My father's a fan."

Horace looked off in a daze. "Have I told you about the service today? Our pandering president assured us God in Heaven was a Democrat, or at least lined up firmly on the side of democracy and the Progressive agenda, and then Russ Rawlins stood up and shamelessly linked his campaign for the White House to the Lord God Jehovah, hot dogs, and apple pie." He turned to Miss Elder. "He tried to strangle me not too long ago, did you know that?"

"Russell Rawlins tried to strangle you?" Miss Elder looked skeptical.

"But I must say, both he and the president were quite attentive to Jane," Horace continued, nodding. "It was a good service. Jane will remember it always." He took another sip of whiskey.

Miss Elder studied Horace's face intently.

"I have nothing against a religious education," Horace said with a far-off look. "'Yea though I walk through the valley of the shadow of death, I will fear no evil; for thou art with me; thy rod and thy staff they comfort me.'" He flashed a smile. "Imagine being able to smite such wonderful phrasing on your IBM Selectric. Are you a religious person, Miss Elder?"

"Yes, I am," Miss Elder said.

"Then you might believe me when I tell you that in church today I saw a shaft of golden light slanting down from the heavens. Ruth, from beyond the grave. She implored me to take care of Jane. I promised I would, of course…" Horace's eyes filled with tears. "I'll give that little girl anything and everything I have…"

"I think I've heard enough," Miss Elder said. "You can go to sleep now, Mr. Button. I'd like to spend a few minutes with Jane, and then I'll be on my way. And thank you for your hospitality. It's been an enlightening day."

"Wait," Horace said. "You say your father's a fan? Jack, in my closet, there's a box of books. Get one for our friend here. And hand me a pen."

"That's very kind of you, Mr. Button," Miss Elder said quickly. "But I don't accept gifts."

"Nonsense. Jack, fetch me a book."

I gave Horace a new hardcover copy of *Speakeasy* and a Sharpie from his desk drawer.

"Please don't ruin that perfectly good book by writing in it," Miss Elder said. "I can't possibly take it."

"Rubbish," Horace said. "You're only taking it to give it to your father. Now you must tell me his name."

Horace inscribed the book to Miss Elder's father. Clarence Elder was a retired oil and gas attorney who lived in Baton Rouge, Louisiana, where Miss Elder was raised.

"Don't say a word to anyone," Miss Elder said, clutching the book. "But I promise you, Dad will treasure this."

While Miss Elder met with Jane in her stateroom, I traded Horace what was left of his double Jack Daniel's for a full glass of Hennessy and soda. I sat with him.

"In the end we find she's all right," Horace said of Miss Elder. "But what's her obsession with the Jesuits?"

I told him about our lunch conversation.

"In short, I lied," I admitted.

Horace occupied his tongue with an ice cube from his brandy and soda.

"It's only a lie if you don't implement the plan," he said. "And I must admit I like the thinking. Build a team to manage the household and deposit our little baroness at the Birkenstocked feet of the Jesuits."

I stood up. "I should let you nap. Is there anything else I can do for you?"

"One last thing. There's a swanky steak house called Potomac and Olive, off Dupont Circle. The maître d's name is Wolfgang. Tell him we'll be a party of six, arriving between eight and nine. I want the big table in the center of the dining room, nearest the wine locker. You and Jane will join us. We'll drop the bombshell on Billy there. It'll be a watershed moment in company annals—lifted glasses, dinner speeches, and long knives, all rolled into one."

FIFTY-ONE

"GIVE 'EM HERE, MAJORDOMO," Wanda said. "I don't want you touching my panties."

"Ever?"

"Ever." She grabbed the lace-trimmed underwear from my hands. They were still warm from the dryer. We resumed folding clothes, picking underwear, socks, and white T-shirts from the muddled pile on the table in front of us. It was four o'clock in the afternoon. For the time being we had the Capitol Blossom Fluff and Fold to ourselves.

"Can we talk about this?" I said.

"Is that why you came? Not to help but to talk?"

"You've been giving me black looks all day. What is it? What's going on?"

"This was two weeks on a train. So we flirted a little. But now you're talking real life. I live in that house in Hillsborough, too, you know."

I stepped behind her and gripped her at the waist, looking at her face in a wall mirror. We locked eyes.

"Why do you think I took the job?" I said.

"I'm telling you, Majordomo. I'm off-limits."

"I like you, Wanda. Why is that so hard to believe?"

She stepped out of my grasp.

"What about your fiancée?" she said.

"Bianca? Bianca's ancient history. She wants nothing to do with me, and to tell you the truth, I want nothing to do with her."

"But you might want something to do with me?"

"That's what I'm saying."

"It's a terrible idea."

"Why is it terrible?"

"Because. It'll never work."

"Why won't it work?"

"For one, I won't risk my career."

"You won't risk a relationship, is what you mean. You know what happens in football when you play it safe? You sit on the ball and you lose the game."

"I'm not interested in football metaphors. You can't win this, Majordomo, so don't even try. From here on out, it's strictly business between us."

"How about this: If it becomes an issue, I'll be the one who resigns."

"More folding and less talking, Romeo," Wanda said. "Don't forget, we still need to pick up the dry cleaning."

As Wanda was pulling a load of towels from the dryer, I took out my phone and checked the time. I couldn't put it off any longer.

"Expecting a call?" Wanda said.

"I am," I said, "an important one, but there's a call I need to make first."

I went out to the sidewalk in front of the Fluff and Fold.

Giselle answered on the third ring.

"Jack! Billy told me he moved your flight up. Are you in Seattle?"

"I'm sorry, Giselle, but I'm not coming."

Two loud motorcycles rumbled past, followed by a wave of cars. I turned my back to the traffic. I watched through the window of the Laundromat as Wanda worked between the long rows of coin-operated dryers.

There was silence on the other end of the line.

"Giselle? Did I lose you?"

"I'm still here."

"Things have gotten complicated," I said. "It just won't work."

"I see," Giselle said. "What happened?"

"I won't waste your time with a long story."

"But you and I had an agreement."

"I know we did."

"It's so odd. For all intents and purposes you're bankrupt, and I was prepared to give you everything. So what happened, Jack? I'd like to know."

"I've been presented with some opportunities."

"Opportunities?"

"Things too good to pass up."

"Better than first-class travel and sex?"

"Giselle, please."

"I'm speechless. I really don't know what to say."

"I don't know what to say, either. Other than I'm sorry it didn't work out."

"I'm sorry, too," Giselle said. In the background a man was talking. The tone of Giselle's voice became oddly detached. "Jack, was it? I don't think there's anything I can do for you. In fact, I don't know how you got this number."

"How I got—"

"You're really quite a bold young man, if not borderline impertinent. The only thing I can suggest is that you call my office in Century City and make an appointment with my producer. You can tell him we've spoken. But I should warn you. We hire strictly on merit."

I listened patiently while Giselle held forth—I owed her that much. I studied the cartoonish painting on the window of the Laundromat. Someone had portrayed the Capitol dome in white surrounded by cherry trees in full bloom, each pink blossom a single dab of paint. *Who had the patience to do these things?*

"I think I've given you enough of my time," Giselle was saying. She spoke to the man in the background. "Yes, Yuri, but it pisses me off. Tell them I'm on my way, and I expect better." She returned to the phone. "And Jack, whoever you are, I'd appreciate your losing this number. This is highly inappropriate."

She ended the call. I stared at the name across the top of the display: Giselle Lebeau.

The sweetheart of America's kitchen. *My* ticket to Easy Street.

Back inside the Laundromat, at a folding station surrounded by dryers, Wanda was cinching the drawstring on a white canvas bag bulging with clothes. She saw me coming, looked away, and began tying a knot.

"Let me guess," Wanda said. "Miss French Made Easy."

"I had to call her," I said. "It was the decent thing to do—"

"And this is where you tell me you've changed your mind and you're catching a cab to the airport."

"No."

Wanda looked up. "What did she say?"

"Nothing I didn't deserve."

"But you made it clear—"

"Wanda, I'm not going anywhere. I'm staying right here."

She lowered a shoulder and prepared to hoist the bag.

"Here," I said, "let me get that."

I took the bag. Wanda turned away. She was crying.

"Hey, what's wrong?" I said.

"Nothing."

I touched her on the shoulder. "Wanda, what is it?"

She wiped her eyes with both hands. "It makes me sad, that's all."

"You're sad that I'm staying?"

"Sad for what will never be. Because even if we had it... however great it was... I'd eventually screw it up."

"Wanda, nothing in life is that preordained."

"At least Giselle stood a chance of making you happy."

I set the laundry bag on the floor and took Wanda in my arms.

"Listen," I said. "You make me happy. We'll take it slow, all right? See where it goes."

"It's a horrible idea. The answer is no."

"At least tell me you'll think about it."

Wanda brushed her tears with her long fingers. She managed a smile. "This is so embarrassing. I don't usually cry over guys."

I pulled her close. We stood there a long minute, my arms wrapped around her. Someone came into the Laundromat. I didn't look to see who. I heard them open a washer and load it with clothes.

My cell phone rang. It was the call I'd been waiting for.

"Good news, buddy," Arthur said. "I have a spot for you on the train."

"You have a spot?" I looked at Wanda. She stared numbly at the wall, and then she looked up at me, curious.

"The bad news is you're going to have a roommate," Arthur said. "But it's a double bedroom on a sleeper, so it's not like you're sharing a bed, you know? You'll have bunk beds. The Secret Service has your name and car assignment. You're on the official manifest."

"That's great, Arthur. Who's my roommate?"

Arthur paused. "You might want to kill me when I tell you."

FIFTY-TWO

AS THE SUN DROPPED LOW, a brown haze settled over the city. Wanda and I made our way back to Columbus Circle. I took the lead, navigating the disjointed sidewalks, forging a path through the oncoming pedestrians, dodging broken glass and panhandlers and black patches of gum. I carried the laundry sack over one shoulder. In my other hand I gripped the dry cleaning. The snarl of wire hangers cut into my fingers.

"I feel like an elf following Santa Claus," Wanda said. She walked a few steps behind, lugging the rest of the dry cleaning.

"Only the North Pole isn't eighty-five degrees with ninety-nine percent humidity," I said.

We arrived to find Columbus Circle closed to traffic. The arched entrances of Union Station were blocked by crowd-control barricades and armored vehicles. Soldiers manned the wide perimeter. They weren't letting anyone through.

I pled our case to a National Guardsman carrying an M-16 rifle.

"Sorry," he said.

"But we just came from inside there," I said. "Not two hours ago."

"Can you call a supervisor?" Wanda said.

"We have our orders, ma'am. The train station is closed."

"Then when can we get back in?" I said.

"I don't have that information," the soldier said.

"I really think you need to call a supervisor," Wanda said.

A Secret Service agent arrived, wearing a flak vest. He reacted to our

Pioneer Mother identification badges with an indifferent shrug. "Train crew boarding doesn't start until ten tonight," he said. "No exceptions, guy. What can I tell you?"

"So what are we supposed to do?" I said.

"Find a place to sit and wait, I guess."

I glanced at Wanda.

"Okay," she said, "but someone has to explain to Horace Button why he doesn't have any clean clothes. And tell little Jane Pepper why she didn't get dinner."

The Secret Service agent scrutinized Wanda.

"Wait a minute," he said. He turned his back to us and spoke into the sleeve of his shirt.

An imposing African American arrived, his tightly tailored suit showing off his muscular physique. He conferred with the Secret Service agent.

"Said Jane Pepper and Horace Button?" The black agent looked at us. He had striking blue eyes. He beckoned us. "All right. You two follow me."

Special Agent Grier led us through the Main Hall. The sound of our footsteps echoed off the high ceiling. The shops and restaurants were dark.

Near the main Amtrak counter, a temporary work space had been fashioned with pipe and black draping. A troop of Secret Service agents assembled identification badges and boarding packets for the funeral train's crew and passengers. They worked with their suit jackets off, their suspenders, badges, and guns in plain view. Special Agent Grier interrupted a female agent and said he needed our ID badges made up right away. She located our names on the manifest.

Wanda and I were photographed and fingerprinted.

Another agent searched our things. He dumped the contents of the laundry bag and stripped every article of dry cleaning from its hanger, checking pockets, turning pant legs and suit jackets inside out, leaving everything in a heap on a long plastic table.

"We're from the government," I whispered to Wanda. "And we're here to help."

"I heard that," Special Agent Grier said.

Twenty minutes later we had permission to board the train and had our bundles back in hand. Our identification badges were affixed to thick black lanyards that said "U.S. Secret Service." I was assigned to the Pullman sleeper *Desert Sands*, Bedroom D.

At the boarding lounge to Track 16, Wanda and I passed through the automatic doors. What we saw ahead stopped us cold.

The train stretched well beyond the length of the shed. The other tracks had been cleared of all equipment. On the widest section of the station platform, parked parallel to the *Pioneer Mother*, were two black hearses. The next railroad car forward was a gray Amtrak baggage car, its two freight doors open. A forklift was loading a flag-draped coffin inside. A second coffin, identical to the one on the forklift, rested on a mortuary stretcher.

Wanda and I set the laundry bag and dry cleaning down on a bench. We ventured a few steps closer and stopped.

There were no photographers or members of the press—only the mortuary assistants in their black suits, two freight handlers, and the forklift operator.

Alongside the *Pioneer Mother*, Horace, Jane, and Pierre stood watching, their backs to us. Horace held Jane's hand. Elephantine, he dwarfed her. Pierre wore his white steward's jacket. The only sound was the efficient hum of the forklift, its back-up alarm sounding, now on, now off, as the tractor deftly lifted its cargo and placed it inside the baggage car. The busyness of the forklift, combined with the lingering scents of diesel exhaust and creosote oil, gave the massive, nearly empty train shed the feel of a factory floor.

A baggage handler inside the railroad car gave the mortuary assistants a thumbs-up. He jumped down and pulled both doors shut.

As if sensing us behind her, Jane glanced over a shoulder and then ran to us. She buried herself in Wanda's embrace and sobbed. I turned away.

We all watched as the hearses left the station platform quietly. Horace and Jane wept. Wanda wiped tears from her eyes.

We boarded the *Pioneer Mother*, bringing our laundry and dry cleaning with us. Wanda made tea. Horace took a Manhattan to his stateroom—a *dresser*, he called the drink. He wanted to shave and shower before our dinner at Potomac and Olive.

While Jane sat in a parlor chair and listened to Taylor Swift on her iPod, Pierre fussed with bottles behind the bar. I watched him from a barstool. He stopped frequently to wipe his forehead with a kitchen towel—his face glistened with sweat.

"I hated Ruth Pepper's politics," he said in a low voice. "And to be honest, I thought I hated her as a person, too. But now that she's gone... I don't know, it's hard to explain. I have to admire her courage, you know? The way she spoke from the heart and didn't worry about being politically correct. I'm sort of sorry she's gone. It's like only in death did she become a real person. Before that, she was just someone who was easy to hate."

On my way to retrieve my duffel from the equipment locker, I passed Wanda in the galley. She was chopping vegetables. I lingered in the doorway until she noticed me.

"Guess this is it," I said.

"You're out?" Wanda said.

"I want to find my bedroom and get settled before dinner." I stood there a moment, watching her chop.

She glanced at me. "Something you want to say?"

"It doesn't feel right—me going out on the town while you're working."

Wanda stopped chopping and looked at me. "It's what I do, Majordomo. Better get used to it. Go enjoy your dinner."

I located the *Desert Sands* three cars ahead of the baggage car. The refurbished Union Pacific sleeper was bright yellow with silver-fluted siding. Duffel in hand, I climbed five steps up to the vestibule and opened the heavy metal door.

The railroad car was silent. Its weighty blue upholstery reeked of tobacco.

I found my bedroom off the narrow hallway. The upper and lower berths were both deployed and kitted out with sheets, blankets, and bath towels. I set my duffel on the top bunk.

I was dressing, buttoning up a clean shirt, when suddenly a woman squealed in the hallway and the door burst open.

Burt Bannister, the mortician, had an arm around Dagny's waist and was pulling her into the bedroom. In his other hand was a magnum of champagne.

Burt stared at me with an open mouth.

"What the hell?" he said.

I quickly turned to my duffel and plucked out the first necktie I found. "Just a minute and I'll be out of your way."

"No, I mean… what are you doing here? It's Jack, right?"

I showed him my ID badge. "I'm your roommate. Arthur didn't tell you?"

Burt glanced at Dagny. "Shit. I guess not."

Dagny backed against a bulkhead, eyes on the ceiling, and crossed her arms.

Burt smiled at me contritely. "Just blowin' off a little steam, you know? It's been a long week."

I draped the tie around my neck and grabbed my blue blazer from the bed.

"This dinner should go late," I said. "The room's all yours."

"Hey," Burt said, "we're not… I mean… no one's sleeping on this thing tonight. Just thought we'd check out the room and enjoy a quick glass of champagne, you know, before we push off." He looked around at Dagny. "Pretty nice room, don't you think?"

"Oh, it's real nice, all right." Dagny spoke to the ceiling. According to her Secret Service badge she'd been assigned *Desert Sands*, Roomette 5.

I zipped my duffle. "Okay, I'm gone. The bottom bunk's yours, Mr. Bannister—"

"Hey, call me Burt!"

"Burt. As I was saying, take the bottom bunk, if that's all right with you."

"Bottom's fine with me," Burt said buoyantly, looking around at Dagny. "I'm a sleep-on-the-bottom type of guy, when you get right down to it."

Dagny shook her head disconsolately.

Burt began opening the champagne. "Don't let us rush you out. C'mon, roomie. Stay and join us for a drink."

"I'll take a rain check," I said.

FIFTY-THREE

WITHOUT SO MUCH AS A GLANCE at the stylish woman behind the hostess stand, without an inkling of apology to the well-heeled patrons waiting in the lobby, and without breaking stride even for Wolfgang, the maître d'hôtel who directed a brigade of servers, bussers, captain waiters, and sommeliers, Horace pushed forward into the spacious dining room and staked a claim on the best table in the house. No establishment underling—indeed, no *propriétaire* in his right mind—would dare ask Horace Button to wait for a table.

The rest of us followed in Horace's wake. The room was elegantly done in dark wood paneling and colorful artwork. A floor-to-ceiling wine vault sparkled behind thick glass. The table Horace claimed sat center stage before the wine vault. Heads turned as we settled into our chairs: Horace and Billy at opposing ends; Dr. Rose and Poppy filling in on one side; Jane and I on the other. Dr. Rose and Poppy were already half-bagged from the ride over in the limousine, where they free-poured from a handle of Bombay Sapphire. At adjacent tables, the diners looked disapprovingly at us—we, these artless yokels, invading their tony chophouse and without waiting to be seated. A few openly scowled at Jane... Why, the nerve of bringing a child into Potomac and Olive! On a Friday night, no less! And seizing the most prestigious table in the house as if this were a Pizza Hut!

And then, a remarkable thing happened.

Across the dining room, a man stood. He faced our table with a somber expression and began clapping his hands in a metronomic cadence. As it sank in that Jane Pepper and Horace Button had entered their midst, the other patrons got to their feet and began to clap. Soon everyone in the dining room was giving Horace and Jane a standing ovation. Even the restaurant staff stopped working and enthusiastically joined the applause.

Jane looked around, surprised. Horace stared straight ahead, his face impassive. At first I thought he was annoyed by this unexpected accolade, but then he reached out and gave Jane's hand a squeeze. His big basset-hound eyes blinked back tears.

By the time the ovation subsided, Wolfgang stood beside our table. He warmly welcomed us while a dark-complected, dignified sommelier poured champagne.

There were toasts to David and Ruth, of course, and to Jane for her courage. Billy saluted Poppy for showing up the flotilla of elegant women at the Naval Observatory.

"Did you catch it?" Billy said. "She had the president staring at her diamond necklace."

"My boobs, more like it!" Poppy said.

"She said *boobs*," Jane whispered to me.

"Mother, please! I'm trying to make a toast." Billy lifted his champagne flute and said to the rest of us, "To Poppy Whitehead, the classiest dame in Washington. At least for one last night."

Dr. Rose looked around restlessly. "Has this noodle shop got a dance floor? I feel like doing the bossa nova."

Poppy slapped him on the arm. "Henry, behave! You're sitting across from a poor orphan, and all you can think about is getting your ashes hauled."

Dr. Rose gazed drunkenly, adoringly at Poppy. He took her hand.

"Have you told them yet?" he asked.

Poppy stared into the old doctor's eyes and gave him a cougar growl.

Billy regarded the two of them warily. "Told us what?"

"I finally wore her down," Dr. Rose said. "The old firehorse and I are going away on a vacation."

"It's true," Poppy said. "We're checking in for a week at a dude ranch in Steamboat Springs. We're going to drive heifers."

"Mother," Billy said, "that's irresponsible. You're too old to be in a relationship, much less driving heifers!"

"Oh, shut it, Billy. I've driven more heifers than you'll ever know."

Jane, her expression turning stormy, planted both elbows on the table and quietly began to cry. She brought her linen napkin to her face.

"Hey." I put an arm around her thin shoulders.

"My dear poor girl," Poppy said. "I can tell you this: We lose people in life. Some leave us way too soon, and there's little rhyme or reason why—"

"But it's all my fault," Jane snuffled. "I'll never see them again."

"Oh, darling," Poppy said. "Don't be so sad. Your uncle has a lovely home in Hillsborough. You'll live like a queen."

Billy smirked at Horace. "Just how many queens can that house accommodate, anyway?"

"Billy," Poppy said. "Zip it!"

Jane kept crying. I finally took her out of the restaurant. We sat on a bench near the glass double doors. The night was warm. All along the tree-lined street, people flowed in and out of the bars and restaurants. Cicadas chirped noisily in the branches overhead.

Jane grasped the linen napkin tightly and held it to her face. She took air in gulps.

"Jane, I want to talk to you," I said. "Can you listen a minute?"

She nodded faintly.

"Those people, the ones who killed your mom and dad, they were predators," I said. "They were hunting them. They would have tracked them down no matter where they were. People that evil would have no problem planting a bomb in a camp full of kids, if that's where they could get their target. For all we know, by staying in New Hampshire an extra week, you saved the lives of a lot of your friends." I put a hand on her back. "Guilt is only appropriate when you've done something wrong. You didn't do anything wrong, okay?"

"Okay." Jane spoke in a tiny voice.

"You had eleven, almost twelve years with two parents who loved you very much," I said. "In that time they taught you a lot: how to love and show compassion, how to be a good friend, how to stand up for yourself and fight for the things you believe in. Those qualities are in you now—they make you who you are. That's a gift from your parents that you'll never lose. Are you following me?"

"Yes," Jane said.

"More than anything," I said, "your mom and dad would want to see you lead a full and happy life. That's how you can honor them—by being the best person you can, by making the most of every day and every opportunity that comes your way. Does that make sense?"

"Yes."

"They wouldn't want to see you consumed by guilt, especially unwarranted guilt." I looked down at her. "So no more guilt, okay?"

"Okay."

"Do you promise?"

"I promise."

I gave her a hug. She hugged me back.

"Can I tell you something?" Jane said, still hanging on.

"Sure."

"I prayed you wouldn't go to Hawaii."

"That makes me happy to hear that," I said. "Happier than you'll ever know."

Jane and I rejoined the others at the table.

"Are we ready to convene the board dinner?" Horace said to me. He sat in his chair like royalty.

Billy looked up from his champagne flute. "What board is that?"

"The *Sunshine Trails* corporate board." Horace turned to Poppy. "I thought your idiot son might like the opportunity to dine with his newest director." He gestured to me.

Poppy scoffed. "Ha! The train steward." She waved her champagne flute at the sommelier. "And this Mexican stable boy's the Pope!"

Billy inspected me hostilely. "I still don't get why you aren't in Hawaii."

"Because he has better things to do," Horace said. "Like vote my father's shares in the company."

Billy froze.

"That's right, Billy," Horace said. "You heard me correctly." He raised his cell phone for everyone to see. "This little thing with no wires, it's amazing and rather useful. I've used it to talk to lawyers on both coasts, including our corporate counsel in San Francisco. He's confirmed everything."

Billy settled back in his chair. He gave Horace a self-satisfied smile and lifted his champagne flute by its stem. "I have to hand it to you, Horace. You're pretty clever. It only took you twelve years to figure it out."

Poppy looked from Horace to Billy. "Billy, what the hell is he talking about?"

"*Sunshine Trails*," Billy said. "Turns out technically you and I don't control the company." He glared at Horace.

"But that's absurd," Poppy said. "Of course we do!"

"Sorry, Mother." Billy forced a smile. "I take it the hundred and sixty shares finally showed up?"

"The estate attorney found the stock certificate in Ruth's strongbox and put two and two together," Horace said. "She's a very savvy lady."

"I suppose now you're going to tell me I work for an eleven-year-old," Billy said.

"No. You work for me and Jack," Horace said. "He'll be voting the Trust's shares."

"Jack? Why Jack?"

"The trust agreement is explicit in its prohibition against self-dealing," Horace said. "I had to find someone with an arm's-length relationship to the magazine. Jack agreed to step in."

"Come on. Jack's a brain-damaged gigolo," Billy said. "This is the *swing vote* you're talking about. He'll effectively control the magazine."

Poppy's eyes bugged. "The steward? Controlling *Sunshine Trails*?"

Dr. Rose turned quickly from Poppy to me. "You go, Jack!"

"I don't understand," Poppy said. "How is that possible?"

"An overlooked detail in the ownership structure, Mother," Billy said. "You and I in fact lack the authority to call the shots."

Poppy's face hardened. "But that's a crock!" she said.

"The year was 1973," Horace began. "Lincoln and I stumbled across the *Pioneer Mother* for sale, and we had to have her. We borrowed the money from my father and secured the loan with a hundred sixty shares of voting common stock. Cash was tight in those days—we had a lot of extra expenses, you know, just getting the old girl fixed up and roadworthy—so, giving my father those stock shares seemed a lot easier than paying off the loan. Then he died, and the shares were passed to Ruth. I'd forgotten all about it until Lisa French brought it up."

Billy said, "My dad told me your father never had an interest in voting those shares."

"What was there to vote on?" Horace said. "The magazine was soon riding high. Your dad ran the business side, I focused on editorial and entertainment. The company grew of its own accord. We were all perfectly contented."

Poppy weighed in. "I'll say. Those were good years!"

Horace stared angrily at Billy. "Now you've run things into the ground."

"*I* have?" Billy said.

"Yes!" Horace said forcefully, pounding the table. "And as fifty-one percent owners, Jack and I have no choice but to take control."

Billy eyeballed me dismissively. "Jack doesn't know the first thing about running a magazine. Do you, Jack?"

"Zero," I agreed.

Billy turned back to Horace. "But he can get to Giselle. That's where we need him most—horizontal in Hawaii."

Horace's face went crimson. "What the hell, Billy. You've known it all along? That those shares were out there in my family's name!"

"Damn right I've known it!" Billy said. "And I didn't tell you for the same reason my father never did. You don't have the discipline to run a magazine. Someone else had to deal with the accountants and lawyers and advertisers while you were out on the town, whooping it up." He turned to me. "You'll learn, Jack. He's like a 300-pound hummingbird. All he wants to do is eat and drink and flit here and there, being the life of the party. He gets away with it, too, because there's always some-one following behind to clean up the mess. But then I imagine you've already gleaned that lovely side to him."

"Don't grovel for your job at the dinner table, Billy," Horace said. "It's unbecoming of a gentleman."

Billy turned to me. "So let me ask you, Jack. What do you know about serving on a board of directors? How does being a bartender qualify you for the position?"

"I can answer that," Horace said.

"No, let him speak for himself." Billy kept his eyes fixed on me. "Go on, Jack. What's your first act as a director?"

Everyone stared. I hesitated for a moment, gathering my thoughts.

"The first thing I'd do," I said, fingering a knife, "is review the board resolutions that were made after those shares were issued, to ensure compliance with the corporate bylaws. Next I'd call for a compensation audit of the executive team. For every dividend or bonus payment that went out, I'd want to make sure the necessary shareholder consent was obtained, and the required board resolutions were made."

Billy appeared dumbstruck.

"Recuperating at Stanford," I said. "I sat in on a lot of classes at the business and law schools."

"I can vouch for that," Dr. Rose said. "I pushed his wheelchair!"

Billy shot Dr. Rose a nasty look. He moved his glass of champagne to another spot, as if it were a piece in a chess match. "That's all water under the bridge," he said to Horace. "Dividends and bonuses—you can't ask people to pay that stuff back."

"In fact, we'll insist on it," Horace said. "We'll pursue it legally if we have to—it's called a clawback provision."

Billy's face reddened. He looked from Horace to me. "What about Giselle?"

"We're putting the deal on hold," Horace said. "Jack and I need to study the merits."

Billy gave me a smug smile. "I think Jack already has a deep understanding of Giselle's merits."

"Another thing, Jack," Horace said. "When we get back to San Francisco, I want you to meet one-on-one with each of those pompous, freeloading editors. I'm afraid they've subordinated their sensibilities to the political flavors of the month. Report back to me with your impressions—who should stay and who should go. That fellow Nigel is a particularly vile little swine."

Billy turned to me. "Trust me, Jack. You don't want Horace running things. He'll leave your little client destitute."

"Who's your client?" Jane asked, looking up at me.

FIFTY-FOUR

"ARE YOU DRUNK?" Pierre asked.

"No," I said. Midnight approached. We worked shoulder to shoulder in the dimly lit galley, making spring rolls for a reception Horace and Rosalind were hosting in the morning.

"A little buzzed?" Pierre said.

I concentrated on cutting cucumber and mango matchsticks. Several glasses of champagne, a dirty gin martini, and too much wine had affected my dexterity.

"Just slow with a knife," I said. "Doesn't mean I'm drunk."

Pierre nimbly assembled the fillings on beds of basil, mint, and cilantro leaves. The responsibility for rolling up the rice paper rested squarely on his shoulders.

"So tell me again," I said. "Why were you so afraid of that Child Services lady?"

"Because she was from Baton Rouge."

"And what's wrong with that?"

"Everyone from Baton Rouge knows Bruneau's GatorWorld. The government's been trying to shut us down for years. If she knew who my family was, she'd have me thrown off this train."

"Your family runs an alligator park?"

The service chime rang. Horace was in the observation lounge, smoking an after-dinner cigar.

"It's my father's thing," Pierre said. "I want no part of it and never did. Alligators are disgusting, opportunistic demons." He quickly rinsed and

319

dried his hands. "Be right back."

Pierre left the galley. I was still cutting matchsticks when Wanda came in. The shoe box she set on the counter was sealed with transparent tape and adorned with stickers and Post-it notes.

"How's it going?" she said.

"Getting there." I reached for another cucumber. "How's Jane?"

"The poor thing's exhausted. Today's hitting her pretty hard."

"Do you want me to stay?"

Wanda stared at me with disbelief. "With Pierre in the upper bunk? Not a chance."

"I meant to help with Jane."

"Oh," she said. "No. One of us might as well get some sleep."

I stopped cutting for a moment. Wanda's face was uncharacteristically pale.

"You feeling okay?" I asked.

"Fine, just a little exhausted myself." She looked at the rice paper rounds. "There is something you can do, though."

"What's that?"

"Put Snickers in the baggage car."

"Snickers?"

Wanda handed me the shoe box. "Jane's dead cat. She wants him in with the caskets."

I tilted the box. Something shifted inside.

"Tell me there isn't a dead cat in here," I said.

"Strictly symbolic—one of her stuffed animals. I promised her that you'd do it tonight."

"Me? Tonight? The Secret Service will probably blow my brains out."

"Come on, Majordomo. It means a lot to Jane."

"Why don't you do it, then?"

"I inherited my mother's fear of ghosts. I make it a point to avoid coffins after dark."

The vestibule of the *Pioneer Mother* was poorly lit and oddly cool. Carrying the shoe box, I crossed the steel ramp that bridged us to the baggage car. I expected—hoped—the door of the baggage car would be locked. To my surprise, the handle swung down freely. I opened the heavy door.

The small, high windows in the side doors yielded a tinge of light. I could make out the two caskets in the center of the car. The air smelled like the dirt cellar of an old house. Behind me the self-closing door swung shut with a loud bang.

"Don't worry, your eyes will adjust," Rosalind said. The sound of her voice made me jump.

"Jesus, you scared me," I said. "Where are you?"

"Over here."

My free hand made contact with the steel shell of the baggage car's interior wall, and I picked my way around the first coffin. Ahead of me on the floor was an indistinct shadow.

"You're on my shit list, you know," Rosalind said. "I specifically told you to stay away from the press."

"I don't think we were wrong," I said. "Do you?"

Rosalind sighed. "Who knows anymore? I've lost the ability to think."

"Mind if I sit?"

"By all means."

I dropped stiffly to the floor and sat against the wall with her.

"What brings you here at this hour?" I said.

"I should ask you the same thing."

"I'm making a delivery. The Snickers memorial shoe box."

I could see Rosalind more plainly now. She wore her hair down and had her arms wrapped around her knees. In the faint light, wearing jeans and a baggy sweatshirt, she appeared younger and much softer—a college-aged camp counselor, maybe.

"What about you?" I said. "Couldn't sleep?"

"They got the guys that did it."

"The terrorists?"

"On Jekyll Island—off the coast of Georgia. A nighttime shoot-out on the golf course. Both dead." Her voice was flat.

"I guess that's good news."

"I felt compelled to come tell Ruth. Hoping for closure, but it didn't really help."

"Do you know who they were?"

"It'll all come out tomorrow. Al-Umer er Raisuli—the AUR. We were pushing to have them classified as a foreign terrorist organization. So they killed Ruth."

"Thereby proving your point. What a bunch of morons."

We sat for a time in silence.

"It wasn't supposed to end this way," Rosalind said.

I looked at her. "Tell me about you and Ruth."

"I first heard her speak at an Ag-Government Summit in Las Vegas," Rosalind said. "That was probably six or seven years ago. She was mayor of Winnemucca. The summit was on ranchland protection and sustainable communities, something sophomoric like that, and Ruth really laid it out on the table. She asked how a handful of thirty-something lawyers from Washington with poli-sci degrees could possibly know more about sustainable ranching than the families who'd been doing it for a hundred years. She was fearless, the way she called out the political ruling classes of both parties for destroying our country. I had to agree with her. The next thing I knew I was running her campaign for the Senate. I lost my marriage over it."

"Your marriage?"

"The man I was married to—he traveled in Washington's inner circles, and he was embarrassed to have a wife who was politically associated with Ruth Pepper."

A long silence. "When did you last see her?" I said.

"I was with her the night she was killed. She appeared at a fundraiser for a former Marine officer running for Congress—this was in Virginia. Ruth's speech was interrupted I don't know how many times by protesters. Afterwards, she was kind of down. She said she should've handled the hecklers better, and it bothered her that the actual candidate never really got a chance to be heard. 'I guess it would've been easier to be a Liberal'—those were the last words I ever heard her speak."

I studied Rosalind's profile. Her eyes glistened.

"That night," she continued, "when my father learned of Ruth's death, he got in his pickup truck and drove from North Carolina straight through to Washington. I met him at the door of my townhouse and did something I hadn't done in twenty years. I wept in his arms." Rosalind wiped her eyes. We sat without speaking for a minute, and then she turned to me. "I don't know what you said to placate D.C. Child and Family Services, but it must've been a whopping piece of fiction."

My gaze settled on the high windows, which were opaque with grime.

"It was you, wasn't it?" I said. "The one who reported Jane being neglected."

"Yes." Rosalind looked up at those same windows. "He was so... awful in those first days. I wanted to petition the court to remove him as guardian. I knew a negative finding from Child Services would bolster my case and make it easier to take Jane away from him."

"And my press conference this morning was just a lot of bluster, like Miss Elder said." I looked at Rosalind. "Are you still going to file the petition?"

"No, Lisa French convinced me it's best that Jane stay with her uncle. How'd you get him to come around, finally?"

"He pretty much did it on his own, once he realized he'd have help. I've decided he's going to give Jane a good life, whether he knows it or not."

"You're taking on a lot, being trustee." Rosalind said. "You have a fiduciary responsibility, you know that, right?"

"Yes."

"And when the time comes, which it inevitably will, you'll stand up to Mr. Button? You'll do what's right for Jane and Jane only?"

"I will, Rosalind. You have my word." I turned to her. "What about you? What's next?"

"I'll probably go home to Winston-Salem. Maybe run for Congress. Someone needs to pick up the torch."

"Well, good for you."

Rosalind looked at me. "Does that mean you'll take my call when I ask for a campaign contribution?"

"Absolutely. So will Jane's uncle."

"I'll hold you to it."

I silently mulled my future. She may have been doing the same.

"Here," I said, "we can't forget this." I scooted forward and placed the shoe box equidistant between the two caskets. "How does it look?"

"Like it belongs," Rosalind said. "I think you should say a few words."

I thought for a moment.

"Rest in peace, Snickers," I said. "Jane says you were a good cat."

FIFTY-FIVE

OUR SATURDAY MORNING DEPARTURE LOOMED. In the double bedroom aboard the *Desert Sands*, I zipped my duffel shut. Burt Bannister stood over my shoulder. A Red Cap waited patiently in the doorway.

"I don't want you thinking Dagny's a trollop," Burt said to me in a low voice. "It's only that Mrs. Bannister and I are going through a bad time."

"Burt, stop," I said. "I'm happy to switch."

"You sure?"

"Of course. What are roommates for?"

Burt turned to the Red Cap. "Throw everything on the bottom bunk."

The Red Cap brought two sets of bags into the bedroom. One soft bag hit the mattress with the distinct sound of bottles clinking together. Burt looked sheepish.

"Okay, so I brought a little scotch," he said.

I carried my duffel out into the narrow hallway, which smelled of fresh coffee. Dagny lurked in the vestibule, her black pebble-leather Coach bag at her feet. She filed her nails and avoided eye contact.

I went down the hallway to find my new quarters. The doorway of each roomette was adorned with a set of blue drapes, which made the hallway seem even narrower. People and luggage filled the aisle. Rock music, ebullient greetings, laughter—the charged atmosphere reminded me of moving into a college dorm.

In the roomette that had been assigned to Dagny, I found a comfortable chair at a large window. On the chair was a boarding packet. The official roster of the Congressional Delegation listed eight senators and seven congressmen, including the Speaker of the House. Russell Rawlins was one of the senators. He was in the dome car *Anchorage*, three cars back.

The packet included a detailed timetable. We were backtracking the way we'd come on the Capitol Limited and Zephyr: Chicago, Denver, then over the Rockies to Utah and Nevada. We were scheduled to arrive in Winnemucca on Tuesday, September 5, at 8:00 a.m. Ruth and David's graveside service would be that morning at eleven.

Tucked in the packet was Dagny's invitation to the ten o'clock open-house reception aboard the *Pioneer Mother*.

Leaving the door open and the curtains pulled back, I unpacked my things, and then I stepped out into the hallway to see what was going on. The girl in the roomette across the way was laying out a laptop computer, an iPad, an expensive pair of Bose headphones, and a tall bottle of water.

"I'm Jack," I said, extending my hand.

"Alexa." We shook. She was about my age and had long black hair. According to her badge, she was a Zone One, which meant she was confined to the public-access carriages—all the sleepers, coaches, bar cars, and dining cars forward of the *Desert Sands*.

"You're on Senator Pepper's staff?" I said.

"I think half the people assigned to this car are."

"What did you do for her?"

"Me? Speech writing and media relations, mainly."

"I'm so sorry. It must be awful to deal with."

"It hasn't really hit me yet," Alexa said. "I still can't believe she's gone." She studied my badge, which I began to realize was something of a status symbol. My three-zone privileges gave me full access to the train. I could pass through the vista dome cars immediately behind the *Desert Sands*, where the Congressional Delegation was housed, and I could travel freely through the baggage car to the *Pioneer Mother*.

"What about you?" Alexa said. "What do you do?"

Her question left me tongue-tied.

"Hello, hello!" said a clownish man with a digital video camera in front of his face. "Smile for the camera!" He was walking the length of the train, capturing footage of the showy and sometimes gaudy interiors of the vintage railroad cars. The *Desert Sands* received a steady stream of these videographers, most of them members of the press. At the end of our sleeper car, a Secret Service agent blocked the way to the rest of the train and told the visitors they'd reached the end of the line.

Twenty minutes before departure time, I disembarked and set out for the *Pioneer Mother*. Track 16 was a flurry of activity. Congressmen, senators, staffers, reporters—everyone I passed seemed to know one another. Skirting the handshakes and backslaps, I walked alongside the delegation's three silver-fluted vista dome cars. Steam shot from underneath their car bodies; air hissed at their coupling apparatuses; generators hummed. There was movement in the filmy windows of the *Anchorage*: the white-uniformed sleeve of a steward working behind a bar and a gloved hand placing a rose in a vase on a table. Up in the dome, a man in a seersucker suit sipped a cocktail.

I boarded the *Pioneer Mother* at the rear, where a crowd of VIPs packed the open platform. They held glasses of champagne and listened to a paunchy, white-haired senator from Georgia describe the raging gun battle that had killed the AUR terrorists. Jekyll Island was a barrier island off the coast of the state, and the senator knew the topography.

"It's where they filmed *Bagger Vance*," he was saying.

I squeezed my way through the knot of men and entered the packed observation lounge. The Speaker of the House was talking to Rosalind, who wore a stylish dress and had her hair down the way I'd seen it in the baggage car the night before. Ahead of me, Horace recounted a story for an audience that included Burt and Dagny.

Arthur found me in the crowd. "So do you want to kill me?"

"No. Why would I?"

"Not worried that your roommate will harvest your organs and embalm you in your sleep?"

"Change of plans," I said. "I traded rooms with his administrative assistant."

"Oh." Arthur looked at Dagny. "Oh!"

Arthur spotted Rosalind talking with the Speaker and then excused himself to join them.

Behind the bar, a second bartender helped Pierre. His slicked-back hair was gray at the temples. He took drink orders without looking up, and he started making the drinks even before the customers finished ordering them. His button-down uniform shirt had *Anchorage* embroidered over the pocket.

"Champagne?" The pretty girl passing a tray of brimming champagne flutes smiled at me. She wore the same button-down *Anchorage* shirt.

"Sure, thanks," I said.

I looked around.

Who *were* all these people?

There was a sudden stir near the galley. The tall man making his way into the observation lounge was Russell Rawlins.

The train had begun inching forward. It was such a smooth and gentle start that some of the people around me expressed skepticism that we were actually underway. Mike Duckworth, who chaired the House Ways and Means Committee, bent down and peered out a window.

"We're moving, all right," he said.

Someone tugged at my hand.

"Take me out there," Jane said. "Please. I want to see us leave!"

We couldn't get past the doorway. The open platform was crowded with sightseers.

"We can try the forward vestibule," I said.

"No, I want to be out there." Jane crossed her arms and glared at the interlopers.

When the senator from Georgia saw Jane standing there, he graciously rounded everyone up and herded them inside. I thanked him for yielding the prime vantage point.

"Hey, she's the important one here," the senator said.

Jane and I stepped to the railing. By this time, we were clear of the train shed. The railroad yard unfolded all around us, rows of empty tracks gleaming in the hazy sun, a snarl of power lines racing above our heads, dipping and diving as we went.

Horace opened the door to the platform.

"I see you've found the best seat in the house," he said. He carried a Manhattan. He held the door open for Rosalind.

"Is there a lot of wind? I don't want my hair getting blown all over," Rosalind said.

"For God's sake," Horace told her. "Let your hair blow."

Rosalind grimaced, donned sunglasses, and joined us at the railing.

Even on the main line, our train maintained a somber pace— Rosalind's hair barely stirred. In the brambles and thick green foliage of the right-of-way, mourners began to appear. They stood silently, hats and caps held over their hearts. Many of them held American flags—too many to count.

"Uncle, what are all these people doing out here?" Jane said.

"They've come to pay their respects to your mom and dad," Horace said.

"Can I wave to them?"

"Certainly."

"Look, Uncle—a man in a tree!" Jane waved eagerly.

Mourners lined both sides of the track. They clustered at grade crossings and amassed on the platforms of urban commuter stations. Lines of police officers and military personnel in uniform stood at attention and saluted our train. American flags hung from overpasses, pedestrian bridges, and the extended ladders of fire trucks. Digital billboards in front of schools and churches offered succinct tributes: "God Bless America!"; "We Love You Ruth!"; "Prayers for the Pepper Family."

With our train's mournful pace, and with people so close to the tracks, we could hear everything that was said, but few words were spoken. On a bluff above the roadbed, a bagpiper played "Danny Boy." At one grade crossing, a sax player gave a stirring rendition of "Amazing Grace." On a whistle-stop train platform, a church choir sang "America the Beautiful."

In a matter of fifteen minutes we must have passed nearly ten thousand people.

Jane flitted back and forth on the open platform, waving.

From behind the anonymity of her black sunglasses, Rosalind watched these scenes unfold. "This must be driving Russ Rawlins mad, not being the center of attention," she said to Horace.

He glanced over his shoulder. "The senator is at the window as we speak, pacing like a caged lion."

Rosalind smiled. "If Ruth were here, she'd boot him off this train."

"Then, in her honor, we should do the next best thing," Horace said. "Let's get him out here."

"God spare me," Rosalind said. "Why would you want that?"

"His political views are rooted in lies and delusion," Horace said. "Let him see for himself how much the world loved Ruth."

"Please tell me you're kidding."

"Come on," Horace said. "It'll be fun." He swallowed the last of his Manhattan, flung the ice onto the tracks, and pushed open the door.

"All right, you grandstanding son of a bitch," Horace said to Senator Rawlins over the din. "Come out here and give the citizenry a sporting chance at a clean head shot."

"My pleasure, thank you," Senator Rawlins said, stepping past Horace to the open platform.

Was he deaf?

The senator went straight to Rosalind and embraced her.

"How you holding up, kid?" he said. "That was a magnificent service you put on yesterday."

Rosalind slipped free of the senator's grasp and took a step back.

"Thank you, Senator," she said. "And thank you again for your kind remarks."

"Heartfelt," Senator Rawlins said. "I meant every word. God, I wish you were a Democrat."

"That isn't going to happen, I'm afraid," Rosalind said.

"No? It'd mean an important post in my White House. First floor of the West Wing."

"Flattering but highly improbable. If you'll excuse me, it's gotten a little blowy out here." Rosalind ducked past Senator Rawlins and went inside.

Senator Rawlins looked after Rosalind for a long moment. He turned and went to Jane. He squatted to her eye level and took both of her hands.

"And what about you, princess?" he said. "How you holding up?"

"Okay, I guess," Jane said.

"You're an inspiration, you know that?" Senator Rawlins said. "Just so gutsy and brave. Tell me, what do you think of our little train here?"

"I think it's very exciting. I never expected to see so many people by the tracks."

Senator Rawlins straightened up. "You've got your mother's populist roots."

"Huh?" Jane wrinkled her nose and looked at me.

"I've been watching you," Senator Rawlins said. "You're a good little waver, you know that? Can you show me how you do it?"

"How I wave?"

"What's your technique? I may be running for president, and I could use a lesson."

We were passing through a small, tree-lined town. Jane turned enthusiastically to the railing and began waving to people on both sides of the tracks.

"You have to be fast," she said to the senator. "Try not to miss anyone."

"Can I do it with you?" Senator Rawlins said.

"If you want."

Senator Rawlins went to the center of the railing and started waving to the mourners. In no time he was singling out certain men and women along the tracks, pointing at them, bugging his eyes, opening his mouth, making the caricature of an astonished face.

"Go back to Rhode Island, jack wagon!" yelled a man in a camouflage jacket holding an American flag.

"Bite me, ass monkey!" Senator Rawlins called back.

The door to the observation lounge swung open, and a Secret Service agent came out to the platform.

"Sorry, Senator, but you need to come inside," the agent said. "You're too exposed out here."

"Nonsense," Senator Rawlins said. "These people love me. See those faces? They're lighting up." He kept waving.

"Really, Senator, you can't be out here. I'm afraid I have to insist—"

"Christ. What a bunch of baloney."

Jane looked at Senator Rawlins. "Why can't you be out here?"

"Too many crazies with Bibles and flags," Senator Rawlins said. "The Secret Service doesn't trust them."

Dismayed, Jane looked at Horace. "Do I have to go inside, too?"

"No," Horace said. "You can stay. As long as someone's out here with you."

"I'll give you some advice, little one," Senator Rawlins said to Jane. "The same thing I once told your mother. Stay out of politics. It'll ruin your life."

As Senator Rawlins was leaving the platform, he stopped to acknowledge me, offering his right hand. "Hiya, sport, Russ Rawlins."

"Jack Marshall," I said.

The senator eyed me curiously. He clasped my hand with a firm grip. "Have we met?" he said.

"You cost him his job," Horace said. "That night at Mount Hollow— Jack was the bartender."

"You don't say." The senator pumped my hand again. "Not one of my finer moments. Sorry."

"Your chief of staff did him a favor, getting him dismissed from the Hollow," Horace said. "Now he sits at my nightly dinner table, above the salt."

Senator Rawlins gave me a bemused grin. "Whatever the hell that means," he said. "I'm glad to hear it." He clapped me on the shoulder. "Come on. I'll buy you a drink."

"Hear that?" Horace said to me. "It's ingrained in the professional Democrat. He'll happily buy you a drink when it's someone else's liquor."

Senator Rawlins laughed. "And I intend to eat you out of house and home and smoke your cigars while I'm at it."

"The time has come to exercise a little government austerity," Horace said.

"Forget it," Senator Rawlins said. "Ain't gonna happen."

"Coming in with us, Jack?" Horace said.

I turned to Jane. She looked at me with pleading eyes and faintly shook her head.

"No thanks," I said to Horace and Senator Rawlins. "I'll stay out here a while."

FIFTY-SIX

AFTER THE RECEPTION, Horace lingered over Bloody Marys at the bar with a small collection of newly minted friends. Their little party flourished until the middle of the afternoon, when they all ran out of gas. Horace invited Russell Rawlins, Burt Bannister, and Dagny to return for dinner.

"The mortician and his mistress I can understand," I said to Horace. "But Senator Rawlins? It was my impression you despised him."

"I do," Horace said. "But if he's going to be president, I thought exposing him to my Conservative sensibilities might elevate his Liberal depravities. Besides, the man tells wonderful lies."

At eight o'clock that evening, we were all gathered again with Horace and Jane at the *Pioneer Mother*'s bar. Vivaldi's "Four Seasons" played over the satellite radio. The dining table was set for six. Looking elegant in his black tie and tails, Pierre mixed martinis. Senator Rawlins had the floor.

"First District of Rhode Island, late sixties, I'm in my first race for a congressional seat. It's midnight. We've got flashlights and notepads, and we're combing a cemetery in Middletown for names and birthdates. We're going to register them all to vote, of course, and they're going to pull the lever for Rawlins. One of the volunteers says he's going to skip a row of headstones, something about overgrowth and the names being too hard to read. 'Like hell you will,' I said. 'Those people have as much right to vote as anyone in this cemetery!'"

The adults around the bar guffawed.

Jane turned to me, perplexed. "Dead people voting?"

Suddenly, the train decelerated. After a series of sharp jolts, we labored along at a sluggish pace. Jane looked eagerly at her uncle.

"Yes. Go," Horace said.

Jane leaped off her barstool and hurried out to the open platform.

I followed.

It was dusk. We were somewhere on the outskirts of Toledo, Ohio. Like the others we'd passed that day, most of these trackside mourners stood in reverential silence, many with their hands and hats over their hearts, but along with their signs and American flags they held cigarette lighters and candles. A barrage of smartphone LED camera lights flashed at us from both sides of the track. Jane went to the railing and began to wave. I moved to a corner of the platform and watched from there. A female Secret Service agent stood in the corner opposite me, facing the tracks. She fixed her gaze on the mourners and never said a word.

Darkness fell and the wooden farmhouses and endless fields gave way to weather-beaten homes and old brick storefronts. The door to the observation lounge swung open. Pierre carried a martini on a tray.

"A drink for you," he said. "Courtesy of the chef."

I thanked him and took the martini.

"I suggest you check the cocktail napkin," Pierre added.

The Secret Service agent glanced in my direction.

I held the napkin up to the light of the window. "Crews quarters. Tonight. 11:00" was in Wanda's handwriting. I pocketed the note and smiled to myself.

Wonderfully wicked Wanda.

The crowds grew as our train approached downtown Toledo. The flames from the mourners' candles floated airily in the night, forming white ribbons of light that bordered the receding tracks. Cameras flashed continuously, lighting Jane up like a runway model.

"I feel like a movie star!" she said, still waving.

We were finally called in to dinner, which became a raucous, festive affair. Wanda's *filet de boeuf Richelieu* garnered rave reviews. Horace told good stories. Burt and Dagny got drunk. Senator Rawlins recounted several hilarious tales involving Washington's biggest personalities on both sides of the aisle. He was a football fan. He asked me to explain a popular defensive scheme called the Cover Two. I diagrammed the concept for him on the back of Wanda's cocktail napkin: two safeties split the field, and the middle linebacker drops back to fill the deep crossing zone.

"It's why there's such a premium on middle linebackers with speed," I said. "Especially at the professional level."

Senator Rawlins shook his head. "The billionaire team owners operate like Robin Hood in reverse. The minuscule amount they pay in taxes is a national disgrace."

"The disgrace is what we pay you pickpockets in Washington," Horace said. He reached for the cocktail napkin, flipped it over, and read Wanda's message. He turned the napkin over again without looking at me.

Coming back from a trip to the restroom, Burt crept up behind Senator Rawlins. He had a cloth measuring tape in his hands.

"Oh boy," Dagny said, rolling her eyes. "It was just a matter of time."

Burt stretched the measuring tape down the back of the senator's jacket. "Ah! A good six-foot-six job. I'd suggest something in eighteen-gauge steel... white velvet interior... gunmetal finish. Costly but in perfect taste!"

Startled, Senator Rawlins looked around as Horace howled with laughter.

After dinner we stayed at the dining table. We lit cigars and drank cognac. Pierre served from a platter of assorted cheeses. Jane laid her head on the table and fell asleep. Wanda came out of the galley. She woke Jane and helped her to bed.

Sometime later the galley went dark and I heard the shower running.

At eleven o'clock I excused myself from the table, said good night to my dinner companions, and made my way up the hallway. At the double bedroom I unlatched the door and slipped inside.

Every light was on.

Wanda sat curled in her terrycloth robe in a corner of the lower berth, her back planted firmly against the bulkhead, her face pensive.

"Something wrong?" I said.

"I've got my answer." She drew her knees to her chest and clutched them with her arms. "Your job as trustee, both of us living in the same house... We need to set some ground rules."

"Ground rules."

"For starters, I won't sleep with you," she said.

The ladder to the upper berth separated me from Wanda. I squeezed around it and sat with her on the bed. I studied her face.

"Care to expand on that?" I said.

"Watching you today... tonight... seeing you interact with all those people... It scares me, Jack. I don't want to be left behind."

"Wanda, nobody's going to leave you behind—"

"I'm asking for a commitment. Right now."

"A commitment?"

"Seven years. That's how long until Jane goes to college. I've decided. I'm prepared to stay... If you'll stay, too."

"Are you talking marriage?"

"I'm talking a stable, two-parent household. Until Jane goes off to college. In the meantime, you and I court."

"*Court?*" I smiled at the outdated term.

"To see if we're a match," Wanda said. "But I won't sleep with you. Not without a ring."

"Isn't that a little extreme?"

"Extreme? No, there'll be a minor child in the house. Don't look at me like that, Majordomo. I'm not some kind of freakish prude—I'm taking a stand here. No more broken homes, no more screwed-up kids. The string ends with you and me."

I considered myself a warrior. How could I argue with that?

"That's not to say we won't get married," Wanda continued. "And if we do, I want children. Raising Jane doesn't mean we give up having a family of our own."

"With all due respect, I think you're putting the cart before the horse—"

"Maybe so. But I want everything on the table. If we're going to date, it has to be with an endgame in mind. Otherwise you're wasting my time."

"You've obviously put a lot of thought into this—"

Wanda pressed her index finger to my upper lip. "I'm not finished yet. I expect us to be exclusive. No pining for your ex-fiancée."

"Bianca?"

"You need to tear up that stupid letter you carry around. It's time to move on—"

"You went through my stuff?"

"Same with Giselle. History."

"But if a business relationship were to develop—"

"Fine. I've got no problem with that. Just don't get any ideas about romance, Romeo. She's too old for you."

"Now you're scaring me."

"I'm merely pointing out the obvious for your own good. Another thing. We hire a governess, like we promised Miss Elder. I can't chef and ride herd on you and Mr. Button and raise a teenage daughter all at the same time, not without losing my mind."

"Enlighten me," I said. "What's the company policy on nepotism?"

"Nepotism?"

"I'm thinking my sister, Libby, would make a great governess—that is, if you and Mr. Button don't have a problem with it."

"If she can do the job, he won't have a problem. I won't, either."

There was a knock at the door. Wanda and I looked at each other.

"Yoo-hoo, lovebirds," Pierre said on the other side of the door. "I have a delivery, compliments of the house. Shall I just leave it in the hallway?"

I went to the door and yanked it open. Pierre stepped back, looking frightened. He held a silver bucket with a bottle of champagne. He looked me up and down.

"*Quelle surprise*," he said. "We're still dressed." He presented the champagne. "This is for the two of you from Mr. Button—a token of his esteem. Shall I open it?"

I looked at Wanda. She raised her eyebrows.

"Yes, Pierre, by all means," I said. "Open it. Thank you."

In the privacy of the double bedroom, sitting side by side on the lower berth, with the old Pullman rocking and swaying, I poured the champagne into two crystal flutes. I stopped for a moment and contemplated the effervescence in my glass.

"You're a million miles away right now," Wanda said. "What are you thinking?"

"I'm thinking how good it is to be going home," I said. I touched my flute to Wanda's. "Here's to the next seven years."

FIFTY-SEVEN

Letter from the Editor
by Horace Button
"December Reflections"

HILLSBOROUGH, CA—For me, winter is a happy time: roaring fire-places, cozy dining rooms and prodigious helpings of lamb served from gleaming silver trolleys. This holiday season the gift-giving and rum toddies bring the promise of new beginnings.

Our December issue reflects the grasp, wisdom and impeccable good taste of our newly revamped editorial staff. For a sample of our improved content, I invite you to check out Etiquette Advisor (p. 13), a column by new contributor Pierre Bruneau. Pierre maintains the rigorous etiquette standards aboard the *Pioneer Mother*, the elegant 1932 Pullman-built private railroad car that has for many years been a hallmark of this magazine (and shall continue to be until my deathbed scene plays out). In Pierre's monthly column you'll get his insight on everything from hosting dinner parties to business dining, restaurant etiquette and more.

The recent—long overdue—restructuring at *Sunshine Trails* presented our most eligible bachelor and party host extraordinaire Billy Whitehead the opportunity to take a well-deserved sabbatical. As I pen this column, Billy is in Vollenhove, Netherlands, about to perform sea trials on his mega motor yacht *Utopia*. Rumor has it Billy's mother, Poppy, has tightened the purse strings on Billy. If anyone has experience sawing 30 feet off a nearly completed, 100-foot motor yacht, please contact Billy directly.

On a personal note, it's been almost four months since we made the westward run from Washington, D.C., to Winnemucca, Nevada, to lay to rest my beloved sister and dear brother-in-law. We continue to receive your thoughtful cards, letters and e-mails every day. Without compromising the little squirt's privacy, I can tell you Jane is doing quite well. She's a happy child, she loves tennis and she's smart as a whip. Start praying now for her future Jesuit educators—she's sure to give them a run for their money. Keeping up with Jane has proven more than a full-time job for Libby, our transplanted coed from Nowheresville, Texas. Libby ostensibly serves as Jane's governess, but she's more accurately Jane's partner in crime. If ever I stop collecting my mail, call the rescue squad—Jane and Libby have me tied to a chair somewhere while they're out boy hunting.

This month hit the Button household like a cyclone. For starters, I never imagined so many stockings hanging from my fireplace mantle. Amid the writing, cooking and general holiday chaos, Jack and Wanda managed to put up the most elaborately ornamented Douglas fir you've ever seen. The night we gathered to trim the massive conifer, Jack asked Wanda for her hand in marriage. In June I will have the honor of walking my much-loved friend and chef par excellence down the aisle in what's shaping up to be a simple backyard ceremony. Jane can't wait to serve as maid of honor.

Jack is putting the finishing touches on a salacious tell-all book about life after football. And speaking of book projects: Wanda's latest effort, *The Pioneer Mother Cookbook*, is slated to debut at next summer's North American Food and Wine Literary Festival. In this exquisite cookbook, Wanda shares the classic menus and gastronomic wonders that make dining aboard the *Pioneer Mother* one of the most memorable and exciting culinary experiences on the planet. I hope you'll join us in Denver for this not-to-be-missed summer symposium.

As I reflect on the year about to come to an end, and look forward to the year ahead, I can honestly tell you that life at the manse in Hillsborough has never been so wild or so much fun. From our household to yours, and from all of us at *Sunshine Trails*, here's wishing you a Merry Christmas and a Happy New Year.

Signed,
Editor-in-Chief and Publisher
HB

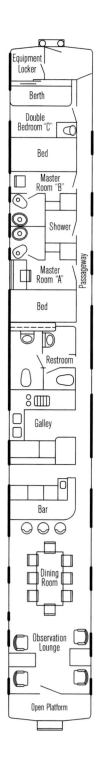

Equipment Locker

Berth

Double Bedroom "C"

Bed

Master Room "B"

Shower

Master Room "A"

Bed

Passageway

Restroom

Galley

Bar

Dining Room

Observation Lounge

Open Platform

Pioneer Mother

Business Car

Features: Open-platform car with comfortable observation lounge. Two master staterooms; each with a queen bed and private lavatory. One double bedroom with day sofa-seating, upper and lower berths, and lav. Guest restroom and separate shower. Dining room seats 8. Spacious walk-behind bar seats 3. Interior paneled in teak and mahogany throughout.

History: Pullman-built in 1932 as AT&SF business car 21. Acquired by Horace Button and Lincoln Whitehead in 1973 for *Sunshine Trails* magazine. Renamed *Pioneer Mother*. Extensively upgraded in 1988 and again in 2014. Richard Nixon used the car one year to travel to the Army-Navy football game.

ACKNOWLEDGMENTS

THIS NOVEL IS IN PART a fictional tribute to the legendary bon vivant, food writer, and social critic Lucius Morris Beebe (1902–1966). Some of the nouns, adjectives, turns of phrase, and colorful stories that appear in this book were inspired by passages found in Beebe's considerable body of work, including *The Lucius Beebe Reader* (Charles Clegg and Duncan Emrich, 1967); *The Provocative Pen of Lucius Beebe, Esq.* (Chronicle Publishing Company, 1966); *The Stork Club Bar Book* (Lucius Beebe, 1946); *The Big Spenders* (Lucius Beebe, 1966); and *Snoot If You Must* (Lucius Beebe, 1943).

Thank you to my brother, Chris Peterson, for bringing Lucius Beebe to my attention. As with so many adventures in my life, this one started with you.

My daughter Katie's senior-year honors thesis at Stanford includes the description of a seventh-grader called, for purposes of the research project, "Dorothy." When I read Katie's account of Dorothy, I felt as if I'd come face-to-face with Jane Pepper. Thank you, Katie, for allowing me to hijack some of Dorothy's wonderful character traits: the short bob haircut, the collection of stuffed animals, a high regard for Eleanor Roosevelt.

Thank you to Wade Pellizzer and to Doug Spinn for your prompt responses to my questions about the ins and outs of travel aboard a private railroad car.

To Roy and Susan Richey, owners of the Piper-Beebe House, Virginia City, Nevada, for graciously allowing us inside your home.

To William (Bill) Morrish for enduring my summer of ineptitude behind the bar at your camp on the Russian River. For the record, the men of that delightful camp were friendly, considerate, and upright — nothing at all like the monsters who inhabit my fictional Mount Hollow in the Santa Cruz Mountains.

To Shelley Cortopassi, Ken Painter, Candace Duecker, and Kristen Bauer for managing affairs of state while the Peterson brothers play.

To Maria Calhoun for your tireless hours worked on behalf of Huckleberry House.

To the gang at Red Deer Systems: Andy Feenstra, Steve Eisler, and Sandi Palermo. Your computer and accounting savvy allow me to concentrate on writing.

To Tommy Cortopassi for introducing me to the intricate world of fine dining.

To Paul Erdman, Tiffany Gunderman, and Jacob Andersen for schooling me in the art of restaurant service.

To my advance readers: Debbie Larson, G. Bruce Dunn, John Cornfield, Pat McGovern, Michelle Tremblay Schulze, and Dr. Edward Brand. Your encouragement kept me going.

To Kathleen Wise for your inspired book cover and crisp interior design.

To Laurie Gibson for your insightful comments and the meticulous attention you paid to the manuscript.

To Jack O'Shea for coming up with the title.

To James Ashley Shea, for your sharp eyes and wisdom.

To Jennifer Silva Redmond for working your magic. First you made the book better. And then you made it a lot better.

To Jill Treadwell Svendsen, my business partner at Huckleberry House, who has been with me every step of the way.

To my father, Gregor G. Peterson, the founder, in 1989, of Huckleberry Press, Lake Tahoe, Nevada: You are greatly missed, but you are always in our thoughts.

Finally, I want to express my heartfelt gratitude to my parents, George F. Russell, Jr., and Dion Peterson Russell. Your love and support make it all possible.

While I often suspect George and Mom are rolling their eyes at my latest book project, the eye rolling, under my immediate roof, has been remarkably restrained, at least from what I can tell. To my beautiful wife, Teresa, and to my daughters Katie and Caroline, I can only say thank you for believing.

Photo: Caroline Peterson

ABOUT THE AUTHOR

A third-generation Californian, Eric Peterson attended UCSD and completed his Communication degree at Stanford. In college, he worked for Amtrak, getting a glimpse into the rarefied world of travel via private railcar, and seeing a few impressive parties on the cars' open platforms. Peterson realized his dream of becoming a novelist in 2009, after years spent working for a venture partnership, founding a software company, and running a fine-dining restaurant. His debut novel, *Life as a Sandwich*, was a finalist in the San Diego Book Awards; *The Dining Car* is his second novel and the fifth book from Huckleberry House.

CPSIA information can be obtained
at www.ICGtesting.com
Printed in the USA
LVOW08*0138250417

532057LV00002B/14/P